3·26·79

The National
Movement
in Scotland

The National Movement in Scotland

Jack Brand

Routledge & Kegan Paul
London, Henley & Boston

First published in 1978
by Routledge & Kegan Paul Ltd
39 Store Street,
London WC1E 7DD,
Broadway House,
Newtown Road,
Henley-on-Thames,
Oxon RG9 1EN and
9 Park Street,
Boston, Mass. 02108, USA
Set in 10/12pt English
and printed in Great Britain by
The Lavenham Press Ltd
Lavenham, Suffolk

British Library Cataloguing in Publication Data

Brand, Jack

The national movement in Scotland.
1. Nationalism — Scotland — History
I. Title
320.5'4'09411   DA765   78-40578

ISBN 0 7100 8866 3

2053246

Mhairi Catriona,
this book is for you

Contents

Preface and Acknowledgments

In this study I have tried to provide an analysis of the rise of the Scottish National Party and the nature of the national movement in Scotland. I should like to thank the many people, too numerous to mention, who have helped me in this with their time and with their collections of papers. I have seen many members of the party and others who have worked for or against the cause of nationalism in Scotland and, without exception, they have been co-operative and interested in this work.

In particular I ought to mention the staff of the National Library of Scotland who have, with great skill, collected many of the papers relating to the development of the national movement. Readers of the notes will notice the wide use which has been made of the National Library resources. The initials NLS in the notes refer to the collections held in the National Library of Scotland. The abbreviation Acc. refers to Accession number, and Dep. refers to a Deposit number. Finally, I have a real debt to Mrs E. Clifford, who struggled through my awful writing and produced a typescript against all the odds. As usual any errors made in the course of this work are wholly my responsibility. The research was partially funded through the generosity of the Carnegie Trust for the Universities of Scotland.

Part One

Part One

1 The Nature of the Problem and its Background

The aims of this book are to describe the nationalist movement in Scotland and to explain why the Scottish National Party (SNP) has become such a prominent factor in British politics. Inevitably these two discussions are interlinked. Any account of the nature of the movement has implications for theories about why it has, over the last fifteen years, been able to attract so many votes.

The situation in Scotland

Before starting the more systematic analysis it is worth while to outline what success the SNP has had in Scotland.[1] From its foundation in 1928 (as the National Party of Scotland: NPS) until the beginning of the 1960s the SNP, dedicated to independent statehood for Scotland, was a tiny fringe party. With a few exceptions, mostly engineered by peripheral organisations rather than the party itself, it made no impact on British or even Scottish politics. At the time of writing this chapter (February 1977) two opinion polls conducted by separate organisations at different times and with different designs have estimated that the SNP has the support of the largest block of voters in Scotland.[2]

On the basis of that information alone, a reader might think that this was remarkable but no more than a flash in the political pan similar to the shortlived successes of the Mouvement Poujadiste, or the Dixiecrats in the United States. The real situation is more akin to that of the Parti Quebecois.[3]

3

Table 1.1   SNP votes and MPs[4]

Election year	Votes for SNP	SNP vote as % of the Scottish vote	SNP MPs
1945	30,595	1·2	—
1950	9,708	0·4	—
1951	7,299	0·3	—
1955	12,112	0·5	—
1959	21,738	0·8	—
1964	64,044	2·4	—
1966	129,112	5·1	—
1970	306,796	11·4	1
1974 Feb.	632,032	21·9	7
1974 Oct.	836,628	30·4	11

A glance at Table 1.1 shows that the SNP has not tumbled suddenly onto the stage. After the disastrous 1950s it has made steady progress in doubling or almost doubling its vote at each election. The party thus seems to be a permanent feature of the Scottish political scene. One further comment on the table ought to be made. The size of the 1970 vote is very largely explained by the fact that, for the first time, the party contested virtually every seat in Scotland (sixty-five out of the seventy-one) where at the previous election it stood in only twenty-three. Thus, the advance it made at this election has to be qualified by this and also by the fact that it lost its deposit in forty-two of the sixty-five seats. In the next general election, however, it maintained the rate of increase of its vote and in the election in October 1974 it fought every seat in Scotland and lost no deposits at all. Indeed in forty-two of the seats in which it did not win, it came second, displacing the Conservative or Labour Party. Thus the SNP is now represented, almost always strongly, in every constituency in Scotland.

As a footnote to this discussion of the importance of the SNP in Scottish politics one should point out that the situation is serious for British politics. Only in the elections of 1945 and 1966 was the Labour Party able to command a majority of seats in England and Wales alone. In other words Labour won the elections of 1950, 1964 and the two elections of 1974 by depending on Scottish seats. If the SNP replaced Labour as the majority party in Scotland, the probability of Labour forming a British government would be seriously diminished.

The natural history of political parties

The rise of a political party is a rare event. In their recent description of party systems Rose and Urwin were able to point to remarkable stability not just since the Second World War, but since the First.[5] Since 1945 there have been some innovations: in France, for example, the Gaullists and the MRP. More recently, in Scandinavia several small parties have appeared. These latter have had mixed fortunes and none of them is likely to transform the nature of politics in their countries.[6] Thus the post-war European scene presents a picture of surprising stability.

There have been several recent pieces of research which suggest the possibility of change in the ground on which political parties are based. Ronald Inglehart has demonstrated the incidence of 'post-bourgeois political values'.[7] Art Miller's work on the decline of political trust in the United States has been followed by studies showing similar trends in Britain[8] and, again in Britain, Butler and Stokes have spoken about 'the decline of the class alignment'.[9] If these assessments are correct, one might expect major changes in the structure of Western politics in the future.

This background of discontent and changing social values is certainly important for the rise of any political movement. The increase in the SNP vote must, in other words, be seen in relation to political changes that are taking place far beyond the borders of Scotland. It is also important to recall that Scotland is not the only country which has a 'separatist' movement and we must see whether there are general tendencies in European society which have given prominence to nationalist movements at this time.[10] I believe that general explanations do give us some guidance for the explanation of this specific phenomenon but that, to understand why a nationalist party has become prominent in Scotland at this particular time, we need to know something about Scottish history and conditions. Several events and processes peculiar to Scotland have affected more general movements in unexpected ways.

The second major preoccupation of this study is to describe the national movement. There are certain obvious characteristics which have to be dealt with: is it in favour of complete independence or Home Rule? Perhaps there is internal disagreement on this point. Is it left wing or right wing? Is the basic philosophy populist and is it, in any case, a movement or has it crossed the invisible line to become a 'real' political party? Although my major focus of attention will be the SNP I do not think that it is possible to give a coherent account of the party other than by understanding its relation to other aspects of Scottish life, including the development of a new consciousness of Scotland.

It is because of the relation between the political and other processes that this book has its particular organisation. In Chapter 2 I shall discuss some past accounts of nationalism and the ways in which this might bring certain characteristics of Scottish nationalism to our attention. In Chapter 3 I shall outline my own explanation for the rise of nationalism in Scotland. This concludes the introductory part.

In the second part I shall trace the development of the new attitude of Scots towards Scotland. I shall describe some domains of Scottish life in which certain sorts of Scottish people have taken a new view of themselves and their country; a view which has led to nationalism for many. I shall devote Chapters 4 and 5 to a discussion of the political and economic history of Scotland from the end of the First World War to the present. I shall demonstrate that, for Scots, and for less affluent Scots in particular, the difficulties of Britain in the 1960s and 1970s have led to a new feeling for the community of Scotland. Chapter 6 will look at the rise of literary nationalism and cultural nationalism. This is a feature which affects only a tiny minority in a direct sense. In an indirect way it has been more influential and has been a mirror of the changing mood of the nation. Perhaps more than any other group the young have been associated with the new wave of nationalism in Scotland. In trying to explain this I shall look at the influence of the folk song movement and the influence of the educational system in Chapter 7. In Chapters 8-10 I shall discuss some Scottish institutions which might have been thought to contribute to the growth of nationalism but which have not done so. These institutions are the Church, the Scottish regiments of the armed forces, football, and the Press.

The third part deals specifically with the rise of nationalism. Its relation to the earlier section is that I shall show the connection between nationalism and other events in Scotland. In Chapters 11-13 the history of the political movement will be described and in Chapter 14 some organisational points will be discussed. Chapter 15 will conclude the book with an attempt to summarise the argument and to expand it.

2 The Substance of Nationalism

In the last twenty years social scientists have been more concerned with the integration of states than with separatism. Major work has been done by such scholars as Stein Rokkan on the relation between the centre and the periphery and there has been work on nation building by Lucien Pye and others.[1] Rokkan's major contribution to this area has been to study the circumstances under which peripheral groups were integrated into the central culture.[2] Lipjhart and several others have contributed to this field.[3] Although there has been some recent work on ethnicity[4] there is no body of political theory of the same weight to explain modern separatism. We are, therefore, forced to turn to more traditional treatments. The studies which concentrate on modern European nationalism, such as those by Kedourie and Kohn, draw most of their examples from the nineteenth-century struggles of such countries as Prussia and Poland.[5] Much of their attitude to nationalism is coloured by the experience of nationalist dictatorships in the 1930s and 1940s. For many of these writers nationalism is an evil, since nationalism is equated with the doctrine that the chosen nation should in some way lead the world.

The dominant attitudes in European politics have also been concerned with integration rather than separatism. NATO and the EEC have been important considerations in political thinking. Where the existence of nationalist movements was acknowledged they were regarded as quaint survivals rather than as serious figures in the political landscape.

In Britain at least, the situation has changed dramatically. The nationalist movement in Scotland is strong and shows signs of becoming stronger.[6] Part of the argument of this chapter is that we need to develop new ways of describing it. I shall argue that Scottish nationalism is a modern movement responding to modern social and political conditions. As such we can more usefully look at it as similar to developments in the new countries of Asia and Africa rather than as a pure descendant of nineteenth-century European nationalism.

Let us, for the sake of argument, say that a classical nationalist position could be summarised in these (rather ambiguous) statements:

All Mankind is divided into nations: it is a natural division.

Each nation has a peculiar character.

A nation has a 'right' to run its own affairs.

Only when nations run their own affairs as independent states will their full potential be realised.

Nation states have the first claim on the loyalties of their members.

Most practising nationalists as opposed to political philosophers would not attempt to defend these concepts of 'rights' or 'nature'. They would take them as self evident. It is not my purpose to discuss them either but simply to point out that they are part of a profession of belief by nationalists and that these appeals take precedence over other arguments.

The SNP would certainly pass the test as a true nationalist party. Its manifesto, prepared for the general election in October 1974 stated:

The vast majority of the people of Scotland recognise that Scotland is a nation and that it should exercise privileges and responsibilities as other nations do, through a Parliament entrusted with the sovereign rights of the people of Scotland.

The booklet assumes the existence of the nation of Scotland, with the right to the same status as other nations.[7] Thus its most recent election programme is built on the basis of a traditional nationalist approach.

There are, however, some problems about this description of what nationalism means in Scotland. One of them is that various other arguments have been used by nationalists to justify their aim: the establishment of an independent government in Scotland. The chief of these is that such a government would run the country's affairs better. This is an argument distinct from one saying that Scotland claims independence as a right. Even though the quality of economic and social life should collapse, it would be more 'moral' for Scotsmen to run themselves rather than be run from London. A related line of reasoning is sometimes used. It is argued that if a country is run by its own people there is released a flood of creative and artistic energy which is repressed by an alien rule, however caring and benevolent.

In practice nationalist movements use both sorts of appeals and it is this which gives rise to the ambiguity which surrounds the phenomenon. Is the nationalist voter responding to the promise of improved material conditions or to the 'spiritual' appeal of the national community?[8] Many commentators have written that the rise in the SNP vote in the 1960s and 1970s was not due to 'true' nationalism.

Although this criticism applies mostly to the nationalist voter it can also be applied to the party members and even the leaders. In a later chapter we shall see that, from the mid-1930s until 1942, there was a strong group in the SNP who were motivated mostly by the second group of arguments: those for efficiency and increased sensitivity to the needs of Scotland. It was significant that such people, who were grouped around Sir Alexander McEwen and the Duke of Montrose, were federalists rather than advocates of complete independence. Often their rhetoric was such that it was difficult to distinguish the real arguments that they were putting forward but we shall see convincing evidence that they were 'Home Rulers' rather than 'separatists'. It is essential to recognise, however, that these same men were deeply committed to the national community of Scotland even though they might not be committed to its independence. Most of their lives were devoted to its service. This point also comes out when one examines the Home Rule movement in Scotland before the First World War. Just as in the case of the Irish Home Rule movement, it did not claim complete independence for its particular country. People like Blackie were perfervid Scots although the emotional claims of national consciousness were linked to a programme for more limited Scottish autonomy.[9]

This ambiguity is related to a distinction made by several writers on nationalism. Kohn indicates two varieties of nationalism.[10] One is in the liberal tradition and is a movement which exists for the people. The people are sovereign rather than the state or the monarch, and the nationalist movement seeks to put power in the hands of the nation (the people) and to take it from the state which has exploited the people for the sake of high politics or in the interests of an aristocratic class.[11] This is a form which is to be found mostly in western Europe. It is associated first with the French Revolution which is seen as a national movement as well as one for the Rights of Man. In either case it was a rebellion against the highly centralised and formalised court politics. In eastern Europe, where the central power was weak and initially unable to sustain the coherence of the state, nationalism was a glorification of that state at the expense of the rights of the people. The history of Prussia is taken as an example of this procedure.[12]

A first point brought out by this distinction is that nationalism is not a single system of beliefs but rather a family of related belief systems. One can appropriate the term for those who advocate independence of the nation state for the betterment of the individual or one can define as nationalists those who believe in the inherent claim of the nation irrespective of the material or individual benefits or disbenefits which this may bring. If one is interested in the development of the phenomenon of nationalism, then it is not helpful to argue too long about the exact meaning of the term because the different interpretations spill over onto each other at all levels from leaders to the most inconstant of voters. Indeed for large parts of the time both leaders and followers may be unclear about their own positions and only the party ideologues are satisfied with a precise definition. Much has been spoken about the 'demonstration' effect in the spread of political and other ideas. This re-emphasises the importance of recognising the 'family likeness' theory of nationalism since the example in one country is almost always perceived differently and applied selectively elsewhere.

What this points to is that, like most other social and political movements, socialism or fascism or populism, nationalism is not one movement founded unambiguously on a clear ideology but is, rather, a group of movements with a family likeness. Even within Scottish nationalism itself there are various interpretations of what nationalism means. This is an important fact about nationalism itself but it has implications for our argument when we come to explain the rise of support for nationalist parties. If people understand different things by nationalism it is unlikely that one simple explanation will account for the rise of nationalism.

One point which brings this out is the enquiry into the origins of nationalism. Up to about ten years ago most writers argued that nationalism was a product of the nineteenth century. A principal factor in its rise was the appeal made by the French Revolutionaries to the people as against the aristocracy. The nation was no longer the king and the nobles but the people as a whole. The Revolution was accomplished in the name of the people and foreign wars were fought in the name of the people. In exactly the same way the lamp of nationalism was lit in other parts of Europe by a spirit of opposition to the imperial pretensions of France, and trimmed by German philosophy.

There can be no doubt that nationalism became a major issue in the nineteenth century. Even among the writers just mentioned, however, there is a recognition that there is no clear starting point. On the contrary, attitudes and movements very similar to nationalism can be identified at various points in history. Kamenka contends that something like national consciousness appeared in France as early as the thirteenth century.[13] The Capetian kings of France were hailed as heroes stopping the German and English invaders. Geoffrey of Monmouth's *History of the Kings of Britain* can be described as showing signs of national pride as can most of Shakespeare's histories. At one level of society, then, there was some sense of a national community. Perhaps it existed only among the literary figures and some noblemen but there was present a feeling that France and England were, in some sense, units which commanded the love, as well as the feudal loyalty, of those who lived there. It is not my intention to argue that the nationalism that exists today is the same as those medieval sentiments. My point is simply that the term does not refer to one tidy theory with a definite genesis and a clear line dividing it from other theories and attitudes. When we turn to Scottish nationalism we shall see that many of its followers are not dogmatic, even in terms of the SNP's aims referred to earlier. When we speak about the rise of nationalism in Scotland since 1960 it might be more appropriate to describe it as the rise of national feeling. To do this would put those events more clearly in the context of Scottish history.

To understand the substance of Scottish nationalism it is necessary to recognise the existence of such feelings at an early stage of

11

Scottish history. It is worth remembering three major points. Up to 1603 Scotland was a kingdom independent of England, with her own monarch. In that year the King of Scotland, James VI, became the head of both states and moved his court to London but until 1707 Scotland retained her own Parliament and other political institutions. In fact, at several points during that hundred years the Scottish and English governments were on very bad terms and on several occasions this broke into open warfare and invasion.[14] The first consideration then, is that 270 years ago Scotland was a separate state and it could not be said that the two kingdoms were good neighbours. The second point is related to this. The English Crown claimed overlordship of Scotland at various points but these claims were decisively overturned during the Wars of Independence of the thirteenth and fourteenth centuries. The high point of this episode is generally taken to be the battle of Bannockburn in 1314 when the Scots under King Robert Bruce routed the English army under King Edward III. Modern history suggests that Bannockburn was not as decisive as was popularly thought but for our purposes the main point is that there were several statements during this period, and slightly after it, showing that a certain stratum of the Scottish people were aware of Scotland as a community to which they had a loyalty. It is, moreover, Scotland in some sense which seems to have this loyalty rather than the Scottish king. The best-known piece of evidence for this is taken from the petition by the Scottish Nobles to the Pope in 1320: the Declaration of Arbroath:

> But if he [the king] were to abandon this task, wishing to subject us or our realm to the King of England or the English, we should instantly set ourselves to expel him as the betrayer of his own rights and ours. For so long as one hundred men of us remain alive we shall never submit under any conditions to the yoke of English domination.

Similarly there are two epic poems about this period written slightly after it. In one of them, John Barbour's *The Bruce*,[15] there are many well-known statements of Scottish sentiment. Perhaps more important for our purposes is Blind Harry's *Schir William Wallace*.[16] It does not have Barbour's literary quality but it was much more widely read among people of all stations in life. Wittig points out that, along with the Bible, it was one of the few books to be found commonly in the houses of literate peasants after the

Reformation.[17] One of the reasons why Wallace may have appealed was that he was more a man of the people than Bruce. He was not a noble but a Renfrewshire laird in a very small way. The fact that ordinary Scottish people were prepared to rally behind him to beat off an invading army which they clearly identified as English suggests, yet again, that there was a belief that the Scottish identity was important and, moreover, that this feeling spread fairly far down through the Scottish population in late medieval times. Blind Harry's sentiments are quite unmistakable.

Finally, in this consideration of national feeling in Scottish history, there is ample evidence that the Union of the Parliaments in 1707 was unpopular.[18] There was a pro-union party but even for them the important argument was that Scotland would prosper as a result. There were angry demonstrations against it both on the part of the Edinburgh mob and of more weighty bodies such as the Convention of Royal Burghs.[19]

The point to be taken out of this discussion is that some sentiment akin to nationalism has a very long history in Scotland. It is pointless to argue for long about whether this was true nationalism since, as I have suggested, nationalism is not one concept but a whole series of related concepts and phenomena.

The variety of national and nationalist feelings makes it doubly unfortunate that traditional writing on the theory of nationalism has tended to identify only two major strands to which I have already referred: on the one hand the liberal or whig tradition founded on an attempt to scrap the traditional, particularistic customs and privileges, and on the other hand what Hayes calls 'integral' nationalism and others have variously described as the 'Eastern' tradition or 'romantic' nationalism. It is important to recognise that these and other traditions of nationalism may be mixed up in the growing national consciousness and nationalism of any country. I shall try to illustrate this in the case of Scotland. It is, for example, undoubtedly true that many of the nineteenth-century figures in Scottish nationalism took a great deal of their symbolism from German nationalism. Professor Blackie of Edinburgh was a leading figure in the Scottish movement. As a scholar of Greek he had spent a great deal of time at German universities and, no doubt, the ideas of Herder, Fichte, Jahn and Arndt were familiar to him. He certainly took seriously the history and traditions of the nation and the primitive culture which was peculiarly Scottish.[20] He was a key figure in the establishment of Celtic studies in Scottish universities and in the study of Highland problems. For him Fichte's idea of the *Ursprache* was translated into the Scottish context. At the same time there was no question of Blackie entertaining those ideas of Fichte or his disciples which spoke about the mission of the Prussian nation. Although many nineteenth- and twentieth-century Scotsmen with nationalist sympathies became interested in Scottish history and the study of Gaelic and many of the other romantic, even Gothic, notions associated with nationalism in eastern Europe, there is no evidence that they also thought in terms of a dominating Scottish state. In a sense we can regard the history of modern Scottish nationalism as a struggle between these two interpretations of nationalism: the 'Whig tradition' and 'integral nationalism'. At the same time it will become clear that, in practice, the nationalist movement in Scotland has consisted of a mixture of the two.

When we are considering the substance of nationalism it is inevitable that there should be some reference to those characteristics of a nation which many have believed to be particularly important. I shall only refer here to the three which have been most frequently mentioned: language, the folk culture and race. It has been argued that, in order to be truly a nation, there must be present a distinctive language or a distinctive culture or that the people must constitute a single race identifiable from those of surrounding countries. In the next three sections each of these characteristics will be described in relation to Scotland. By identifying the issue or its absence we shall, once again, be able to see what sort of nationalism exists in Scotland.

Language

Many writers have referred to the central part that language has played in the extension of political nationalism. For the earliest theorists like Herder, language was the most important mark of the nation.[21] It expressed the thoughts and personality of the people and was itself a formative influence. Later theorists of nationalism like Fichte took the argument a stage further by asserting that the nation which spoke an original and pure language, an *Ursprache*, held the highest position and had a mission to lead the others.[22] In several countries the early leaders paid a great deal of attention to the teaching, or even the creation, of the national language. In Norway Nynorsk was put together as an alternative to the Danish based

Riksmaal.[23] The Czech language was resuscitated in something of the same way and, best known of all, Hebrew, from being an almost exclusively liturgical language, became the modern speech of Israel.[24]

Broadly speaking, two languages are spoken as the native everyday speech in modern Scotland. English is spoken by the vast majority and Gaelic by a diminishing minority, at least as everyday speech.[25]

In later chapters we shall see that there was a language issue in the early days of nationalism. It had two forms. For many of the earliest nationalists, the Celtic culture of Scotland was what distinguished it particularly. For nationalists like Erskine of Marr, Scotland would be truly herself only when all Scotsmen used Gaelic as their everyday speech. The use of English was a weapon of assimilation and even moral degeneration. Later on, certain literary figures and, most prominently, C. M. Grieve (writing as Hugh MacDiarmid) argued that the true speech of the Scots should be Lallans.[26] He argued, accurately, that, although from a common root, the English of England and the Scots of Scotland had become quite different. In the centuries prior to the Union of the Crowns, Scots (and before it Gaelic) had been the language of the Court and, down to the Union of the Parliaments at least, Scots was the language of intellectual, cultural and legal discourse. The move south of the king and nobles meant the loss of patrons for the poets who wrote in Scots. The eighteenth-century bourgeoisie aped English accents even to the extent of hiring teachers of elocution, and Scots degenerated into the dialects which we know today. Given this situation MacDiarmid thought that Scots might be re-created.[27]

What MacDiarmid did, as we shall see, was to write some fine poetry in Lallans as he conceived the re-creation of the Scots tongue. Other followed him, some of them gifted but none with his stature. What MacDiarmid did not do was to encourage the Scots to *speak* Lallans. Very few even tried to use it in anything other than poetry. We cannot say, then, that the creation or re-creation of Scots constituted a language issue even on the limited scale of the situation in Wales or Ireland. There can be no question at all that, for the vast majority of Scottish nationalists, the language issue hardly existed. They might be happy that they spoke with a Scots accent. The more literate might encourage the study of Scottish poetry as a school subject. They would demand that Gaelic should be given an equal place with English in the rapidly diminishing areas where Gaelic was still generally spoken. On the other hand there was no concentrated effort to develop the language as the badge of the nation.

Part One

Folk culture

Another aspect of some nationalist movements is their interest in and concern for the health of the folk culture. Kedourie associates this with the continental type of nationalism typical in Slav or German countries.[28] These peoples did not, it is argued, have the great literary traditions or other forms of 'high' culture. Although they envied the achievements of western Europe they wanted to express their own uniqueness.

Again there can be no doubt that in the nineteenth and twentieth centuries there was an interest in Scottish folk cultures. Part of this was expressed in the collections of folk songs, of which Sir Walter Scott was one of the initiators.[29] The folk museums set up in the twentieth century have been well nurtured. Some nationalists have been known for their interest in these fields but this cannot be said to be a characteristic of Scottish nationalism. It is crucial to recognise that the most obvious and romantic folk tradition of the kilted, bagpipe-playing Highlander was vigorously rejected by nationalists from the beginning. There were special reasons for this as we shall see but the crucial point is that the picture of the twentieth-century Scottish nationalist as the romantic crypto-Jacobite could not be further from the truth. Such people existed but not in the SNP: or at least not for long. Thus, the national movement in Scotland is not characterised by an appeal to the memory of a dying peasant society any more than it is by reference to a dying language. This also distinguishes it rather vividly from populist movements.

Race

One may dismiss some of the other bases of national consciousness and the rise of nationalism in Scotland more briefly. The reference to the tradition and values of the people is often accompanied in nationalist movements with an appeal to the race. This is well known in German nationalism but it is an ever-present factor in many parts of Africa and Asia.[30] While there have been Scottish nationalists who have been anti-English, a glance through nationalist literature in every phase shows that there have been few feelings of racial hatred.[31] The policy of the SNP is that Scottish citizenship is the right of all who live in Scotland and not only of those who can in some sense claim to belong to the Scottish race.[32]

16

Up to now Scottish nationalism has been described by saying what it is not. It does not base itself seriously on language, race, national culture or character. What does seem important is that national feeling has been present in Scotland for a very long time. At the time when Scotland was about to lose her Parliament it was expressed very strongly as an opposition to this loss. In other words, one of the most important factors for understanding nationalism is the history of the community. There are many factors which can create a sense of that community. A peculiar language or culture certainly helps but there are many countries in Asia and Africa, for example, which are strongly nationalistic but do not have any of the traditional props. What is more common is an historical process which establishes for these people a sense of their own separateness. Most writers on modern nationalism would agree that this is the critical consideration: 'true' nationalism is defined, not by the presence of a peculiar language, culture or race, but by a feeling that the community is separate. History made the Scot very conscious of this separateness. What has to be resolved is why this consciousness was translated into a demand for political separation. It had, after all, lasted all through the eighteenth and nineteenth centuries without producing a nationalist movement. Why was there little or no Scottish nationalism in the classical period of nationalism, the nineteenth century? Why did it take off in the 1960s?

In order to answer these questions one other characteristic concomitant of nationalist movements has to be mentioned: modernisation. It has often been remarked of nationalist movements in Africa and Asia in the 1950s and 1960s that they abandon their own histories and even the great pieces of art and architecture in order to create a modern state.[33] The symbols of the new Nigeria or Ghana have been the modern buildings of the capital cities, the national army and so on. In discussing the relation of culture to Scottish nationalism I pointed out that it was not an antiquarian movement but, on the contrary, sought to create in Scotland a modern state. The models for Scottish nationalism from its early days have been the Scandinavian countries. This was the epitome of the small prosperous European democracy with little time to spend on its history. The character of Scottish nationalism has been to bring Scotland out of the wreck of nineteenth-century industry and the 'Gothic' mists sponsored by the tourist interests. In this it was like the movements in Quebec and the new countries of Asia and Africa. It is on this basis that it has to be judged. Just as the Parti

17

Quebecois revolted against the traditionalism of Quebec society with its dominance by priests and the traditional middle class, so the Scottish nationalists revolted against the tradition of Scottish life and the extent to which the industrial complex of Clydeside had been frozen in the nineteenth century. The substance of nationalism in Scotland is that of a modernising movement committed against the authority of the political, social and economic powers that dominate Scotland.

One final point must be made about Scottish nationalism. It started as a social movement and still bears many of the characteristics of the social movement. We should remember that people join social movements for many reasons. Once the movement gets on the way these reasons may be even more diverse and the character of the social movement itself becomes more complex. Once again then, it is worth putting up a warning sign to say that no simple approach will describe the national movement and no simple explanation will account for its rise. To this account we now turn.

3   The Rise of the SNP: Some Theories

The critical question which lies behind this whole study is put very simply. Given that a modern nationalist movement was found in Scotland in 1928, why did it move from being a tiny fringe party only in 1961? What accounts for its growth since that time? The purpose of this chapter is to examine the answers which have been given by various analysts and to propose an explanation.

Most of the work which has been done on the development of social movements has concentrated on non-political cases.[1] There are several very honourable exceptions including many studies of the rise of the Nazi Party in Germany but more recently, and more important for my purposes, there is Maurice Pinard's fine study of the rise of Social Credit in Quebec.[2] Both Pinard and the authors of the works on the Nazi Party are forced to look upon their subjects not as political parties in the conventional sense but as social movements. At the beginning of their careers these organisations were unambiguously social movements rather than political parties in the usual definition of the former term. Wilson, for example, defines such a movement as a conscious, collective, organised attempt to bring about or to resist large-scale change in the social order by non-institutionalised means.[3] The interesting point about these new political parties is that they do operate to some extent outside the institutionalised processes of politics. One need go no further than to say that such parties often want to overturn the entire social or political order rather than to work within a set of rules in order to achieve certain limited ends. This latter description better describes the Conservative and Liberal Parties in the British system and it also describes what the Labour Party has become. From being a movement which sought sweeping changes in society, the early socialist movement allied itself with trade union interests so that the extent to which the movement looked for 'large scale change' diminished. It concentrated on the amelioration of social and economic life. It might be argued that the SNP has travelled down the same road. Whereas at the beginning Scottish nationalism was a movement operating outside the recognised institutions of British politics, it has now accepted the conventions of party politics and operates in the same ways as other parties. It should still be noticed, however, that, unlike the other political parties, its whole aim lies in changing some very basic rules of the political game. In its ordinary operations there are traces of behaviour more common to movements than to the institutionalised political parties. There is an employment of tactics which are not in common use by the other parties. More than anything else it is important that support for the party is regarded more as a crusade, whereas the emotive force supporting other parties is not nearly so strong. Later in this book data will be brought forward to support these propositions. For the moment it is sufficient to say that the approaches of those who have studied the rise of non-political social movements have proved to be very helpful in the analysis of the SNP.

One of the most useful approaches in the rise of social movements has been outlined by Neil Smelser.[4] In his 'Value Added Approach' he outlines several stages for the specification of the causes of a social movement. It is not my purpose to construct a general theory here and I certainly do not agree in every way with Smelser's assumptions. When all is said and done, however, the Value Added Approach is an extremely useful heuristic device. Pinard has already illustrated its usefulness and, although the development of the SNP is radically different in many ways from that of the Ralliement des Creditistes, many of the same categories apply.[5]

The logic of Smelser's approach is that, at every stage of the explanation, the conditions of the development of the social movement are specified more precisely. To put it another way, the early stages of the explanation indicate the general possibilities for the development of a social movement but, with each stage, the nature of the movement which is to develop is more clearly specified until we understand why this train of events rather than any other took place.

The first necessity is the presence of 'structural conduciveness'. By this Smelser means that the system should be such as to offer conditions which would allow such a movement to grow. Pinard interprets this as the existence of constituencies where the minority party was very weak. Structural conduciveness existed in the sense that there was no adequate vehicle for the expression of protest against the existing majority party. Under these circumstances it was easier for a third party to appear to the voter as a serious political proposition. Structural conduciveness can exist in other forms which I shall discuss later.

The next stage is that 'strain' arises in the system. Again strain can take many forms, one of the most common being economic deprivation of some sort. The system no longer operates to provide the level of reward to which its members have been accustomed. If a 'generalised belief' is formulated to identify the trouble and to explain why it has come about then the next stage of the process is achieved. In the case of the working class movement the generalised belief might be that the cause of their trouble was the greed of the factory owners or the inefficiency and venality of a capitalist system. 'Precipitating events' will next specify in a dramatic and, for the individuals caught up in the situation, an unambiguous way, the nature of the case and the need for action. Next 'mobilisation' of the participants is a function of leadership and is necessary if the movement is to be effective. Finally 'social controls' operate to ensure that the movement does not overstep certain basic rules and social understandings.

Of the advantages of using this approach I shall mention only three. First, it brings out the fact that the development of a social or political movement is a process, not a sudden event, and there is a building-up to the establishment of the organisation concerned. In our study of the nationalist movement in Scotland we shall see how the process unfolded. Another point well brought out is that social movements are related to a series of causes or previous events no one of which is sufficient to produce the results which follow. Thus, while relative deprivation or the need to make a protest may explain one phase of the process, perhaps the final and most decisive one, it is still true that the protest would not have taken this particular form if other factors had not also been present. In other words, the Value Added Approach brings out the extent to which the social movements are the culmination of many causes. If we are to understand them we have to know something about their history. A further and again a related point is that different explanations for the rise of social movements may be applicable at different times. The reasons why the party grew in the 1960s may be entirely different from the reasons why it grew in the 1970s, and the reasons why one group supported it may be quite different from the explanation that accounts for the support of other groups.

For all these reasons I shall use Smelser's approach as a method of approaching the problem. I do not argue that Smelser has provided a theory of the rise of social movements. Rather, he gives us a framework on which theories can be constructed. Even though, as a structuralist, Smelser rejects a conflict model of society, it is in no way incumbent on anyone using his approach also to reject the conflict model. It is possible to use Smelser for the insights he gives into the way in which these events take place.

The argument of the book

Given this as a general background, I shall state my explanation for the rise of the SNP in general terms. My argument is that the rise in support for the SNP is explained by two processes which took place at the same time. On the one hand there is the European phenomenon of distrust towards established political parties and towards the political system itself. In Britain as a whole this had several effects but the most obvious of them was the increase in the Liberal vote. The overall situation is well described by Butler and Stokes as 'the decline of the class alignment'. In other countries there may have been different reasons for the growth of distrust but in Britain it is at least arguable that a major cause was the repeated failure of governments of both colours to do anything about the economic situation. To a very large extent governments had brought the situation upon their own heads. Whereas in the nineteenth century they had not claimed to be able to deal with economic problems, now they were active with many measures and the whole philosophy of government was that it could be an effective economic force. In Scotland, as we shall see, the economic difficulties seemed particularly intransigent and the efforts of the government served to depress its credibility.

So far, we have to see the rise of the SNP as part of a European, or at least an all-British, trend. This does not, however, take us to the point of explaining why the discontent should have taken the form of supporting the SNP. Why should the discontented voters not have supported the Liberals who were, after all, fairly well represented in Scotland proportionately and who had a long tradition in Scotland? Why did the tradition of Red Clydeside not turn into support for the Communist Party? The fact that neither of these possibilities took place and that, instead, Scottish voters turned to a hitherto obscure and ridiculed party needs a further strand in the argument. Given the conduciveness for supporting a new party why should that party have been the nationalists? The link between rejection of the old parties and support for a new one is given by the rise in interest in Scottish affairs which, I shall argue, took place in the years from the 1920s onwards. In subsequent chapters I shall show that this development took various forms and is to be observed in political, cultural and other fields. The same economic events which led people to reject the old political parties also led them to be more aware of Scotland as a unit on its own.

The vote for nationalism was a vote to establish a modern prosperous society where there were problems of unemployment and industrial decay. Out of the various alternative explanations and their attendant solutions offered by political parties, that of the SNP was accepted because of the way in which it fitted within this renewed interest in Scotland and also because of its basic simplicity. I shall also argue that the decline in the 'class alignment' of Scottish politics and the growth of interest in Scottish affairs would not have been sufficient to account for the rise of the SNP had it not been for some extremely skilled organisers who worked for the SNP.

Before restating the argument in more detail one or two of its characteristics should be noticed. It identifies Scottish nationalism as a modernising movement, not as an attempt to re-create a Scottish Golden Age but as a determination to work for a technologically advanced, prosperous, modern, small nation state. Traditions may be used for propaganda purposes but their preservation is not the heart of the nationalist appeal. It is tempting to regard Scottish nationalism as an example of the move away from such material concerns as have been documented by Ronald Inglehart in several European countries.[6] Nothing could be further from the truth. The SNP appeals precisely because Scottish people are worried about unemployment and declining industry. Secondly, the argument assumes a feeling of alienation on the part of the Scottish electorate and this is alienation from the major parties and from some of the rules of the game of politics in Britain. I do not, however, want to argue that the rise of the SNP can be explained by any kind of 'mass society' model. There is no evidence that the Scottish voters are 'atomised' as well as alienated and that these atomised voters turn to the nationalists. Finally, the argument identifies one of the important reasons for change, an endogenous change in Scottish society: a greater concern for the condition of Scotland leading to political action to achieve improvement.

This study concentrates on the development of Scottish nationalism after 1919. It is part of my argument that a new development took place then. This development is identifiable in an institutional form by the setting up of an organisation called the Scots National League: the first organisation to advocate complete independence for Scotland. The new movement was not only different in the degree of independence it wanted for Scotland, it also rejected the existing order. In this it was close to the emerging socialist movements. It called for a new society in which people would live happier and fuller lives. As we study the rise of the nationalist movement we shall see that there were two main trends. On the one side stood the Scots National League, but the Scottish Home Rule Association was for a much more limited devolution of power to Scotland. In this it represented an older tradition and it is important to be aware of this for two reasons. On the one hand it identifies the differences between the two movements and on the other hand it indicates the extent to which different strands have come together to make the movement. Once again modern Scottish nationalism is not a single phenomenon which can be explained with one neat theory. We have to look at history to see why various developments took place and why they eventually coalesced.

A little history

We have seen that up to the Union of the Scottish and English Parliaments in 1707, Scotland was an independent state united with England under one crown. The nature of the Union was that, although Scotland lost her own Parliament as a result of that treaty, many of the characteristic Scottish institutions were retained.[7] The most important of these institutions were the Presbyterian Church, the peculiar system of Scots Law, local government and the university system. The important consideration was that these élite groups in Scottish society were guaranteed a future and, in fact, the Union also catered for the interests of other groups in Scottish society: the majority of the landowners for example, and those merchants who were keen to break into the English overseas markets. Thus, however unpopular the Union was among many people in Scotland, certain key élites were given guarantees and advantages or, in the case of the merchants, the promise of advantage. In a society where most public business was carried out by local government, the élites in Scotland, clerical and lay, were able to control Scottish affairs without a Parliament and did so. In the course of the nineteenth century Britain became prosperous and also became the centre of a world empire. Scotland shared in this success, and the industrialisation of the Clyde Valley meant that, from 1850 until about 1919, the west of Scotland was one of the most prosperous parts of Britain. At the same time changes were taking place in British politics. The state began to take a more active part in the life of society. The parliamentary timetable became crowded with legislation to provide education, housing, sanitation and many other services which before had not been a public service, or had been provided by local government. By this time the informal arrangements which had existed to look after Scottish business in Parliament had disappeared and the extent to which the Scottish élites were able to manage Scottish life had declined.[8] Scottish business was crowded out of the parliamentary timetable and many of those in Scottish society who had, for practical purposes, been left alone to look after Scottish affairs began to feel that their needs were not being recognised. This would probably have been the case under any circumstances but with the increase in state activity the feeling became even more acute. It was widely felt that legislation was passed with England in mind, so that it was often inappropriate for Scottish conditions.

As a result of this there was considerable disquiet in Scottish society. These concerned groups represented middle and even upper class interests. It is extremely significant that one of their leaders was the Earl of Rosebery, a Scottish grandee later to become a British Prime Minister.

Hanham has shown that, from the 1850s onwards, a series of organisations was set up in Scotland which demanded more Scottish control over Scottish affairs.[9] These organisations were firmly linked to powerful groups in Scottish society even if they did not enjoy the support of all sections of that establishment. We shall see later that the clergy of the Church of Scotland were important exceptions. The Scottish Home Rule Association, which was established in 1886, drew its membership from the Liberal Party, and in general the movement for Home Rule before 1914 could count on the support of such organisations as the Convention of Royal Burghs and the Scottish Trade Union Congress.

The First World War in this, as in other things, was a watershed. There were many who still supported Home Rule but one essential difference was that the policy no longer had the support of powerful interests in Scottish society. It quietly ceased to be an issue of importance in British politics great enough to be supported by a major political party. It is at this point that the Scots National League came on to the scene. Whereas before the war, there had been talk of the shortage of parliamentary time for Scottish affairs, the major concern now was the worsening economic condition of Scotland. More than this, what now developed was a nationalist movement of a modern type quite different from the pre-war organisations.

My first point is that the demand for more Scottish control over Scottish affairs has been a discontinuous development. Before 1914 it was an attempt by certain important sections of Scottish society to re-establish Scottish control in the ways in which this had existed in the earlier parts of the nineteenth century. The groups which had controlled Scottish affairs attempted to reassume this role. After the war the support of these groups for this policy faded and nationalism became the concern of a minority which had no backing from anyone controlling any Scottish power base. Nationalism was, in a sense, the equivalent of the pre-war Home Rule movement but it was markedly shorn of its important supporters.

Why had they deserted? The major reason was that British politics became defined in a different way. Instead of being a fight between the Liberals and the Conservatives in which Home Rule was one of the traditional areas of difference, the central debate became that between capital and the workers and this was expressed by the Conservative and Labour Parties. With the help of the trade unions Labour was able to overtake the Liberals as a major party, and the economic conditions of the 1920s and 1930s pointed up the salience of the economic issues in a particularly uncomfortable way.

Inevitably this meant that the question of how Scotland was to be governed faded. At least as important as this was the way in which the issue was eclipsed. The nineteenth century had given birth to two great movements which challenged the old order: socialism and nationalism. In Britain as a whole and in Scotland in particular, it was socialism which became the major channel for those who wanted to challenge the established order. For various reasons it was in opposition to the other major approach, that of nationalism and thus, while socialism was dominant, nationalism had little chance. Nevertheless, the new nationalist movement was, like socialism and the working class movement generally, an attempt to challenge the existing social order. In this it was quite different from the pre-war Home Rule movement, which did not challenge the basic social order but rather requested a modification of it in order to re-establish Scottish control of Scottish affairs. The articles and speeches of the 'new' nationalists constantly refer to new forms of social justice, the possibility of a republic and the destruction of the British Empire (see Chapter 4). Their arrival was very much the result of the immense trauma suffered by European society as a result of the First World War.

It is the post-1918 nationalist movement that will be studied in this book. It is of this movement that the questions will be asked: why did it arise when it did and why has it taken so long to make any kind of impact? Before we could do this, however, it was important to distinguish it from what had gone on before. It was important to draw the line of distinction because there is an historical overlap. Many of those who were prominent in the cause of Home Rule were not solid members of the Scottish establishment but rather marginal figures who spoke about Scotland in the romantic imagery of central European nationalism. Hanham draws our attention to the interests of people like Professor Blackie or T. D. Wanliss.[10] They were concerned about the status of Gaelic as a language and about the history of Scotland. They shared with German nationalists a fascination for folk ways and for the promotion of a peculiarly Scottish culture. Although they did not propose complete independence for Scotland they had an emotional approach to Scottish nationhood. This was an attitude which was shared by many of the members of the Scots National League. One's thoughts are naturally drawn to events in Ireland where even Sinn Fein started life demanding Home Rule while at the same time presenting the most uncompromising programme for the establishment of a distinctive Irish culture.[11] As in Ireland, so in Scotland a movement existed before 1914 alongside the pressure group heavily based on powerful Scottish interests. This movement tended, however, to be cultural and to be overshadowed in the thrust for Home Rule by the pressure group. After the war it was the movement which became dominant and in a relatively few years it gathered to itself the remnants of those who had had sympathy with the pressure group. This then, was the second confusion between the pre-war and the post-war situations. Not only was there an overlap in language and the imagery used but there were also many individuals who drifted between the two organisations.

There were, however, certain differences which characterised the post-war movement alone. The first was that the element of antiquarian and romantic nationalism was quickly stripped away by Scotland's sudden economic decline. The modern character of the new movement was emphasised not only by its challenging of authority but also by its concentration on the building of a new, stable Scottish economy. The other difference was that the movement lacked leadership which could make a sufficient impact. In the years before the war the Home Rulers could call upon well-known Liberal spokesmen, provosts of the major cities, noblemen, lawyers and clergymen. After the war this support disappeared. For a few years the ILP, in the form of the Clyde group, were speakers at rallies for the SHRA but never for the Scots National League. After that, as in many other spheres of Scottish life, leadership was lacking and leadership with political contacts and feel was really non-existent.

What was Scottish nationalism after 1918? We might expect the nationalism of the post-war years to be a movement of alienation from the existing society, as the socialist movement was. I have suggested that socialism was the more important. Nationalism came to rival socialism, or at least the Labour Party, when Labour itself was seen as part of the established system in Britain. This is not, however, a sufficient explanation. Why should alienation be expressed in terms of nationalism rather than in terms of a more extreme socialism—support for the Communist Party for example? The reason why the nationalist movement rather than any other became important had, I believe, to do with the background of a renewed interest of the Scots in Scotland. In the nineteenth century there were several waves of interest. It was made possible because the Treaty of Union left Scotland as a discrete entity in many senses. In the 1920s and 1930s there was another wave of interest which had few political implications. Indeed, one could say that the National Party of Scotland was one symptom along with others such as the founding of the Royal Scottish Country Dance Society and the publication of a large number of topographical and historical books about Scotland. It was these non-political and political developments which created a general interest in Scotland.

Scottish nationalism as a social movement

In what ways can this account of the rise of nationalism in Scotland use Smelser's framework for studying the development of social movements? In the beginning Smelser argues that we should take note of any aspects of structural conduciveness. In his analysis of Social Credit in Quebec, Pinard uses this idea to identify conditions in certain constituencies. Where the opposition party was particularly weak the new party had a better chance of establishing itself. In other words, the situation was particularly conducive to the rise of the third party in these areas because the major opposition party could not be regarded as a serious alternative. In Scotland we shall see some trace of this feature but there were other aspects of structural conduciveness which were at least as important. The separate nature of Scotland was recognised at the Union and, in the late nineteenth century, there began the building up of modern Scottish institutions whereby administrative powers were devolved to a Department of State in Edinburgh. By the time that the SNP had begun to grow in the early 1960s it was accepted that public affairs in Scotland should be conducted in a special way. Whether this way was satisfactory or not, it was ground on which the nationalists could build. Whereas in the nineteenth century many of the native élites remained important in Scotland, in the twentieth century there was a massive exodus from all strata of the population including those who could have assumed leadership roles. More precisely, decisions about Scottish matters were taken out of Scotland while at the same time institutions were built up. Decisions about social welfare were no longer made by local government but by the Scottish Office, which was regarded as an arm of Whitehall. By the twentieth century the social leaders, in the persons of the landowners and leaders of large businesses, had practically all gone from permanent residence in Scotland. Rokkan notes a difference between Scandinavia and Britain in that the British central culture was upheld and reinforced by a network of landed families whereas in Scandinavia the central culture was essentially a matter for an élite of central officials.[12] For Scotland that merging of the two roles of local leader and representative of the central culture had disappeared by 1919. Few of the gentry lived long enough on their estates to command civic allegiance. The leadership roles were open to a vigorous group of nationalists.

It will be recalled that the second important concept in Smelser's scheme is 'strain'. In Scotland, as in many other places, the dominant strain was economic. In Chapter 5 we shall see that the Scottish economy collapsed immediately after the First World War and, apart from a short period around the Second World War, it has never picked up again. There has, therefore, been widespread continuous unemployment and many firms have been taken over or been closed down. Whereas before 1914 the Clyde valley was an industrial heartland it has now become a derelict ruin of nineteenth century industrialism. This was the dominant concern or strain that absorbed the attention of the nationalists.

I shall argue that the system strain in Scotland has other components. Strain was resolved in the early part of this century by the institutionalisation of social conflict in the Labour and Conservative Parties. In the early 1960s there arose disenchantment with these parties and one aspect of structural strain was that voters no longer understood the major cleavages in society.

It should be underlined, however, that the situation in Britain, or Scotland in particular, cannot be assimilated to those models which have been widely discussed in recent literature. Inglehart's influential article on 'post-bourgeois' politics has very important referents in other parts of Europe but nationalist voters are very much concerned with material questions and the drop in the standard of living.[13] On the other hand, as we shall see, the level of discontent with the existing parties is very like that referred to by Art Miller and many others.[14] It can be said that the support for nationalism arises from strains in certain new groups in Scottish society and that these groups to some extent come from 'post-industrial' situations in the sense that nationalism has tended to grow at an early stage in the new towns. As in the classical 'post-industrial' model, there is a growth in the presence of industrial workers and the dominant industries are based in technology and demand higher levels of education. On the other hand only a small part of the growth in nationalist votes was in constituencies which could be described in this way. I shall argue further that strain in Scotland does not arise from the development of a 'mass society' in which the individual is atomised and intermediate organisations disappear. On the contrary I believe that intermediate organisations have been important in the building up of nationalism.[15] There is one particular group in Scotland which has been attracted to nationalism more than others and for whom alienation has been particularly important. The young have come over to Scottish nationalism in very obvious ways.[16]

I shall argue that their case illustrates very well what has happened in Scotland as a whole. They are alienated from the existing political arrangements, the parties and many of the rules of the game, but this is not because they have become 'atomised'. Pinard notes the importance of young voters for the rise of Social Credit.[17] MacKenzie and Silver, and Butler and Stokes point to the fact that young voters are politically more flexible than their elders for whom the 'habit of voting' is more pronounced,[18] but in Scotland their alienation was expressed in terms of nationalism. I shall try to show that the reason it was expressed in this way was that a new culture was built up. Part of this was the 'youth culture' common to all European youth since the Second World War but part of it involved a new awareness of aspects of Scottish life. Just as for large sections of Scottish youth the folk movement used Scottish symbols, so for other parts of the population other aspects of conditions in Scotland began to concern them more and more.

These new worries over Scotland's economic condition and the deterioration of respect for British institutions constituted severe strains on the Scottish system. The nature of this strain brings our attention to another aspect of nationalism. Gellner and several others have drawn our attention to what nationalism is: 'a movement characteristic of modernisation'.[19] Part of the appeal of the SNP to the young was certainly that the SNP wanted to get rid of the old institutions. We shall see that this applied to Scottish as well as to English institutions. As Kedourie has pointed out, nationalism is a secularising movement which works for the dissolution of traditional institutions that have functioned under the old order.[20] The strain in Scottish society was based on a desire to turn Scotland into a modern prosperous state rather than to remain as a traditional society: rural and industrial, with major economic problems.

It may have been objected that if strain is a major feature in the development of a social movement then those who have suffered most in Scotland have not been the ones to support the party. The nationalist vote has been very low on Clydeside, which has suffered some of the worst conditions in Scotland. One may reply to this that many writers have noticed that it is not those in the worst conditions who lead a new movement.[21] It is at this point that we must discuss the phenomenon of relative deprivation. The danger for social revolt occurs when a group believes itself to be deprived and has expectations of a situation better than its own. This expectation can arise from a comparison with the conditions of another group or it can be based on a comparison of their present experience with past prosperity. We shall explore what data there is on relative deprivation in Scotland.

One of the most interesting stages of Smelser's framework is his development of the 'generalised belief system'. In this the nature of the 'strain' is identified and a remedy is proposed. Scotland is suffering from high levels of unemployment. One explanation of the situation might be that Scottish workers are of a particularly bad quality and manufacturers are trying to leave for this reason. Another might be that the working class in Scotland as elsewhere was suffering from the exploitation of the capitalist system. Finally, the explanation might be that Scotland suffered from being a peripheral part of the British Isles and was ignored by the British government. For each of these explanations there is a range of solutions. For our purposes the most interesting is the final explanation, for which one solution would be that Scotland should take affairs into her own hands by becoming an independent state.

The major argument in the next few chapters will be that the last explanation was widely accepted—that Scotland's troubles came from English negelect—and equally the solution was accepted that greater Scottish control would improve the situation. Greater concern in Scotland for Scottish affairs was fostered by economic, political and social events and this concern concentrated on Scottish explanations and solutions rather than on any of the alternatives, such as the 'class' explanation.

Even given that there was this new emphasis we may ask why the nationalist solution in particular was accepted by so many. It might also be pointed out that many who voted for the SNP did so without apparently supporting the programme of full independence for Scotland. Part of the answer to these questions may be found in examining the nature of generalised belief systems. The other part will become clear when we discuss another of Smelser's stages: the nature of mobilisation.

It is well known that the relation between the ideology of a movement and the attitudes of its followers is not clear. Campbell has remarked:[22]

Most discussions of this problem share an underlying assumption that there need be some basic congruence between the ideology proposed by the élite and the motivation of the mass base. . . . Certainly such movements must have points of strong attractions. But to presume that the mass base is endorsing the ideology as the analyst conceives it, is to presume that such programs—that usually call for change in the pattern of political and economic relationships—are in some real sense comprehended by more than a handful within the mass base. . . . This assumption [is called] into question even for the moderately educated and moderately involved voter.

Pinard argues that it is not necessary for the masses to agree with the ideology of the social movement.[23]

but simply require the development of a generalised belief which identifies the sources of strains in the system and envisages an overall cure. Often in our culture this simply involves identifying the government leaders as evil, and embracing a new slate of leaders who claim to have found all encompassing solutions.

We should also recall a positive reason why voters should have supported the SNP policy. It was a policy which was simple; it provided an easily understood account of the situation and it was available in the sense that an organisation existed to put forward the policy. At the beginning of this century, too, there was discontent with the existing system and, I shall argue, two alternative explanations and solutions existed: the socialist and the nationalist. The socialist explanation was better put and thus had an early success in electoral terms. When the Labour Party became less convincing as a vehicle of protest, the nationalist version of the situation was more acceptable.

The final strand in my argument to explain the rise of the SNP has to do with the stage of mobilisation described by Smelser. Without good organisers the SNP would have got nowhere. When the history of the party is reviewed in the later chapters it will be seen that these highly competent organisers were lacking in the early 1930s when the SNP had some success. Mobilisation on the basis of the belief system was possible because a grass roots organisation was carefully built up. Once the party had achieved its first near misses or even successes, these successes operated as further reasons for supporting the party. It was no longer perceived as useless to cast a vote for the SNP. Thus we may look on the victory at Hamilton as a precipitating event in Smelser's terms. An event like Mrs Ewing's win at Hamilton demonstrated vividly that it was possible for the SNP to be a success. Earlier there was a whole series of precipitating events in many

33

different constituencies. In West Lothian the event which increased the vote for Billy Wolfe was almost certainly the closing of the shale oil workings in 1962.

In conclusion, one may say that Smelser's approach helps us to work through the stages of development of a social movement and to fit an explanation to these stages. The rest of the book is devoted to analysing such an explanation and examining the evidence for it.

Part Two

The chapters in this part of the book examine the development of a new interest in Scottish affairs outside the nationalist movement. It is important to examine these developments, since they formed part of the base from which the SNP upsurge took off. Without them discontent with the British political system might have taken a different form. I shall look, first of all, at the development of interest in Scottish politics, then at the concern for the Scottish economy. These are linked, of course, and in particular have important implications for the future of class politics. Later we shall see how cultural considerations contributed to the development of interest in Scotland and how certain events may have mobilised Scottish youth. We shall also see how other sections of Scottish society—religious and sporting interests, for example—did or did not contribute to these events.

4 The Political Background

The purpose of this chapter is to discuss the political background of Scottish nationalism. A whole set of political events in Scotland, in Britain and in other parts of the world have determined the ways in which Scottish nationalism has developed. It is difficult to be sure that they have had specific effects but this study would be incomplete if it did not draw attention to them. I shall argue that, in the development of politics in the last hundred years, there is both the structural conduciveness for the rise of nationalism and the development of new strains.

A particularly important part of this analysis will be to look at the policies of other parties with regard to decentralisation, Home Rule and Scotland. First, this is important because the decline in support for these parties gave the Nationalists a chance. Secondly, it is necessary to emphasise that the Nationalists are not the only group with an interest in Scotland nor are they the only one who have made plans for a Scottish Parliament. The claim that Scotland in some way merited special treatment was kept alive by at least a minority in the other parties and contributed to the revival of interest in Scotland. What are the relations between these various attitudes? What part does Scotland play in the thinking of other British parties?

I shall review the political background historically starting with the years after the First World War. It is useful to summarise the main points which will be brought out in order to give some idea of the argument.

Historically the first important factor is the collapse after 1918 of the Liberals: the party which had nurtured the policy of Home Rule. This happened for reasons far removed from the ideas of parliamentary devolution but, if this had not happened, the story of Scottish nationalism might have been quite different. With the collapse of the Liberals came the rise of Labour and a 'class' interpretation of the issues in British politics. For the critical years in which national feeling was becoming political in Scotland, the dominant model was one which had little room for national differences. The nature of this approach to politics was heavily underlined by the economic crises. Nationalism's chance came when the 'class alignment' in British politics began to collapse. The saliency of these class issues was no longer as great in the winning and losing of elections and a vacuum was created which, in Scotland, was filled by nationalism.

In the international field two major features were important. The first was that for a great part of the twentieth century when Scottish nationalism was growing, the situation in Europe, or the world as a whole, was such that thoughts of Scottish Home Rule simply seemed irrelevant. The economic crisis was world wide and not confined to Britain. Even more dramatically, the 1920s and 1930s were the time of the rise of the Dictators. The world was too preoccupied by thoughts of fighting a new war to pay much attention to the affairs of Scotland. Home Rule was certainly not on the 'agenda' of British politics. After 1945 there were fears of a third war and these worries seemed less real only at the end of the 1950s. The final point to be brought out is the collapse of Britain as a first class power. Up to the end of the Second World War it was still possible to think of Britain as the centre of an empire. By the beginning of the 1960s the empire had gone. I shall argue that respect for the central authorities of the British state was deeply affected. The structure and attitudes which held British politics together were seriously eroded.

The general account which will be given is, therefore, of a political climate which inhibited, but could not prevent, the rise of nationalism in Scotland. When we look at the history of the movement we shall see that there was a great deal of interest in Scottish Home Rule at the beginning of the century. This did not necessarily express itself in terms of a demand for an independent Scottish state but the plans of Muirhead and Barr called for very generous devolution (see below, Chapter 11). The striking feature of this inter-war period is that the interest died away in the early 1930s and only came back strongly in the 1960s. In approaching the problem of the rise of a social movement I will, therefore, follow Vander Zander in emphasising the importance of examining its opponents.[1] Thus in terms of the 'Value Added Approach' this chapter tackles two stages. It illustrates how British politics was structurally conducive to treating Scottish politics as a separate issue. We shall consider the building up of separate institutions which emphasise this, as well as the failure of the traditional parties to retain control. This chapter will also present evidence to suggest that there were certain political strains which also contributed to the rise of the nationalist vote.

The fate of Home Rule

This study takes the end of the First World War as its starting point. Nevertheless, some events in our period cannot be understood except in terms of their nineteenth century background. A most important part of this background is the issue of Home Rule in British politics. Although there were stirrings of Scottish interest from the 1850s onwards, the source of this policy was Ireland. To solve the 'Irish Question' Gladstone committed the Liberals to a policy of Home Rule first for Ireland and subsequently 'all round'. On this the Liberal Party split between those who followed the leader and those who became Liberal Unionists. In Scotland, as elsewhere, this latter group moved nearer to and eventually joined with the Conservatives. It was this alliance which removed the Liberals from office and with them the likelihood that a separate Parliament would be set up in Scotland. Thus, Home Rule was a major issue of British politics in the 1880s but it was obscured by the dominance of the Conservatives following the Liberal defeat.[2]

There was no doubt, however, that the Liberal Party remained, up to 1914, the only hope for Scottish devolution. It was within this party that the Young Scots were set up: a group of Liberals whose main aim was to encourage Home Rule legislation. It is significant that several of the early members of the nationalist movement, R. E. Muirhead and Tom Gibson prominent among them, were Young Scots. It was also primarily from the Liberals that the pre-war Scottish Home Rule Association drew its members. By 1906, however, when the Liberals came sweeping back into power, the SHRA was moribund and it was the Young Scots who ran meetings and gathered support all over Scotland. They were primarily responsible for setting up the 'Scottish Home Rule Council' consisting of the Scottish Liberal MPs, the leaders of the Scottish Liberal Association and the Young Scots. Perhaps the high water mark of their efforts came when a Scottish Home Rule Bill received its second reading in 1913. It is, however, significant that these organisations were brought into being. If the Liberal Party had been solidly behind Home Rule there would have been no need for them. Their presence is a strong indication of the marginal nature of devolution for the party as a whole.

It was not only in terms of a Parliament for Scotland that the Liberals were important. The present Scottish Office is derived from the establishment by Gladstone of an Under Secretary at the Home Office with responsibility for Scottish affairs. It was the Liberal government which introduced the Secretary for Scotland Bill in 1884 although it was finally enacted by the Conservatives in 1885.

It cannot be said that the Conservatives were thus converted to Home Rule. Although the first Secretaries for Scotland were Tories this represented a desire for administrative devolution and no more. The core of the Tories' policy was opposition to Home Rule in Ireland and it would have been difficult for them to run alongside this a policy for Scottish devolution. Thus, in the period of Conservative power from 1885 to 1906 and again after the war, when there was relatively strong Scottish support for Home Rule, the party in power was the very one which had set its face against this legislation. When Lloyd George agreed to become Prime Minister in 1916 he split the Liberal Party. With the 'Coupon Election' of December 1918, the Liberal Party was effectively destroyed. Those Liberals (a majority) who were refused the 'Coupon', or letter of endorsement, suffered a major setback and many of them were defeated. The Liberal Party strength in Parliament was halved and with this went any serious hope of Home Rule legislation.

The other party to suffer badly in the Coupon Election was Labour. Partly because of previous associations with the Liberals the Labour Party was also associated with support for Home Rule. It was certainly true that a fair proportion of the leaders of the Labour movement in the late nineteenth and early twentieth centuries had been Scots and several of them were prominent Home Rulers. Keir Hardie himself had spoken many times in favour of Home Rule. During the 1888 Mid Lanark by-election he said:[3]

I am strongly in favour of Home Rule being convinced that until we have a Parliament of our own, we cannot obtain the

many and great reforms on which I believe the people of
Scotland have set their hearts.

Another person among the older generation, Bob Smillie, was
consistently associated with this policy. Ramsay MacDonald was a
member of the Scottish Home Rule Association and many of the less
well-known leaders of the Labour movement could also be found
supporting demonstrations and appeals for a Scottish Parliament.[4]
It should not be thought, however, that Home Rule was a
particularly important policy for Labour. Although Scotland was
disproportionately represented in the Labour movement at the
beginning, probably because Clydeside was one of the most exten-
sively industrialised areas in Britain, the majority in the party were
English and the issue of a Scottish Parliament must have been
marginal for them. More than this, important streams of thinking
among socialists denied that nationalism or even decentralisation
had any part in a socialist programme. On the one hand, the
majority of the Marxists agreed that 'the working man has no
country'.[5] Nationalism was a bourgeois movement and between
exploitation by foreigners and exploitation by their fellow nationals
there was not much to choose.[6] Although internationally important,
this point of view did not have much following in Britain. More
important was the thinking exemplified by the Webbs. In *Labour
and the New Social Order* no place was given to separate Parliaments
for Scotland or Wales.[7] For the Webbs, and those like them, a
socialist government would centralise power so that the problems of
capitalism could be dealt with by a powerful and unified force and in
order that the standards of living of workers, wherever they lived in
Britain, could be raised. It was certainly true that into the 1920s and
1930s there were some Scottish socialists who still made speeches
about Home Rule. The most prominent among these were members
of the ILP and in particular the Clydesiders. This was the group
which most consistently kept up their references to a Scottish
Parliament in election literature: in some cases right up to 1945.[8] As
always, James Maxton was the most articulate on this subject. At
times it almost seemed that he was in favour of complete independence for Scotland as when he said at a meeting of the Scottish
Home Rule Association, 'No people of high moral standing with any
soul in them would submit to the domination of an English
Parliament.'[9] As the 1920s wore on, however, there was less and less
of this sort of talk. The Clydesiders who had gone down to their first

Parliament with the promise, at Glasgow's St Enoch Station, that they would soon be back, presumably to work in a Scottish Parliament for Scottish socialism, became a picturesque but powerless sideshow at Westminster.[10]

Just how ineffectual they were in the cause of Home Rule came out when they or their close colleagues introduced two Home Rule Bills. The first was Buchanan's Bill in 1924. George Buchanan was the Labour MP for Glasgow, Gorbals, and had been associated with the Scottish Home Rule Association. The failure of this Bill, despite the support of a majority of Scottish members, made many who favoured Home Rule begin to think of independence. The second Bill was introduced in May 1927 by Rev. James Barr, Labour MP for Motherwell and a very prominent supporter of Home Rule. He was seconded by Tom Johnston, later a distinguished Secretary of State and the editor of the Scottish socialist journal *Forward*. Table 4.1 shows that under Labour and Liberal governments, both in theory committed to establishing a Scottish legislature, the outcome was

Table 4.1   Some Home Rule Bills and Motions

Date	Nature	Result	Scottish vote For	Against
1889	Scottish Home Rule Motion	Defeat	19	22
1893	Scottish Home Rule Motion	Defeat	37	22
1894	Scottish Home Rule Motion	Carried	35	21
1908	Scottish Home Rule Bill	1st reading carried	44	9
1911	Scottish Home Rule Bill	1st reading carried	31	4
1912	Scottish Home Rule Motion	Carried	43	6
1913	Scottish Home Rule Bill	2nd reading carried	45	8
1914	Scottish Home Rule Bill	2nd reading adjourned	—	—
1919	Scottish Home Rule Bill	2nd reading counted out	—	—
1920	Scottish Home Rule Bill	Closure carried	38	9
1922	Government of Scotland Bill	2nd reading talked out		
1924	Government of Scotland Bill	2nd reading talked out		
1926	Government of Scotland Bill	Introduced		
1927	Government of Scotland Bill	2nd reading talked out		

the same. Despite some majorities in the House for motions and even for second readings and despite the regular support of a majority of Scottish members, neither party made the major effort needed to get the legislation through.

Admittedly, in the case of the minority Labour government in 1924 under which Buchanan introduced his Bill as Private Members' Business, there was not much chance of getting a sufficient majority for it but some arrangement could have been made with the Liberals—together with Labour they had a majority in the House. When Barr and Johnston introduced their measure it would have been easier, but Prime Minister MacDonald, a past official in the Scottish Home Rule Association, clearly did not think that this was a measure which was important enough to warrant a commitment of government time. Given the make-up of the Labour Party then and the crises through which Britain was passing he had a good case.

We could not leave this section on the decline of interest in Home Rule without saying something about John Maclean. Until the end of the First World War Maclean was perhaps the most popular of communist propagandists and educators working in and around Glasgow. He was imprisoned several times and the fact that he was prepared to suffer in this way seems to have given him a particular place in the regard of his working class audiences. The fact that is best remembered about him is that he broke away from the British Socialist Party (the forerunner of the Communist Party) by arguing for the establishment of a Scottish workers' republic. In a later chapter dealing with the beginnings of the national movement I shall refer to his contacts with Erskine of Marr, a co-founder of the first organisation working for Scottish independence. Maclean seems to have been brought to this position partly because his Highland background made him believe that Scotland should go back to a kind of primitive Celtic communism. Much more important, however, was his belief that the Scottish proletariat was more advanced than the workers of England and consequently socialism had a better and earlier chance north of the Tweed. The first strike of the war had been in 1915 on Clydeside, considerably earlier than the better-known Welsh miners' strike. The wartime Clyde Workers Committee was notoriously militant and had pressed, not simply for better pay but also for social and economic policies which touched many parts of the national life.[11] Maclean summed up this argument in his election address when standing in Glasgow, Gorbals, in 1922:[12]

Scotland's wisest policy is to declare for a Republic in Scotland so that the youth of Scotland will not be forced out to die for England's markets. I accordingly stand out as a Scottish Republican candidate feeling sure that, if Scotland had to elect a parliament to sit in Scotland it would vote for a working class Parliament . . . The Social Revolution is possible sooner in Scotland than in England. The working class policy ought to be to break up the Empire to avert war and to enable the workers to triumph in every country and colony. Scottish separation is part of the process of England's imperial disintegration and is a help toward the ultimate triumph of the workers of the world.

Maclean's daughter, Mrs Nan Milton, has argued that his ideas were first formed around 1919 with the feeling that the Scottish workers had been betrayed by their leaders in London. She draws attention to the final *Strike Bulletin*[13] of the Clyde Workers Committee which said,[14]

London Executives don't understand our aspirations here and never take the trouble to find out what is wrong when a strike occurs. We have to emancipate ourselves from the dictatorship of the London junta by building an organisation which will be under our control.

Whether this was the precise start of Maclean's thinking on this matter or not, these were important arguments for him.

After the Second World War and especially in the 1960s, Maclean became a cult figure in the Scottish left. Although he was popular while he lived, there is no evidence to suggest that many followed him in his ideas of a Scottish Workers' Republic and, despite the annual Silent March to commemorate his death, his name was known to fewer and fewer until a Rally sponsored by the British-Soviet Friendship Society in 1948. The Communist Party itself rejected the idea of an independent Scotland.

To sum up, the parties which supported Home Rule at the beginning of the century were either smashed as in the case of the Liberals or gave less and less attention to it as in the case of Labour. Although individual Conservatives and Communists were favourable, the policy of their parties was opposed to the idea. It was not surprising that the Speaker's Conference on Home Rule reported in 1920 in favour of a very much watered down and awkward form of devolution. The proposals were quickly forgotten.[15]

Part Two

Crisis in Britain, crisis in the world

The world of 1914 was significantly different from that of 1920 when the first nationalist organisations were founded. Some of these differences provide the background for understanding these latter events.

At the beginning of the century Britain controlled a worldwide empire, her fleet was still able to control the sea lanes all over the world and, although both her naval power and her industries were challenged, she was one of the three major industrial world powers if not the first of all. At home the pomp and self-satisfaction of empire had been encapsulated in the Queen's Jubilee. Most of the anti-monarchist and anti-establishment feeling of the mid-century had given way to an unquestioned pride in being British and, for most people, the Boer War saw a rise in fervid British jingoism.

The Boer War was also the time when the self-confidence of the empire began to show a few cracks. The British army was challenged by a handful of Dutch farmers. It was after 1918, however, that Britain's world position began to crumble. Her survival had depended largely on the entry into the war of the United States. Britain could not ignore the fact that this great country was now on the way to a world position which would only be obscured by the United States' own hesitation in exploiting it.

There can be no doubt that the First World War was a horrific experience for those who went through it. There were not many British families that did not lose a son or a father, and the privations and the carnage suffered by the men in the trenches now seem almost unbelievable. A general reaction rejecting authority was very evident. Among the rich, social life became hectic and the 'abandoned' dances of the period mark the change very clearly. Among the poets and intellectuals there was a spate of writing which expressed disillusion with the conduct of the war and those who were still conducting the nation's business. It was a time when many of the best European intellects drew attention to the decay of western European civilisation. There was a distinct rejection of the idea of patriotism and the sacredness of authority. Among ordinary people the end of the war also brought turmoil. Some of this is clearly remembered such as the Troubles in Ireland but there was also mutiny in the army and the navy, a police strike and many soldiers and sailors, returning from the war to a housing shortage, squatted in empty property. Abroad, the Russian Revolution and similar episodes in Germany and Hungary formed the background to the rise of a revolutionary movement: the British Communist Party. With this political and social turmoil it is not surprising to find that new movements were founded and, among them, an organisation working for Scottish independence was not out of place. As MacDiarmid and others pointed out, the war was supposed to be for the rights of little nations. Apart from this, however, the decline of the old structures of authority must have led people to think of other possibilities.

The possibility of Scotland as a small independent nation might have been brought to mind by what was happening in Ireland. One of the curious features of the early Scottish nationalist literature is that Ireland is relatively seldom mentioned. One reason is that, by 1928 when the National Party of Scotland was founded, Ireland was a dead issue in British politics. The early papers of the Scots National League and the Scottish Home Rule Association do refer to Ireland: to the principle of Irish independence, to the atrocities committed by the Black and Tans and so forth. We shall see that there were individual members of the SNL especially who learnt from what had happened in Ireland but the interesting point is that Ireland is not a recurring theme for the nationalists. On the contrary, the model which is held up again and again is that of modern Scandinavian democracy. Norway, which gained its independence in 1906, and later Denmark and Sweden are used again and again by nationalists like Muirhead, Kinloch and Dr Archie Lamont as the types of society that the new Scotland should become.[16]

One may speculate that the events in Ireland had other effects on Scotland. There have been many who feared for Scotland a repetition of the violence in Ireland. What happened in Ireland probably encouraged the Conservatives to set their faces even harder against Scottish Home Rule. The Scottish business community seems to have believed that independence for Scotland, as for Ireland, would lead to economic stagnation. All these reasons may have contributed to the playing down of Ireland by the Scottish nationalists. I shall argue that other factors including the very nature of the nationalist movement, were also important.

The range of these possibilities was, however, strictly limited by what happened next. By 1921 the economic situation was extremely grave. I shall discuss this in Chapter 5 but here it is sufficient to say that unemployment became the dominating issue of politics. Before the war, it had been low. Suddenly it became extremely high and nowhere was this more true than in Scotland. For men lucky enough to have jobs, wages were low and, in general, the major political concerns of the time were those of economic survival rather than national pride. The nationalists were to draw attention to the extent of the economic trouble in Scotland but their solutions did not seem directly relevant to many voters.

The Marxist analysis of the class situation was accepted by only a minority. On the other hand, the whole rhetoric of British politics was now to be couched in class terms and post-war events went on emphasising the importance of this interpretation. Although the Labour Party lost its most prominent leaders in the Coupon election; MacDonald, Snowden and Henderson were all defeated, it actually increased the number of seats from forty-two to fifty-nine. Despite temporary drawbacks, Labour was to go on increasing its representation at Westminster. The trade union support for Labour consolidated with the further growth of trade union strength. A series of amalgamations resulted in the setting up of very large unions: the Amalgamated Engineering Union in 1920, the Transport and General Workers and the General and Municipal Workers in 1924. In 1926 the General Strike again underlined the saliency of economic issues rather than national issues and the slumps of 1929 and the years immediately following did more to establish the class model as the dominant model of British politics. In Scotland events were often violent. Mowat has exploded the myth that the General Strike was carried on in an atmosphere of strikers and policemen playing an eternal game of football. Food lorries were stoned, hand-to-hand fighting was common and, on 5 May Glasgow police charged crowds of demonstrators. The pages of the *British Gazette* are witnesses of the depth of class feeling that was engendered.[17]

For Scotland, the effect of this was much the same as for other parts of Britain which had founded their prosperity on heavy industry but there was another dimension. A great many of those who had given some of their early energies to the cause of Home Rule effectively abandoned it. If we compare those Scots who led the national movement with those who were in the first ranks of the Labour leaders it is difficult to avoid the impression that the latter were more able. Where the nationalists had one outstanding public speaker, MacCormick, the Labour Party could put forward MacDonald, Maxton, Kirkwood and many others. The nationalists had no journalist to compare with Tom Johnston and, in general, it is difficult to argue that they had many at all who had a firm grasp of the nature of politics. On the question of leadership it is difficult to be conclusive but it is also unrealistic to ignore the impression that a large proportion of those early nationalists lived in a political Never-Never land at a time when the socialists were coming into the real world.

The crises outside Britain

The real world of international relations also contributed to the political background of nationalism. I have argued that, had there been no war, some measure of Home Rule would have been on the statute book by 1920. In the same way the rise of the Dictators in Europe led to an international situation in which Scots, in common with other British people, worried more about the threat of a new war than a new Parliament in Edinburgh. By the time that the SNP was founded in 1934 Italy and Germany were effectively in the hands of men who planned to use war in order to secure their ends. If many hoped that there would be no war, almost everyone knew that it was a possibility. As the world drifted towards 1939, Abyssinia, Spain and Czechoslovakia were only a few of the countries which absorbed the attention of those at home. With the start of the war public attention was fixed firmly on the battle front and, for all too long, on the battle for survival. We shall see that this was also a time when the SNP did particularly well at by-elections. Their vote was ephemeral: a protest vote and with the peace there came a return to traditional political loyalties. More than any previous election the one in 1945 was fought as a contest between Labour and Conservative.

While we are looking at the international position it is worth remembering that fear of war did not end with 1945. On the contrary the Cold War soon raised the fear that a 'hot' war might soon come along. This did come in the shape of the Korean War and the fear died away only in the late 1950s. In fact, as far as the international situation was concerned, the late 1950s was the first time when home affairs were unrivalled by worry about the possibility of foreign wars. For the first time the people of this country were at the centre of their own stage. It may be significant that, in the first years of the 1960s, the nationalist movement started to expand.

There were two other types of external event which had little to do with world wars but which seem to have affected Britain's conception of herself. I have drawn attention to the fact that this kingdom had started the century as the centre of a large empire. The years after 1945 saw its break up. Most traumatically, India went in 1947 and by the early 1960s the African possessions, the Gold Coast, Nigeria, Kenya and the others had also gone. There was no question that Britain was any longer an imperial power. Scotsmen and other Britons who once felt that their own status was increased by being citizens of an empire, could no longer feel this way.

As if to underline the change in Britain's status, the Suez affair in 1956 showed how Britain was dependent on the goodwill of the United States. The disgrace of this unsuccessful adventure was reflected in the British Press. Although its direct importance may not have got through to the man in the Clydebank Shipyard or the ploughman in the parks of the Mearns, Suez was an outward and visible sign of Britain's decline as a great power. From now on, whatever the *Scottish Daily Express* might think, the United Kingdom was to have a very restricted role in world affairs.

Thus Britain went into the 1960s shorn of her imperial splendour. At the same time she became more prosperous than for many years. The austerities of the 1940s and 1950s had gone but the new wealth existed alongside a feeling almost of irresponsibility. This was, after all, the swinging sixties. Britain seemed released from the cares and self-consciousness of being a world power.

Politics in Scotland: the parties' attitudes to Home Rule

Let us now retrace our steps and look at what was happening in Scotland and at the attitudes of the parties to Scotland.

Despite all the external events which drew the Scots' attention from Scotland, things did happen in Scotland and to Scotland. In the years from the end of Home Rule as a serious issue in British politics to the 1960s when the SNP expanded dramatically, several points are worth noticing.

First, and most directly, the government was aware of Scotland as a part of Britain which had to have some special treatment. This was over and above the development of a regional policy for the relief of unemployment. A committee was established under Sir Geoffrey Collins. This recommended, among other things, that the Scottish Office should be concentrated in Edinburgh instead of having its main offices in Dover House in London. As a result of this St Andrew's House was opened in Edinburgh in 1939. For the Conservatives, however, this was as far as devolution should go. It cannot be said that the other British parties were, in practice, any more enthusiastic about a Scottish Parliament.

Let us look first at the Liberal Party. It played a less and less important role in Scottish politics and the story is quickly told. It was probably always true that although a Scottish Parliament was official Liberal policy the English majority of MPs were much less convinced of its importance. The Liberal Party was able to keep Home Rule as a part of its programme while never being put to the test as to whether it would actually work for the measure. As far as the Scottish Liberals were concerned there was a large number who were convinced of the need for a Scottish Parliament. It is worth noticing that there was a separate Scottish Liberal Party set-up.[18] The leader of the Scottish Liberals in the inter-war years, Sir Archibald Sinclair, was sympathetic to the idea of Scottish Home Rule[19] and Lady Glen-coats was a collaborator with John MacCormick both when he was in the SNP and later in the Covenant Movement. Many Liberals were prominent in Scottish Convention after 1945, including the author Nigel Tranter and some Liberals who first came into Scottish politics through the Covenant later joined the SNP. This last point is probably one of the reasons why, in 1966, after having hardly mentioned Scottish Home Rule for many years, the Liberal MP for Inverness, Russell Johnston, introduced the first Home Rule Bill since 1926. It contained provisions for a Scottish Parliament with power over domestic and financial affairs as part of a 'federalisation' of Britain. The reaction to this proposal was a fascinating comment on the attitudes of the major parties and on the way they have changed. The Bill was supported by all the Liberal MPs, but the general reaction in the House was one of hilarious amusement. Characteristic of the comments was the suggestion that a second Hadrian's Wall should be built. Johnson's introduction of the first reading was greeted with catcalls and jeers. The Bill failed to get a second reading when, in May of the following year, a government whip objected.

It is more interesting to follow the course of the Labour Party's policy for Scotland. In the election of 1931 they were heavily defeated. The number of seats held by them declined from 287 to 52 and few of the leaders of the party were returned. Under these circumstances Labour, like any other party out of power, could appeal to as many interests as possible. One such was Scotland. It cannot be said that there were problems in Scotland at this time which were peculiar to Scotland and which called forth a peculiar

Labour policy. It was certainly true that some prominent Labour people were strong Home Rulers and the Labour Party made sympathetic gestures in this direction but this did not include any mention of Home Rule in Labour election manifestos at the 1935 election.

No one in the Labour Party was more identified with Home Rule than was Tom Johnston. He was, moreover, a person with experience of government having been Under Secretary for Scotland in the 1929 administration. In the years immediately before the war Labour's real interest in Scottish devolution was low but Johnston, along with some colleagues, established the London Scots Self-Government Committee in about 1937. At the beginning of their first publication was a quotation from a speech made by Johnston in Edinburgh in 1936, 'Scotland must have a legislative assembly of its own to deal with its own special grievances and meet its own special needs.' This organisation owed a great deal to the energies of Mrs Norrie Fraser, a Scots woman living in London at that time. Although Johnston may have been the first president and the inspiration, it was Mrs Fraser who held the committee together and who was responsible for much of its publishing. Its aim was stated in a pamphlet, *The New Scotland*.[20]

> This committee takes its stand on a framework of British Federalism with individual legislation for the internal affairs of each nation and a Federal Parliament at Westminster for Commonwealth business. . . . Under this Federal Plan economic separation would be avoided. Equally, this committee believes that it is only through Labour and progressive politics that Scots self government can be brought about.

It seems quite clear that the legislation which was being proposed for Scotland was very much along the lines of the Bills of Barr and Buchanan. Indeed, there seems to have been an attempt to resurrect Barr's Bill in 1939 but the war intervened. We should recognise, however, that the London Scots Self-Government Committee were a left wing socialist group which, like Maclean, saw self-government as an opportunity to establish socialism. In her introduction to *The New Scotland* Mrs Fraser wrote, 'I believe that the only way for Scotland is socialism applied by a Scottish Parliament.' This also came out quite clearly from the scorn that was poured on the Scottish Development Council which had been set up by industrialists.[21] The committee recognised that it was not going to bring in Home Rule by working on that platform alone.[22]

For ten years National candidates have been standing on the self-government issue alone and none have yet been elected. The reason is not far to seek. Electors do not vote on purely political issues, however admirable the unself-seeking enthusiasms of a party like the SNP which propounds them, but on bread and butter economic issues.

It often seems as if members of the committee rather regretted this and stood near to the SNP position on independence. Tom Burns, one of its most prominent members, said, for example:

The only federation Scotland should aim at entering and establishing and to which she should consider yielding up any portion of her sovereignty is a free union of equal self-governing democracies not dominated or led by any benevolent Big Power.

It was also notable that several of the articles in *The New Scotland* and later in their journal[23] were written by nationalists, for example, Robert Hurd and Hugh MacDiarmid.

In this committee there was therefore a group of Scottish members of the Labour Party who were working for a very considerable measure of Home Rule. It should be noticed that, at the beginning, they were Scots in London. Their strategy was that, if anything was to be achieved, London was the place to apply the pressure. In London were the major decision makers of the Labour Party and, indeed, the centres of government generally. They held meetings in Gatti's restaurant and in the house of Naomi Mitchison, whose husband was then an MP. She was a Vice-Chairman of the committee. They were very concerned to enlist support from non-Scottish members of the Labour Party. Both Herbert Morrison and Clement Attlee came to one or other of their meetings and Attlee, then the Leader of the Labour Party, wrote the preface to *The New Scotland*.

There was at one time a tendency among Socialists to underrate the force of national sentiment. Today we ought all to recognise that nationalism has an immense attractive force for good or evil. Suppressed it may poison the political life of a nation. Given its proper place it can enrich it. The London Scots Self-Government Committee and Mr Tom Burns are to be

53

commended for having got down to practical proposals as a
basis of discussion.

This was a long way short of a commitment of Labour to a
Scottish Parliament but it is interesting that Attlee should have
thought it worthwhile to write the preface at all.

At the outset the committee found some difficulty in making
contacts and getting support in Scotland itself but, with the war,
many of its members, including Mrs Fraser, went back to Scotland.
Johnston himself had dropped out of active membership of the
committee when he became Secretary of State for Scotland but it
was significant that in 1941, for the first time in many years, the
Labour Party Conference in Scotland passed a resolution in favour
of a Scottish Parliament. This was expressed in a handout circulated
at the conference. 'We advocate the establishment of an executive
authority in Scotland with legislative and administrative powers to
deal a) with matters which have solely Scottish importance, b) with
the Scottish aspects of social and industrial legislation.'[24] During
these war years, and for a short time after this, the committee's
journal had many articles from Labour MPs and general support in
the country. In 1942 it changed its name to 'The Scottish
Reconstruction Committee' and a rising proportion of journal
articles was concerned with the exploitation of Scotland's natural
resources and other questions dealing with the Scottish economy.
What is equally interesting is that the proportion of articles directly
mentioning a Scottish Parliament had diminished by 1948 when
their journal ceased publication. There is little evidence that the
Scottish Reconstruction Committee retained much of an interest in
Scottish Home Rule although it was deeply concerned about
Scotland. The emphasis of national politics and, indeed, Labour
politics in the nation had changed and we must now turn to see why
this had happened.

One reason was the change in the attitude of Johnston himself.
When he first became Secretary of State in the War Cabinet he was
keen to set up institutional means for self-government. Perhaps the
best known was his Scottish Advisory Council of Ex-Secretaries of
State, called 'The Council of State' by the press. In this he brought
together politicians of all parties such as Lord Alness, Sir Archibald
Sinclair and Walter Elliot. Johnston says of it:[25]

We promised to collaborate in surveying problems of post-war
reconstruction in Scotland and it was understood that one

binding article of association was that, when we got unanimity, we would each of us do our utmost with our political associates outside to get concurrence from them too.

Johnston also arranged for the Scottish Members of Parliament to meet together in Edinburgh to discuss Scottish affairs and to meet the Scottish civil servants working in St Andrew's House. The fact was, however, that both these innovations were abortive. The 'Council of State' hardly ever met and achieved nothing. The meeting of Scottish MPs which seems to have been intended to inaugurate a series of meetings of the Scottish Grand Committee in Scotland, attracted only twenty-eight of the seventy-four Scots MPs and the experiment was abandoned. Johnston may have lost his enthusiasm for legislative innovation as a result of these failures. Others of his innovations were more successful. He set up a series of committees dealing with various aspects of the Scottish economy: on the herring industry, on white fish, on hydro-electric power and so forth, and asked a wide selection of Scots to serve on them. Apart from the information and proposals that they brought in, this was a clear indication that there was an enthusiasm in Scotland for post-war reconstruction. This mood prevailed during the war and for several years after and a great deal of its strength must be put down to Johnston's enthusiasm and organising ability. It also meant that he postponed the legislative reform of Scotland in favour of an economic one. He expressed this quite clearly in his autobiography.[26]

For many years past I have become increasingly more uneasy lest we should get political power without first having or at least simultaneously having, an adequate economy to administer. What purpose would there be in getting a Scots Parliament in Edinburgh if it has to administer an emigration system, a glorified Poor Law and a graveyard. . . . Hence the reason why, although I seconded my friend the Rev. James Barr's Home Rule Bill . . . I also was resolved upon the establishment of the Council of Industry.

This last is a reference to the fact that another of Johnston's achievements was the establishment of 'The Scottish Council' which elaborated 'The Scottish Development Council' by adding trade union and government representatives to the industrialists.

By the end of the war Johnston had effectively abandoned the idea of a Scottish legislature in favour of the rebuilding of the Scottish economy. It was significant that he resigned as Secretary of State in order to become Chairman of the Hydro-Electric Board whose aim was to bring prosperity to the Highlands while exploiting a new source of energy.

Johnston's change of heart helped to weaken Home Rule sentiment in the Labour Party. Nevertheless, there were sufficient people interested in devolution to pass by ninety-seven to sixty-seven a resolution at the Conference of the Scottish Council of the Labour Party in 1945 urging that the possibility of Home Rule should be examined. At the 1946 conference there was no reference to this and in 1947 a resolution was passed by 119 to 82 regretting that the Executive had not taken action on the basis of the 1945 resolution.

Three things seem to have happened. Johnston no longer gave the leadership necessary to the Home Rule cause, the country was taken up with the establishment of the Welfare State and the Scottish Convention, set up by the ex-secretary of the SNP, John MacCormick, was seen as a criticism of, and threat to, the Labour government. With the government so hard pressed Labour MPs and activists were urged not to take an active part in the Convention and not to press for Home Rule which was very peripheral to the interests of the majority of people in the Labour movement. The comments of P. J. Dolan, Scottish editor of the *Daily Herald*, were particularly bitter in their criticism of the Convention. For him Home Rule was irrelevant to the needs of Scotland. Interest in Home Rule did not die away altogether in the Labour Party. At the 1955 conference of the Scottish Council of the Labour Party and again in 1958 resolutions were put forward but it was not until the late 1960s that the issue was again taken up.

Before we move to that it is interesting to reflect on the role of the Scottish Reconstruction Committee. It spearheaded a revival of Labour interest in a Scottish Parliament in the 1940s and up to 1945 it maintained this interest. It did, for example, send questionnaires to candidates at the 1945 election: 'As a Scottish MP would you support a measure to establish a legislature in Scotland?'[27] The post-war conditions made this inappropriate and the Committee took refuge in studies of the Scottish economy. It may have been one of the fruits of these efforts as well as of more direct political pressure from the Scottish Convention that the White Paper *Scottish Affairs* was issued.[28] Following this, House of Commons Standing Orders were amended so that technical and non-controversial Bills affecting Scotland only went to a Scottish Standing Committee if there was no objection by ten or more MPs.

In the long years of opposition between 1951 and 1964 Labour did not even flirt with the Home Rule vote. A few isolated voices were raised at Conference of the Scottish Council of the Labour Party. In 1958 John Bayne tried to get a discussion on Home Rule but for practical purposes Labour ignored the issue of a Scottish Parliament.

These were years of great bitterness for the Labour movement. Especially after their defeat at the 1959 election many despaired of ever winning office.[29] One effect of this was the renewed power of radical organisations outside the Labour Party in the New Left Club and the Campaign for Nuclear Disarmament. For many people there was the feeling that radical changes in the party had to come from these sources. It is worth noticing that quite a few of those later prominent in the SNP, the Chairman, Billy Wolfe, the winner of the Hamilton by-election in 1967, Mrs Ewing, and several others, were prominent in CND and several of them still are. There was a general feeling especially among middle class radicals that the Labour Party was foundering and that leadership had to come from outside. In general these were days when there was an enormous excitement in Britain for new policies but, on the whole, the excitement was sited outside the party.

In 1964 Labour came in again preaching the 'Technological Revolution'. This might not be an entrancing slogan but even less entrancing was the fact that the British economy did not pick up. There were a few years of prosperity but by the end of the 1960s it was quite clear that the economy was troubled and that unemployment was rising. The Labour government, which had had such a honeymoon only a few years before, lost the 1970 election apparently because it was not able to deliver the economic goods which it had promised.

Labour's position on devolution while it was in office was clear. When the Prime Minister was asked in April 1967 in the Commons what measure of legislative devolution was planned by his government, Mr Wilson replied, 'If you mean plans for separate Parliaments for Scotland and Wales, the answer is none.' This answer stood in sharp contrast to the early Labour Party position.

By November 1967, however, the finality of Mr Wilson's parliamentary answer was being eroded. Cabinet level consideration was given to devolution for Scotland and Wales. The major impetus for this radical alteration was a SNP by-election victory in Hamilton. While the British Labour Party was moving in a devolutionist direction, the Labour Party in Scotland, under the leadership of

William Ross, the Secretary of State for Scotland, was loath to support Home Rule. Indeed, it was the National Executive of the Labour Party, in December 1967, which asked the Scottish Executive to make a pronouncement on devolution. At the Scottish Conference in March 1968 a resolution was passed deploring separation. No call was made for a Scottish Parliament or Assembly. Broadly speaking, the Scottish Labour Party asked that the maximum freedom over her own decisions should be given to Scotland within the existing constitutional arrangements. A call was not even made for the Scottish Grand Committee to sit in Edinburgh.

In its evidence to the Crowther (later the Kilbrandon) Commission on the Constitution, set up by the Labour government in 1968, the Labour Party in Scotland also rejected the principle of a separate Scottish Parliament or Assembly.[30] They supported 'the principle of maximum self-government for Scotland with the right to remain in the United Kingdom Parliament and to continue full representation there'. To implement this principle they suggested that the Scottish Grand Committee should have some sittings in Edinburgh and that there should be more power given to the Scottish Economic Planning Council. They also suggested that the Wheatley reform of local government would mean, in practice, more devolution of decision making to Scotland through the new regional governments. In short, the party had decided that some institutional expression should be given to devolutionist sentiment.

In October 1973, several days before the Kilbrandon Commission report was published, the Labour Party in Scotland published a further document calling for an expanded role for the Scottish Grand Committee. They suggested that this committee, or its descendant, should take the important stages of Scottish legislation and also fulfil the function of the Select Committee on Scottish Affairs. Despite the growth of support within the party for devolution, the Executive's proposal underlined the fact that 'we are of the opinion that an Assembly other than a Committee of the UK Parliament would be a mere talking shop and would not attract the right calibre of people'.[31] This remained official party policy, despite considerable debate within the party, until after the general election of February 1974.

The success of the SNP in February convinced the National Executive of the party that more account must be taken of the demand for devolution. Once again, they asked the Scottish Executive to prepare a statement on devolution. In March 1974 the

Scottish Labour Conference adopted a resolution in favour of a Scottish Assembly.[32] In June 1974, however, the Scottish Executive narrowly rejected the idea. This was followed by an endorsement of an assembly by the National Executive Committee. In this confused situation, it was decided to have a special Scottish Conference solely to decide the policy on devolution. The Scottish Executive prepared a number of propositions for this conference to accept or reject. Propositions 3 and 5 were mutually contradictory. Proposition 3 read: 'This conference opposes the setting up of a Scottish Assembly as being irrelevant to the needs and aspirations of the people of Scotland.' This was, in other words, the position of the Labour Party in the February election.

The other proposition (5) represented the policy pressed on the Scottish Executive by both the NEC and elements within the Labour Party in Scotland.

This conference recognises the desire of the Scottish people for a greater say in the running of the country and welcomes the setting up of a directly elected Scottish Assembly with legislative powers within the context of the political and economic unity of the United Kingdom.

On 18 August 1974, this latter proposition was supported by a four to one majority at the special conference.[33] In September, the Labour government issued a white paper on 'Democracy and Devolution' committing themselves to the establishment of a directly elected Scottish Assembly with considerable control over domestic affairs.[34] The Assembly was to be financed by bloc grants from the UK government, however, and the degree of control over the economy was not specified. The Labour Party in Scotland also issued a manifesto which promised an Assembly. Labour was, once again, a party of devolution.

We have seen that the Labour Party was not a willing exponent of the idea of Home Rule. There were always people in it who supported the proposition that Scotland should have its own Parliament but they were seldom in the majority until the early 1970s. In the Conservative Party we shall find even less enthusiasm.

When the Labour government fell in 1951 the Conservatives had not even flirted with Scottish devolution as a tactic. We have seen that the whole history of the party was opposed to the idea but at this point some other points might be made. As we should expect from a party largely led by the upper class, it was very anglicised. The majority of these leaders might be of Scottish origin but they were largely educated in England and their orientation was towards the centre of government which was, obviously, in London. There is little evidence before the war of any specifically Scottish interest by a Scottish Conservative MP. Some of them were diligent and popular constituency MPs but the Scottish dimension was one that they hardly touched. This does not mean that they did not speak about Scotland but, when they did, there is hardly anything to show that they considered serious answers to Scottish problems. They occasionally expressed a pride in being Scottish but these sentiments were seldom linked to practical measures for Scotland in particular. Robert Boothby, though more articulate than most of them, is typical.[35]

> We [Scotland] continue to produce the best ships, the best beef, the best oats and the best whisky known to man. Our engineers, craftsmen, miners, farmers and fishermen still hold their own against all-comers. And when all is said and done, no nation of her size has ever exercised a comparable impact and influence upon the outside world.

There is little evidence that Scotland's economic situation is even recognised.

Another indication of a lack of the Scottish dimension in Conservative thinking lies in the fact that, up to 1965, the main organisation of the party was on the basis of two divisional councils; one with its headquarters in Glasgow and the other in Edinburgh. The two secretaries of the two Divisional Councils were extremely powerful and, although there was a central Council of the Unionist Party in Scotland, it rarely met. There was a brief annual meeting before the Conference each year but usually the business there was formal. The two Divisional Councils raised their own finance and decided on their own tactics. Relations between the two councils were not close. A more powerful co-ordinating force was exercised through the Office of the Scottish Whip. The Secretary to the Scottish Whip was, before 1965 at least, the major link between Scottish opinion and the Parliamentary Party. After 1965 when the party was reformed the major co-ordinating body became the office of the Chairman of the Party in Scotland. Previous to this there had been a President of the Unionist Association, a post which was held alternatively by the Conveners of each Divisional Council. After 1965 the administration of the party was concentrated in Edinburgh.

These organisational points do, however, run ahead of an account of Conservative policy for Scotland and the actions of Conservative governments after 1965.

One of the early actions of the Conservative administration when it came to power in 1951 was to set up a Royal Commission on Scottish Affairs: the Balfour Commission.[36] This reported in 1954 and recommended that 'Scotland's needs and points of view should be known and brought into account at all stages in the formation and execution of policies'. In effect, very little was accomplished by the report of this commission other than the addition of a new Minister of State at the Scottish Office, a commitment which had been in the 1950 Conservative party policy statement for the general election.

The 1950s perhaps saw the lowest point in the fortunes of the SNP. They were years of austerity and drabness, although unemployment in Scotland was not particularly bad partly because of the need for re-armament.[37] In the late 1950s prosperity began to return to the whole of Britain. This was the era of 'Butskellism'[38] and what appeared to be a narrowing gap between the policies of the two major parties.

It cannot be said that the Conservative government, any more than the Labour opposition, took special steps to attend to the situation in Scotland. When the Conservatives won yet again at the 1959 election a great deal of the heat went out of Labour in Scotland as elsewhere. It would have to be said, however, that the Conservatives had pulled and pushed some major industries into Scotland: the building of the car factories at Linwood and Bathgate, for example. From the point of view of effectiveness one might have been forgiven for thinking that Conservative governments were as good for Scotland as Labour ones. Nevertheless, Labour did better in Scotland than in the whole country at the 1959 election. In 1964, despite the presence of a Scottish Prime Minister, Sir Alec Douglas-Home, the Conservatives lost the election.

Perhaps because of their position in opposition the Conservatives, uncharacteristically, were the first to react to the situation with proposals for devolution. Mr Heath, the Conservative Opposition leader, proposed at the Scottish Conference of the Conservative Party in 1969 that an elected Scottish Assembly should be established with substantial power over domestic affairs. This was the

'Declaration of Perth'. The proposal had a mixed reception. Never-theless, a Constitutional Commission under the chairmanship of Sir Alec Douglas-Home was set up to consider the matter. This unofficial commission proposed in March 1970 that a directly elected assembly be established with 125 members to meet in Edinburgh for forty days a year and discuss Scottish legislation. Subsequently, the Scottish Tories endorsed the general motion of an Assembly by large, if unenthusiastic, majorities.

They were not in a hurry to implement these proposals. At the Scottish Conservative Conference in May 1973 a motion calling for the Conservative government to hasten the establishment of a Scottish Assembly was defeated decisively. The then Secretary of State for Scotland, Gordon Campbell, indicated that there was no possibility of setting up such as assembly in the life of the present Parliament. The rejection of the motion was widely interpreted as a severe setback for the proposal. Mr Heath stated, however, that his government would continue with plans for the establishment of an assembly and promised to issue a Green Paper at the earliest opportunity.

The Conservative Party leadership were convinced by the February 1974 election results that the party must offer a concrete proposal for action in the October election. In order to obtain this a deal was struck between the leadership of the British Conservative Party and the Conservative Party in Scotland. The Scottish MPs favoured a Scottish Assembly or Council, which was to be an *indirectly* elected body. The members of this Council were to be selected by the new regional authorities. The Council would have control over many Scottish domestic affairs, but remain responsible to the UK Parliament. In order to obtain a concrete commitment on devolution the principle of direct elections was sacrificed.

The position of the Conservatives in Scotland after 1974 was very much changed from that of the late 1950s. Then they held the majority of seats but after October 1974 they were reduced to sixteen seats and a status of the third party in votes after Labour and the SNP. Probably the Three Day Week had a great deal to do with that particular defeat but for a long time the image of the Scottish Conservatives had been much more traditional than that of their colleagues south of the border. From 1975 onwards it became clear that the old landowning élite had been cleared out of the leadership in order to make way for more aggressive and more middle class Conservatives.

The parties and Scotland

The major points about the political background to the rise of nationalism have already been made and it is as well to refer here to their significance.

The first stage of the argument was to say that some form of self-government for Scotland was an issue which was taken off the British political agenda when the elements which supported it were weakened or destroyed at the beginning of the century. Instead the ruling image became that of class politics. This replacement was important both because some special treatment of the Scottish case at that time might have meant that the issue of independence was defused as has been the case of Bavaria within Germany or even Sicily within Italy. The fact that it was not dealt with meant that it was potentially an issue upon which a new interpretation of politics might be based. The other important point about the victory of quasi-socialist class politics was that, when the promises of the class parties to deliver increased prosperity were not redeemed, a vacuum was created into which a party with another interpretation and solution might step.

The evidence for this lack of trust in the larger parties comes from several sources. The first of these is the fall in the level of turnout at general elections since the war (see Table 4.2).

Table 4.2 Turnout at general elections

	UK %	Scottish %
1945	72·7	68·9
1950	83·9	80·9
1951	82·6	81·1
1955	76·8	75·1
1959	78·7	78·1
1964	77·1	77·6
1966	75·8	75·9
1970	72·0	73·9
1974 Feb.	78·8	79·0
1974 Oct.	72·8	74·8

It may be significant that, with the arrival of the SNP as more than a totally marginal party, Scotland begins to show turnout percentages higher than that for the United Kingdom as a whole. Again, since 1945, the Conservative and Labour voters added together have accounted for a lower and lower proportion of the total vote in Britain. In other words, the share going to third parties has risen rather dramatically. The results are shown in Table 4.3.

Table 4.3 Percentage share of total vote at general elections

	Conservative	Labour	Other
1951	48	49	3
1955	49	46	4
1959	49	44	7
1964	43	44	3
1966	42	48	10
1970	46	43	11
1974 Feb.	38	37	25
1974 Oct.	36	39	25

In short, in 1951, 97 per cent of the total vote went to one or other of the two major parties. In both elections in 1974 only 75 per cent of the vote was placed with them. For some reason the party system in Britain is much less dominantly a two-party system. One interpretation of these figures is that, just as Home Rule ceased to be an issue and consequently destroyed a crucial difference between the Liberals and the Conservatives, so the idea of class politics is no longer as important in Britain and the parties whose appeal is based on this will suffer. Butler and Stokes, we have seen, have drawn attention to the decline in importance of the 'class alignment' as have Crewe and Särlvik.[39] Although there are signs that class issues are, once again, becoming important in some aspects of British politics, it does seem that they were less important in the political arguments of the 1960s. The burden of the argument then seemed to be about modernisation and technological advance. Harold Wilson gave the impression of fighting the elections of 1964, 1966 and 1970 on the contention that Labour was technically more capable of managing a complex modern state.

When the level of unemployment started to rise in the late 1960s and the Labour Party did not seem to know how to cope, it was not surprising that many of its supporters started to look for an alternative. The SNP had, by this time, organised its way into being this alternative in Scotland, just as the Liberals had, to some extent, done in England. Much the same process seems to have occurred when a Conservative government came into office.

Scotland as a political system

In the previous section I have sketched in the changing fortunes of the major political parties and their changing attitudes to a Scottish Parliament. I have suggested that the lack of trust in these parties has created a situation where a new party might step in. I have also suggested that the devolution policies of these parties were encouraged by their fear of losing votes to this new party but, at the same time, they may have developed a greater interest in devolution. In the final section of this chapter I should like to describe and analyse the extent to which Scotland operated on its own as a political system or sub-system. We have seen that there has been a growing party interest in devolution. To what extent was this preceded by the development of specific ways for carrying on Scottish political business? To what extent did those responsible for Scottish political business believe that there was a set of peculiarly Scottish problems as opposed to British problems on the one hand and local problems, for example Dundee or Highland, on the other hand? I shall argue, with Keating,[40] that such a system can be discerned. It is dependent on the overall British system but it nevertheless operates as a distinct context in which British decision makers operate.

The institutional bases of this political sub-system have been mentioned already. They are the Scottish committees of the House of Commons and the Scottish Office. Very briefly, from the establishment of the Scottish Office and the institution of a Secretary for Scotland in the late nineteenth century, this part of the British government has expanded in its responsibility for the affairs of Scotland. It is quite different from most of the rest of the great departments of state in Britain in that it is, of course, responsible for a territory rather than a function and it operates in order to bring the demands of that part of the United Kingdom to the attention of the Cabinet. Especially with the establishment of the Scottish Development Department and the Scottish Economic Planning Department within the Scottish Office it has a wide range over the life of Scotland and by far the largest part of government business in Scotland is carried out through it. This is not the place to give detailed examples of the ways in which it operates but Keating brings a great deal of evidence to show its role as a pressure group on Cabinet priorities.[41] This is not to argue that all government decisions which affected Scotland were channelled through the Scottish Office. It is to argue that a large administrative unit had, as its particular task, the care of Scottish affairs. With the further addition of the Scottish Development Department in 1962 and the Scottish Economic Planning Department in 1973 the Scottish Office took on a development role for Scotland over and above simple administration. Thus the Scottish Office could say:[42]

> The Secretary of State for Scotland's increasing involvement in problems of economic development flowing from increasing expectation by Scottish opinion generally that he should interest himself in any matter affecting Scotland, whether or not it comes within the scope of his statutory function led, in 1964 to his being assigned more explicit responsibilities in the comprehensive machinery for economic planning which was introduced on the advent of the new administration.

Thus on the administrative side it was certainly the case that, by the 1960s a very distinct political sub-system was established.

On the political or parliamentary side this is also true. The Scottish Grand Committee, a committee of the House of Commons which considers various stages of purely Scottish legislation, was set up on a regular basis in 1907. There had been earlier experiments in the parliamentary sessions of 1894 and 1895. In 1948 it was agreed that the second reading of certain non-controversial bills could also be taken by the committee.[43] In 1957 a first Scottish Standing Committee was set up and in 1962 a second one was established to deal with the Committee stage of Bills because business was increasing so greatly. By 1965 the situation was, therefore, that most of the Scottish business of the House of Commons was dealt with in one or other of these Scottish Committees. Edwards has estimated that, of the seventy-four Scottish Bills considered in the years 1958 to 1976, fifty-one were, for practical purposes, dealt with exclusively by one of these Scottish Committees and the remainder were considered elsewhere for purely technical reasons.[44] Further than this, Keating demonstrates that the work of Scottish MPs is more and more in these committees and that they have taken a sharply decreasing interest in the other work of the House including foreign and UK business.[45] In all, the Scottish legislators have formed themselves into a political sub-system corresponding to the work of the administrators.

Conclusion

We may sum up this section by saying that, by 1966 when the nationalist movement was well under way, there was a parallel concentration on Scottish affairs in non-nationalist political spheres. For the first time since the late 1920s Scotland was the centre of her own stage undistracted by foreign wars or worries. There had been a growth of Scottish institutions, among the parties, in administration and in Parliament. The rise of a nationalist movement was not wholly out of line with these developments and, most important of all, this rise was facilitated by the lack of trust in British institutions and parties. Despite the fact that these 'Unionist' elements had presided over the move to a more Scottish way of dealing with Scottish affairs, their efforts did not seem to help them.

In terms of Smelser's approach, it can be seen that the British political structure has become more and more conducive to a concentration on Scottish events. In a sense the political separateness of Scotland may have declined during the last century but various events conspired together to focus the interests of certain sections of the parties on Scotland and legislative and administrative arrangements contributed to this result. In terms of an overall explanation, this chapter has demonstrated the ways in which those interested in Scottish politics, even outside nationalist circles, have come to have a greater interest in Scottish affairs. This was to be one of the foundations on which the rise in the nationalist vote is based.

5 The Scottish Economy

It is in the field of economics that the major strains in the Scottish system are to be found. Have these strains created groups in Scotland with a particular consciousness of Scotland as a political unit? Is there any evidence that a form of relative deprivation has initiated a move towards the nationalists?

The core of modern nationalist propaganda in Scotland has been the state of the Scottish economy. The closing or take over of Scottish businesses, the mounting levels of unemployment, the squalid social conditions have all been the subjects of regular articles and speeches. Apart from this, one is forced to look at the economy of Scotland since various theoretical approaches to nationalism give such an important place to economic considerations. Marxism is the best known example of this[1] but the importance of the economy is also crucial to Hechter's approach.[2] My own view is that the state of the economy is important at various stages in the development of the nationalist movement but it is not the only thing to be considered. What makes Scottish nationalism peculiar in the study of modern nationalist movements is its particular emphasis on questions such as unemployment but this is not to say that these are the strains which create the sole conditions for the development of nationalism. In this chapter I shall outline the development and the present condition of the Scottish economy and, in doing so, I shall try to show the points at which the rise of nationalism may have been affected.

It is as well to summarise the argument before beginning. I shall argue that Scotland was, historically, a poor country and that after a short rise in its standard of living then experienced a severe decline in its productive base. With the political centre of power in London and the major British industrial areas far to the south, it is difficult to devise any policy which can ensure prosperity for Scotland. (It can be argued that British membership of the EEC makes things even worse.) Various efforts have been made to improve the situation but none of them have had a long-term success. The effect has been that many Scottish people have despaired of a better life. Some have left. Others stayed and many experienced the steadily worsening conditions of the 1960s after the good years of the 1950s when there was little unemployment. It may be significant that the SNP gathered votes at a time when many Scots must have felt poorer than they had been in the immediate past.

The Scottish economy and the union

The major economic argument in favour of Union with England was that this poor, under-developed country, remote from the European markets and denied access to the English colonies in the New World, would become prosperous through trade and exporting. It is easy to see why Scotland is traditionally a poor country if one flies from Glasgow to Wick on a clear day. The dominating impression is of many miles of moorland and hillside. There is little cultivation other than in the east and in the rich central belt. Two hundred and fifty years ago the situation was worse. There was a larger proportion of the population in the Highlands and in the countryside generally tending the black cattle but the improvements which were under way in English agriculture were virtually unknown.[3] As for the towns, they were few and small and there was little industry or trade. Studies of Scottish economic history emphasise the poverty of the country by comparison with England. Even in the nineteenth century, when the balance was more equal, the memory of these many centuries as a poor relation on the remote border of a great European power was never far from the Scottish consciousness.[4]

After the Union Scotland did prosper. There is room for argument about the relation between the political settlement and the economic development. Prosperity did not come directly after the Union but, for whatever reasons, life in Scotland became a little easier towards the end of the eighteenth century.

It was Glasgow and the west of Scotland which was in the

forefront of this development. The first period of prosperity came with the tobacco trade which was centred in Glasgow.[5] After this had gone, a more important development took place. Lanarkshire became one of the major centres of the industrial revolution. Glasgow, its major town, became one of the first industrial cities.

The prosperity of the west of Scotland in the nineteenth century was based on two, or perhaps three, factors. One of these was a very large deposit of high quality coking coal in the Lanarkshire mines. Another was a very rich seam of low phosphorus iron ore. Iron and later steel could be made using cheap good fuel which was also available locally. The third natural advantage was that Glasgow and some of the other important towns of this period were on a large river, the Clyde, which could, with an effort, be dredged to make it navigable for large ships. This had been important when Glasgow's prosperity was first built on the tobacco trade but when the industrial complex was developed it led to the concentration of industrial activity in shipbuilding and many ancilliary industries. The core of the industrial life of Glasgow was shipbuilding and the heavy engineering which was largely linked to shipbuilding but which developed to other fields such as the building of locomotives and industrial plant.

In a way it is misleading to speak about the Scottish economy in terms of Glasgow. There were other towns in the west such as Paisley, Clydebank, Motherwell and Greenock which also contributed. There were developments in other parts of Scotland, but the west of Scotland was the industrial powerhouse and Glasgow dominated it. Scotsmen came in from the countryside to work in places all over west central Scotland creating the population imbalance which we still have today but it was Glasgow which became an urban monster.[6] This era of prosperity for the west of Scotland started towards the end of the 1850s.[7] The 1850s themselves were years of depression but, although there were fluctuations, the latter half of the nineteenth century was a peak period. 1873 was a year of depression and unemployment. Until about 1885 the growth of the Scottish economy was retarded, prices fell and competition began to make itself felt but, from 1885 onwards until the beginning of the First World War, there was a recovery.

This industrial growth had its effect on rural society. In 1831 half of the population worked in agriculture but by 1890 only a quarter did so. There was massive rural depopulation caused both by people emigrating, going to the towns to work and, to a much lesser extent, by the 'clearances' when landowners moved their tenants, sometimes forcibly, so that their crofts and farms could be converted into sheep runs. This last cause of depopulation applied only to certain parts of the Highlands whereas rural depopulation applied to the whole of Scotland. Later in the century, after Queen Victoria had publicised the 'Gothick' joys of Highland life, slaughtering Scottish game became fashionable.[8] The gentry and those who hoped to pass for such flocked north in the season and it became very obvious that the red deer and the pheasant were even more valuable beasts than the sheep. In many cases the small number of shepherds who had been brought to the Highlands in the middle of the century were replaced by even smaller numbers of gamekeepers. Thus the process of rural, and especially Highland, depopulation speeded up. For the richer and economically more important lowland agricultural areas new farming methods also contributed to the fall in population.

If the countryside was losing population some towns had become very overcrowded. Scottish towns had never been particularly salubrious[9] but the condition of Glasgow in the nineteenth century attracted many comments.[10] Unbelievable overcrowding and appalling sanitation seem to have been the characteristics of the towns. Nevertheless, for many skilled manual workers as for the bourgeoisie this was also a time of improvement in the standard of living. There was some time to attend the Mechanics Institutes and philosophical societies and the skilled workers were not so crushed down that they could not organise trade unions and co-operative societies to protect their standards of living. The end of the century was a key time in the development of modern unions,[11] and co-operative societies had been established rather earlier. St Cuthbert's Co-operative Society was established in the 1850s in Edinburgh and, in 1858, the King's Park Society was established in Glasgow.

Despite its prosperity at the end of the century, the first signs of trouble for Scotland could be discerned. The most obvious sign of trouble was the rise of foreign competition. Earlier in the century Britain was virtually the only industrial nation and the west of Scotland had been a major centre. Towards the end of the century both Germany and the United States began to compete: Glasgow was particularly hit by the competition in shipbuilding. At home conditions were also less favourable. The large Lanarkshire coal field started to run out and, although there was plenty of coal, for example, in Fife, it was not as favourably placed and the varieties

71

now available were not as suitable. Iron ore deposits also began to run out and both these circumstances added up to the fact that the iron and steel industry, the large engineering works and the shipbuilding on the Clyde were not nearly as favourably situated *vis-à-vis* their natural resources as had once been the case. As Campbell says: 'Until the 1870s, the comparative cost of industrial production in Scotland was so favourable that the economy rested on an apparently sure foundation of buoyant foreign demand.'[12] Towards the end of the century, the natural advantages which had placed Scotland in such a competitive position began to disappear.

Perhaps because of their long domination of the markets, perhaps for other reasons, the Scottish entrepreneurs seemed to be unwilling to face the new conditions and take action. Naturally they did not invest at a time when the terms of trade were so heavily against them but in the 1880s when they should have been renewing their plant and looking for innovation they did not do so. The main problem seems to have been that the traditional sectors such as shipbuilding, were buoyant enough not to create a need for investment in other fields.

Another factor to be borne in mind was the condition of the labour force. The industrial economy of Scotland depended not only on cheap raw material but also on cheap labour and a great proportion of this was Irish. Irish labourers were driven to Scotland by the conditions existing in their home country. After the potato famine, however, the nature of the Irish immigration changed. As Handley says: 'Self-improvement was the impulse that transported him to Scotland in the pre-famine days. Self-preservation was the urge that drove him onwards in the black night of the pestilence.'[13] Thus, the west of Scotland experienced an enormous flood of very poor immigrants who had no industrial skills and indeed only primitive rural ones. Even in the days of the famine the better-off who could afford the £4 passage sailed to America and only the very poorest came to Scotland. The jobs which they took were those which required little skill or were very unpleasant. At first this reservoir of labour was a benefit to the west of Scotland. On the other hand various factors including trade union restrictions on dilution ensured that the new workers were not given many opportunities for training. This was not the labour force on which to build a modern rapidly changing industrial base. The new workers, Irish and Scottish, could have been trained and made adaptable but they were there in such numbers that few saw the necessity for doing so and this added to the conservatism and lack of adaptability of the Scottish economy.

The sudden growth of the industrial population and the arrival of the Irish immigrants also added to the insalubrious living conditions. The census of 1861 shows that 226,723 families, or one third of the Scottish population, lived in houses of one room only and there were 7,964 families in houses without windows. The regulations aimed at overcoming this situation were difficult to enforce and it was only after the typhus epidemic of 1866 that serious thought was given to these conditions. It was not until the council housing programmes of the twentieth century that something was really done about them.

Thus by the third quarter of the nineteenth century when Scotland was still a world industrial leader, the social conditions were established which were to linger on to the present day. There were other places like Birmingham and Manchester which were as important for the development of European industry as Glasgow. In Glasgow, however, we still have enormous areas of slums and, even in the housing estates built after the Second World War, slum conditions exist.[14] This situation led some into nationalism. The early pages of the *Scots Independent* make regular references to housing in the west of Scotland and to the general plight of the industrial population.

Even if the standard of living could have been raised, however, there were serious problems with the very nature of Scottish industry. I have already mentioned the low level of investment. More than this, the very nature of the industrial base invited disaster.

First, the economy of Scotland was and is dependent on the production of capital goods. In times of boom this is not a problem but in times of recession the problems arise. The production of consumer goods cannot be so easily halted because there is still a mass demand but manufacturers will find it much easier to neglect the renewal of machinery and trade can almost as easily be carried on in old ships as in new ones. In short an economy built on the production of capital goods will be badly hit in times of depression. The early 1870s were bad for the west of Scotland and the inter-war years were to be even worse.

A second factor which eventually was shown to be a disadvantage was the integrated nature of Scottish industry. As Slaven says, 'The steel industry [in Scotland] failed to have an independent source or stimulus for growth but became an integral part of the industrial complex, which appeared in Scotland at the beginning of the

73

twentieth century.'[15] The steel mills produced for the shipbuilding industry and for the engineering works which were largely ancillary to the shipbuilders. Thus, when the market for ships disappeared the whole industrial system declined.

A related point must also be remembered. Scottish industry produced overwhelmingly for the export market. Between 1900 and 1916 four-fifths of the tweeds, one-third of the coal and two-thirds of the locomotives were exported. In markets abroad these industries were competing with foreign producers in a way that would not have been true of the home market. When the competition of German and American manufacturers became important the saleability of Scottish items suffered.

Finally, it is worth mentioning that Scotland's industry was heavily concentrated in a restricted area. One consequence of this, the appalling housing conditions, has already been discussed, but the other side of this was that bad times for one part of the industrial complex also meant bad times for the rest of that small region.

Up to and including the First World War there were few signs that things were going wrong. In the preparation for the war it was precisely the heavy industries which were in demand and the shipyards were busy with orders for the Royal Navy. In the one or two years after the war the situation was still not clear because merchant shipping lost during the war had to be replaced. By the end of 1921, however, it was clear that things were very wrong.

In part, the problems of the inter-war years were world problems. There was a general recession which did not ease until the mid-1930s and Scotland suffered along with everyone else. I have mentioned that the economy of Scotland, based on capital goods, would feel the world economic situation particularly acutely but it would not be alone in this. In part the problem was a British problem in that Britain had been an industrial leader, the workshop of the world, and was now having to face competition from other countries. Britain as a whole suffered from the effects of the war and Scotland suffered with her.

While it is true, therefore, that Scotland's situation has to be seen in the context of the world economy and of the British economy, there were still aspects of the situation north of the Tweed which made Scotland's situation worse and which ensured that Scotland would not recover with the rest of the world. These Scottish characteristics have already been described but there are several points that can be noted here.

Other areas in Britain had specialised in heavy engineering but recovered after the war because of diversification. One is bound to ask why Scotland suffered so badly. One answer is that the concentration on shipbuilding was particularly disastrous. The downturn in world trade after the war meant a fall in freights and therefore there was no need to build new ships. With shipbuilding the rest of the industrial complex also went down. A great deal of coal was still exported from the Fife fields to Europe but by now there was greater competition from Poland and elsewhere. With all this difficulty for the traditional industries very little money was put into new ones. By the 1920s it was, of course, too late because industrial confidence had sagged but there is little sign that thought was given to investment earlier. There had been some attempt to build up a motor car industry including the famous 'Argyll' works but this had failed. A major consumer industry like this would have put the west of Scotland on a level of prosperity equal to the west Midlands and would have provided a market for the steel industry.

Manufacturing industry was not the only sector of the Scottish economy to be hit. After the Russian Revolution the British government for a time severed the trade links between Britain and Russia. This was a heavy blow to the east of Scotland herring fishermen who had always regarded Russia as a major market.

Other processes which spelled trouble for Scotland began to build up in the early 1920s. This was the beginning of the so called 'branch factory' syndrome. Broadly the development was away from industrial units owned and managed in Scotland to one in which these factories and works had been sold out to firms controlled from outside Scotland. The effect of this was twofold. The Scottish factories themselves became mere production units with the work of higher management, research and development, marketing and so forth done at the head office generally in England and increasingly from abroad, mainly North America. Thus, if a young person wanted promotion within the firm, he was forced to leave Scotland and thus the stock of ability and trained manpower at the highest levels was gradually depleted. The second effect was that when the recession came it was the branch factories and especially the new branch factories which were closed first. Thus the unemployment figures were likely to be affected more quickly and more dramatically in areas showing the 'branch factory syndrome' than in areas where the management of these firms was carried on.

One of the best known examples of this process took place in the railways. In order to help the war effort it was considered necessary to coordinate the railway system and plans were made to reduce the large number of companies operating them. One scheme sponsored by Sir Eric Geddes was for the amalgamation of all the Scottish railway companies but this was rejected in favour of consolidating the Scottish lines with the two major companies which ran up the west and east sides of Britain: the London Midland and Scottish and the London and North Eastern Railway. Thus, the control of the Scottish railway network passed out of Scottish hands. One of the effects of this was that locomotive building in Inverness was closed down with a loss of 8,000 jobs and the work was concentrated in England in Crewe and Derby.[16] Later, locomotive works at Carstairs and Inverurie were also to disappear.

Another well-known example of this process is shown in the story of the Scottish banks, Just after the war some of the major Scottish clearing banks were taken over by English banks. In 1919 Lloyds took over the National Bank. Barclays took over the British Linen Bank and the Midland took over the Clydesdale.

It should not be thought that the process wholly depended on the war. In 1899 John Brown's of Sheffield took over the Clydebank Shipyard, and Lloyds of Birmingham amalgamated with A. & J. Stewart to create the steel firm of Stewart and Lloyds. In 1934 this duly emigrated south to Corby in Northamptonshire. By the 1930s, a very large part of the industrial complex in the west of Scotland was owned by firms from outside Scotland and a very large part was not working at all.

This feature of external control of Scottish business was to become even more important. Firn has pointed out that in the 1970s, in the five fastest growing sectors of the Scottish economy only 13·5 per cent was in native control.[17] There has been an enormous amount of American intervention in Scottish companies and overall there are few firms today which have their headquarters in Scotland.

The overall picture of the economy of the west of Scotland is that, up to the First World War, Scotland shared in the booms and slumps of the rest of Britain. After 1919 it began to fall seriously behind. As late as 1907 Scotland had 12·5 per cent of British industrial production. By 1924 it had fallen to 10·5 per cent and by 1930 it was 9·5 per cent.[18] By these and by virtually every other economic indicator it is plain that the gap between Scottish and English economic performance widened. Scotland had little part in the development of new industry which characterised the British economy as a whole. There were several parts of England which had roughly the same problems as Scotland: the north west and Teesside come immediately to mind but the scale of the problem was greater on Clydeside and it was unlikely that economic disaster on the Mersey would spark off a call for political independence. This was the crucial difference as far as Scotland was concerned. Many people who did not support nationalism for historical or even political reasons began to feel that the economic situation in Scotland called for special measures. For some it was a short step to some sort of political solution.

One of the hurdles to be overcome was to agree that Scotland was a special case. In the 1920s the government and a large proportion of industrial leaders in Scotland seemed to believe that Scotland was experiencing the same sort of crisis as the rest of the United Kingdom. Practically the only people to say publicly that there were severe long-term problems in the Scottish economy were the nationalists. They certainly had no sophisticated understanding of economic processes but a large number of them lived in or near Glasgow and it was difficult to ignore the human misery which unemployment had brought along. Being nationalists they believed that Scotland was a particularly bad case and, probably by luck, their emphasis proved to be correct. There were, however, several nationalists who had more than a passing knowledge of the situation. From the beginning of his involvement with the *Scots Independent*, then the newspaper of the Scots National League, it was obvious that Tom Gibson had an intimate knowledge of industry in the west of Scotland. More influential than Gibson's articles, however, were the writings of G. M. Thomson. In *Scotland, that Distressed Area*[19] and other writings[20] he drew attention to the disastrous state of the Scottish economy. It was significant that when his first book was published it was not reviewed at the time of publication either in the *Scotsman* or the *Glasgow Herald*. It was, however, very quickly sold out[21] and made a considerable impact. It became well known outside nationalist circles and contributed to the recognition of these acute problems. Among professional economists only Dr Bowie of the Dundee School of Economics wrote and spoke along the same lines.[22] Perhaps the publication which brought the nature of the situation home most vividly to the Scottish business community was the publication of the first *Clydesdale Bank Review*.[23] In this the peculiar nature of the Scottish situation was spelled out, not for the first time (Thomson had published several years before that) but in a form that was widely read by the Scottish business community. In 1936 and 1937 the *Review* showed clearly how Scotland had gone deeper into the depression in the early 1930s than any other part of Great Britain.

One of the first signs that the Scottish business community was seriously concerned by the situation was the establishment of the Scottish Development Council in 1931. This was a purely voluntary body made up of businessmen and led by Sir James Lithgow and Sir Stephen Bilsland. It is probably significant that the main figure, Lithgow, was a major shipbuilder and must have been one of the first to recognise the changed economic conditions. This Council in turn set up the Scottish Economic Committee in 1936 which produced a number of well-documented studies of Scotland's natural resources.[24] The Secretary of this committee, James A. A. Porteous, although by no means a nationalist at this time, later became a leading member of Scottish Convention and later still joined the SNP.

The government too was forced to act. In 1934 they set up a committee under the chairmanship of Sir Arnold Rose.[25] At the same time, for the whole of Britain the Special Areas Act 1934 was passed allowing for special government aid to areas of high unemployment. Both these measures may partly have been responsible for the arrival of the Scottish Party and its amalgamation with the NPS to form the SNP, but they were also part of a realisation that some parts of Britain had suffered particularly badly and that Scotland had suffered in particular. The Special Areas Act was the first of a series of measures arising out of the belief that governments could manipulate the economy by way of a regional policy. Up to the 1960s this regional policy was directed almost exclusively at reducing unemployment. It was as a result of these measures that industrial estates were first set up. Hillington was the first followed in 1938 by Carfin, Chapelhall and Larkhall. As Campbell points out, however, their establishment only dealt with a part of the problem.[26] Rose's committee recommended the need for 'an authoritative Scottish body with suitable experience and knowledge financed by the government'.[27] The government would not accept this recommendation and Rose resigned but the Gilmour Committee[28] was appointed and reported, among other things, in favour of consolidating the various parts of the Scottish administration in the Scottish Office and establishing its headquarters in Edinburgh. St Andrew's House was built for this department in 1939.

Another sign that the government was aware of Scotland's problems came in the form of a government sponsored emigration scheme which sought to solve the unemployment problem by cutting down the numbers of employable men in Scotland. As one might expect this was not popular with the nationalists and, in this case, they appear to have been right. The Dominions, which were the interested recipients of the emigrants, would only take people of excellent health and skill. These were precisely the people who would have to be kept in Scotland if the economy was to be rebuilt. It was precisely this group which was, in any case, leaving in the greatest numbers because they were the ones with the initiative and intelligence to look in all places for employment.

In the later 1930s the building up of armaments meant employment and a return of prosperity for the Clyde. In broad terms the situation was similar to that before the First World War in that it masked the perilous real condition of Scottish industry. The building up was due to government contracts for the war effort and not to the demands of a normal market. Nevertheless, it has to be said that this period was a time of prosperity for Clydeside.

In the period between the wars Scotland's agriculture, the other major portion of her economy, did not do too well either. I have already pointed out that agriculture was more important to Scotland than to Britain as a whole because, though this proportion was diminishing, agriculture still employed a larger percentage of the Scottish work force than of the British work force. Agriculture was particularly affected by the traditional British policy of Free Trade and thus the Scottish economy once again was affected by this to a greater degree than the British economy as a whole. It was also notable that the government subsidies which were given to agriculture in 1931 were for wheat and sugar beet, characteristically English crops, and for oats, a characteristically Scottish crop, only in 1937. The major concentration of Scottish agriculture was, of course, on fatstock and whereas Scottish beef had been supreme in the earlier part of the century, in the inter-war years the development of refrigeration techniques meant that beef could be brought from as far away as Latin America for the British market and still be cheaper than Scottish beef. This was a heavy blow. As far as sheep were concerned the extensions of the deer forests meant that this sector of agriculture also declined.

We may sum up the situation between the wars by saying that Scotland was driven deeper into the depression in the 1930s than was the case for the whole of Great Britain. The Scottish economy began to diverge in its performance from that of Britain as a whole. Whereas at the beginning of the century Scotland had been one of the most prosperous regions in Britain, in the 1930s economic indicators showed that Scotland's performance was lagging in virtually every sector. The indicator which most closely affected peoples' lives is worth quoting. In the inter-war years the percentage of the working population out of work varied between 9·5 and 22 per cent in the United Kingdom whereas in Scotland it varied between 10·3 and 27 per cent. The flurry of activity from 1938 to the end of the war was not a sign that the Scottish economy had become healthier. The world had become sicker.

The war years 1939-45

During the war some steps were taken which were to have long-term effects. Some of these were harmful and were continuations of pre-war trends. Non-essential industries all over Britain were closed down and for Scotland this meant that units which were closed down were simply used for storage. Given the general state of industry in Scotland it would be difficult to get them going again when peace returned. Inevitably the war also meant the removal of the able-bodied in the population. Some of them were never to come back and others, having been uprooted once, did not go back to their original jobs after 1945. Up to 1942 a system of industrial conscription was enforced whereby men and women were directed to labour. While some English workers came to Scotland it was believed that proportionately more Scots had to leave the homeland. These arrangements were extremely unpopular and were eventually brought to an end. The other bad effect which has already been mentioned was that the concentration on heavy engineering prevented the development of new, lighter, consumer orientated industries.

There were some positive developments during the war. One of them was that, despite the primary concern to win the war, many people began to take a new interest in rebuilding Scotland after the fighting was over. They were led by Tom Johnston, the Secretary of State for Scotland. Up to the 1930s as we have seen, he had been an active Home Ruler but his later view, that the Scottish economy should be rebuilt first, led him to take certain measures. One of these was the establishment of the Scottish Council on Industry.

Unlike the earlier Scottish Development Council this included trade union representatives as well as owners and management. The two bodies were later merged in the Scottish Council which is still active. This was not Johnston's only importance. He established a section in the Scottish Office to look after economic planning and this was much later to become the Scottish Economic Planning Department. In his personal contacts and encouragement of individual industrialists and trade unionists he ensured that a vigorous interest would be taken in the post-war reconstruction of Scotland. In 1943 he became the Chairman of the North of Scotland Hydro-Electric Board and by this agency provided a very important source of energy to the Highlands and elsewhere. He was also interested in the building of the Forth Road Bridge, the development of Prestwick Airport and many other projects which established an infra-structure on which new Scottish industries could grow.

Johnston was not alone in planning for a new Scotland. There was a general interest in the reconstruction of Scotland and, by contrast with the situation after the First World War, the government felt that it was able to intervene and manipulate the economy. More industrial estates were opened including one on the outskirts of Dundee. In Scotland, as in England, new towns were planned to take the surplus population away from the overgrown urban centres. East Kilbride and later Cumbernauld were meant to deal with the overcrowding of Glasgow.[29] In 1945 a Distribution of Industry Act was passed which designated a large part of Scotland as a series of Development Areas in which special encouragement was given to industry. As important as this was the fact that the new Labour government's policy of nationalisation meant that a very high proportion of the Scottish working population was employed in public enterprise. With the final nationalisation of the steel industry this became even more important and gave stability of employment if it did not give dynamism.

Thus, after the war, in the economy as elsewhere, Scottish people were in a mood to plan for the future. The Scottish Convention Movement which built up in the late 1940s was very much part of this mood. Among the leaders of the Convention, James Porteous and Dr John Macdonald were both interested in economic problems. There was little fervour that could be described as revolutionary but the chance to build a prosperous Scotland had its implications for politics.

Later economic developments were also to have these consequences. There were major shortages of building materials and of certain types of food. Rationing was not relaxed, indeed bread rationing was only introduced after the war. Over the whole British economic scene was the dark cloud of the 'Dollar Gap'. Every conceivable effort had to be put into manufacturing goods for export. In Scotland, as elsewhere in Britain, the government became extremely unpopular as a result of the economic restrictions and this probably had something to do with the large proportions of Scottish voters who signed the Covenant in 1949 and 1950. It is very possible that many saw the Home Rule proposals of the Covenant as a way of getting some control over a difficult economic situation. In the long run other factors were probably as important but we should not ignore the economic situation.

The austerities of the 1940s did pass away with time and for the west of Scotland the traditional industries were once again propped up by production for the Korean War. This meant another period of short-lived prosperity for the Clyde but the phase was over by about 1957. It would have to be said, however, that economic conditions were distinctly better for the majority of Scotland than they were before the war. The establishment of a Welfare State by the 1945 Labour government meant that one's health was not determined by ability to pay medical bills and the implementation of Beveridge's proposals and other measures meant that people would not fall to the pre-war depths of degradation through unemployment or other forms of human misfortune. In any case levels of unemployment comparable to those that had existed in the 1930s simply did not occur except in very small areas. A. D. Campbell estimated that in 1932 real income per head in Scotland was 90 per cent of what it had been in 1929 while in 1948 it was 50 per cent greater than it had been in 1932.[30] The *Clydesdale Bank Annual Survey of Economic Conditions in Scotland* estimated in 1958 that real income per head in Scotland in that year was 75 per cent higher than it was in 1934 when the first review was produced.[31] Thus, although the real economic state of Scotland might be grave, these were the years of Butskellism and 'You've never had it so good'. By comparison with what many people had experienced before the war, living had become much easier. These were not years in which there was a great deal of public support for radical political change in terms of left wing programmes or nationalist ones and this may have been related to the general bromide of the political and economic climate relieved only by Suez in 1956 and the CND marches towards the end of the period. The major interest of most families seems to have been in building up comfortable homes and a decent standard of living.

Towards the end of the 1950s, however, the situation was to change. 1958 was a year of sharp recession and Scotland suffered along with the rest of the UK, but in 1959 and 1960 the UK economy began to recover. Scottish recovery was much less marked. The effort to sustain military production for the Korean War ended about 1953 and heavy industry inevitably suffered. It was from this time onwards that the traditional Scottish industries began to show that, for them, there was to be a major contraction and a very bleak time ahead. It was this sector of the economy which mostly accounted for Scottish GDP. MacCrone points out that up to 1953 this sector kept up with that of the rest of the UK.[32] After that Scotland began to fall behind but in later years, especially in 1959-60, there was an even larger divergence. It is easy to understand the causes of this downward slide. There was no longer the artificially high demand for the products of heavy engineering caused by the international situation. It has already been noted that there was much less diversification and in particular, less of a move towards the production of consumer goods as compared to other British industrial areas. MacCrone also points out, as does Alexander, that even those new technically advanced industries which were established did not seem to share in the prosperity enjoyed in similar industries elsewhere.[33] In other words, Scotland's grim economic situation was caused, not only by the collapse of heavy industries including shipbuilding, but also by the disturbing fact that the more modern industries did not do well either.

The government had, of course, taken steps to deal with the Scottish economic situation as with that in all the declining industrial areas. As early as 1952 Cairncross and Mair had challenged the idea that industry had come to Scotland after the war as a result of government action.[34] They agreed that these moves had been affected at least as much by labour and housing shortages in the south east. By the end of the 1950s it seemed that neither government aid nor the operations of any other economic or political forces was of particular advantage to Scotland.

In 1957, however, Harold Macmillan became Prime Minister and this heralded a change in the government's attitude to the economy. The most dramatic indication of this was directly linked to the recession and unemployment of 1957-8, when Peter Thorneycroft, Nigel Birch and Enoch Powell resigned from Macmillan's administration because they wanted to pursue much 'tougher' economic policies than did the Prime Minister. He, by contrast, was more concerned about the level of unemployment. It was inevitable, therefore, that his attention would be turned to the areas where unemployment was high and Scotland was certainly among these. The year 1958-9 was the first since the war with Scottish unemployment in excess of 100,000 and something had to be done.

One thing which was done was the building of a pulp and paper mill by Wiggins Teape in Fort William. This was followed by the building of a steel strip mill for Colville's at Ravenscraig. The British motor industry had recently gone into an expansive phase and the reasoning behind the government's action at Ravenscraig was that the new mill would provide the raw material which would tempt car manufacturers to set up plant in Scotland. This development did not take place until 1961 when BMC came up to Bathgate and when Rootes (now Chrysler) came to Linwood in 1963.

Thus we can say that from 1958 onwards the British government became much more concerned with problems of unemployment than it had since the war. Since unemployment was concentrated in particular parts of the country which had industries in trouble this meant that the regional element in economic policy emerged strongly. Since Scotland was an area with particularly intransigent economic problems generally, and problems of unemployment in particular, Scotland came to public attention. This meant that Scottish people came to realise that particular measures had to be taken to deal with their situation. With these 'Macmillan' measures, primarily aimed at unemployment, the 'declining' condition of the Scottish economy was brought home to larger and larger numbers of Scots men and women. New pressures started to build up to ensure that the government would do something. In other words there was a new consciousness of Scotland and the needs of Scotland. I shall argue that it is not coincidence that this development only preceded by a few years the first stirrings of new life in the SNP. Most important of all was the fact that this new emphasis on Scotland came at a time when there was a decline in prosperity after the high employment and hopefulness of the 1950s.

Both the unions and the employers in Scotland were concerned about the situation. Although the Scottish economy did pick up in the early 1960s the Scottish Council, representing both sides of industry, set up an enquiry whose recommendations were embodied in the Toothill Report.[35]

This was not the first report of the Council but it was an important one in that the situation was grave and the government's attitude was shown by the appointment of a committee of Assessors from the Scottish Office. The Committee had a semi-official status. The central point of its analysis was the slow rate of growth of the Scottish economy. Its main recommendation was that a series of growth points should be selected and that, instead of a direct concern for levels of unemployment, these growth points should be used to move the Scottish economy so that unemployment would fall as a result of general improvements. This was to be the major suggestion which the government was to take from Toothill. Other recommendations were influential. The importance of diversification was emphasised as was the need for government help in training personnel for new skills and for a more scientific approach towards management. In government policy generally Toothill recommended the setting up of a full Scottish Economic Department within the Scottish Office and for overspill to be emphasised in housing policy. The New Towns were to be among the major growth points. Toothill also drew attention to emigration from Scotland as an indicator of the sickness of the Scottish economy. Emigration had always been an important feature of Scottish life since at least the eighteenth century but in the period from 1931 to 1951 it accounted for 44 per cent of the natural increase of Scotland. In the years 1951-61 it accounted for 76 per cent of the natural increase. In this way the young and economically most active and most skilled of the population were leaving when they were most needed to rebuild their own country. Toothill agreed that something had to be done to stop this drain.

The Toothill Report was both an indication of the awakening consciousness of Scotland and a means of extending this consciousness. Very soon after its publication the rate of unemployment again climbed and in the winter of 1962-3 was particularly bad. As a result two white papers were published, one for the north east (of England) and one for central Scotland, and in them the philosophy of growth points was accepted.[36] Where before aid was given only to areas where there was a high level of unemployment, in practice 4·5 per cent or over, grants of 10 per cent of the value of plant and machinery irrespective of management level were made to new employers who would come to Scotland and other areas affected.

Thus the beginning of the 1960s was a time of new departure for the economy as well as for politics in Scotland. It was a time when the traditional industries went into rapid and obvious decline and when new industries were brought in. The policy of 'growth points' led to an emphasis on help for the New Towns and communities other than those which had been major centres of the traditional industries. We should notice that several of them later became centres of nationalism. Cumbernauld New Town is the best known example since it was the first local authority to come under SNP control but the SNP also became strong in East Kilbride and Glenrothes. It is possible to see parallels between the growth of nationalism in the modernised parts of the Scottish economy and the growth of nationalism after the 'Quiet Revolution' in Quebec.[37] It is also worth remembering that nationalism was very slow to become established in areas where the traditional industries hung on.

The Labour government of 1966 went a further step along the road of this new economic policy by making the whole of Scotland, except Edinburgh and Leith, a Development Area. This action was precipitated by the fact that economic indicators showed that although things had got better for Scotland in the early 1960s there was a down-turn later on. Alexander comments:[38]

Census of production figures for 1968 now becoming available suggest that the effect of regional policies since 1963 with investment incentives . . . has led to a relatively greater investment than in the UK as a whole, but that this has not substantially strengthened the competitive position of manufacturing industry on Clydeside.

Thus in the later 1960s the situation that emerged was that the government followed a regional policy which generally raised the level of consciousness of Scotland as an economic unit. A clear indication of this was the setting up of the Regional Economic Planning Councils and Boards in Scotland and in the regions of England. At the same time it appeared that government action was not working to improve matters and this, put together with the establishment of the regional institutes, could have led to a feeling of hostility to the government based on a regional consciousness. Where this consciousness might not have a ready political vehicle in the English regions, this vehicle certainly existed in Scotland.

The closing years of the decade and the early 1970s saw new economic problems for Britain. Scotland, as always, shared them although more fortunate areas like the west Midlands also experienced recession and unemployment and, by comparison,

Scotland did not do quite so badly. Emigration rates from Scotland were also lower in these years but this was largely due to the fact that, with the world recession, there were not as many job opportunities abroad for the Scots. This may also have contributed to the rise of support for nationalism. Those who had previously emigrated now had no alternative but to exercise their votes.[39]

The one light in this economic darkness was the discovery of oil in the North Sea.[40] BP made the first strike at the end of 1969 but oil did not come to public attention until 1971 when commercial exploitation was started. It is worth emphasising these dates again. The success of the SNP is often put down to the discovery of North Sea oil but in fact the nationalist machine and the major part of its vote had been put together by the time that oil became an issue.

For the British government these strikes have been a major bonanza. They are regarded as one, if not the only, source of wealth with which to tackle the British balance of payments problem. There can be no doubt that they are regarded as a crucial asset which could not be handed over to a Scottish government. Not unnaturally, the nationalists see the oil deposits in a different light.

For Scotland the present and future benefits of oil are unknown. The problem is that exploitation of this resource does not create a large number of jobs, except in the early stages when sites are being built, pipe lines laid and drilling platforms constructed. When the oil is actually flowing 'on stream' the whole operation is virtually on a 'care and maintenance' basis. Alexander estimates that directly and indirectly a maximum of 60,000 jobs will be created and the minimum will be much lower.[41] There have been hopes that new industries would grow up around the shore installations but there appears to be no real reason why this should happen on any significant scale. The oil simply flows along the pipeline to a refinery. In Scotland there is a large refinery complex at Grangemouth but even refining does not provide a large number of jobs except in so far as oil by-products can be manufactured. North Sea oil is a 'sweet' oil with very few impurities and, since it is from these impurities that the by-products can be manufactured, the employment implications of North Sea oil do not seem to be great in a direct sense. As the Mackays point out, the only way in which oil can be used in this way is by using the revenue to invest in new industries.[42]

What has been the impact of oil on the Scottish economy? There has been a lot of activity generated from oil in the north east and in various other parts of Scotland. In places like Aberdeen and

Peterhead unemployment has virtually disappeared. How long will this last? The probable answer seems to be 'not very long'. Not only will fewer people be required to work in the industry and its ancillaries but the traditional industries, such as fishing, have lost large parts of their labour force to the higher paid but short-term oil projects. They are unlikely to get them all back. In the short run, however, the discovery of oil has led to an optimism in many parts of Scotland and it may not be a coincidence that most of the constituencies which returned a Nationalist MP in 1974 are on the 'oil' side of Scotland. Once again it may be that economic and social modernisation is the soil for the development of nationalism.

Conclusion

Whether they have been aware of good or bad times, the events of the last seventy years have made Scottish people more and more conscious of Scotland as an economic unit. At the beginning of the century people were aware of themselves as Scots and there was a certain pride in this. With economic decline came the awareness that Scotland had certain acute needs and particular government action was required. In the 1940s and 1950s various institutions were built up which spoke for Scotland. Apart from those which have been mentioned already we should also remember that the Scottish Trade Union Congress has also taken on the role as a 'spokesman for Scotland'.[43] Apart from these voluntary institutions, the government itself developed a regional economic policy which ensured that Scottish concerns would be accentuated. The political parties, and not least the SNP, have brought forward consciousness of the problems and possibilities of the Scottish economy. In the 1970s the arrival of oil exploitation has made the Scottish economy a first class politico-economic issue.

There is another side to Scottish economic performance. With the downturn of the early 1920s, after many years of prosperity, Scottish voters turned to the Labour Party. Whereas in the 1918 election the Labour Party in Scotland was able to capture only nine seats, at the next election, when the economic situation had become worse, they took twenty-nine. In what may be the same way the Scottish voters began to turn to the Nationalists in the 1960s when the good years of the 1950s were over. In a later chapter we shall examine survey data to see whether relative deprivation was related to nationalist voting. Here we can only say that such a relationship seems likely.

6 The Effects of Literary Nationalism

Nationalist movements are often influenced by poets or novelists who express the national ideals. In Ireland there was, at various points in the nineteenth century, an intellectual movement which was sympathetic to the political movement. One has only to think of the brilliant group of Yeats, Synge, George Moore and others at the beginning of the century.[1] In more recent years Senghor is not only a prominent politician but one of the most distinguished of French African poets.[2] In the development of nationalism in Europe in the mid-nineteenth century intellectuals of various sorts had their part. Among the Germans there was a direct contribution to nationalism by writers like Arndt or Auerbach.[3] In Russia, by contrast, perhaps the greatest contribution of the intellectuals was through the novel. Tolstoy and Dostoevsky, although they also wrote on overtly political subjects, were most powerful when they were writing fiction. Novels like *Anna Karenina* or *The Brothers Karamazov* helped to determine the whole concept of what it was to be Russian.

It is therefore not necessary for a literary movement to be made up of people who were active nationalists or even sympathetic to the nationalist cause. What is important is that there should be some writing which is set in the nation, or, at an even further range, which deals with problems symbolically the same. One may see the contribution to English nationalism made by Shakespeare. His histories elicit national pride in their portrayal of struggles against the French. In a somewhat different way, the Icelandic sagas have made an undoubted contribution to the sense of being Icelandic and from thence to Icelandic nationalism.

89

It is the argument of this section that there is a literary history in this century which is specifically Scottish. Some figures in this history have been directly linked to the nationalist cause and others have rejected it. The important effect, however, has been that Scottish people have been made aware that it was possible to have a literature which was peculiarly Scottish and Scottish in a modern sense rather than in a romantic or antiquarian vein. Something could be written about Scotland other than Jacobite historical novels and bucolic remembrances. These developments were important for a small but influential section in the Scottish intelligentsia. There has, however, been an important difference between the situation in the 1920s and 1930s and the situation after 1945. I shall argue that, for the poets and other writers of the first period, nationalism was a key issue: even *the* key issue. It is difficult to think of a single Scottish writer working in Scotland who did not take up a position. In the post-war world the situation has been quite different. There are still some figures of the 1920s and 1930s and their disciples. Many of these have become a sort of Scottish literary establishment. For the younger writers the concern with Scotland as a nation is often hardly discernible. Most of them have written about persons or situations which were identifiably Scottish but this did not have the implication of being concerned with the political issue. This change, therefore, meant that, in the field of literature as in other fields, the Scots people were left without leaders. Where poets like MacDiarmid, who wrote most of his poetry in the 1930s, wrote about politics and social conditions from a nationalist point of view, poets like Ian Crichton Smith or Tom Buchan hardly seem to raise the subject. When political or social questions are raised, for example by Alan Sharp, they are seen in terms of a sort of left-right split. This question of literary leadership is brought out more obviously by the fact that since the war there has been no one to compare with MacDiarmid in terms of his influence on Scottish letters. Thus, from the point of view of literary stature and from that of the direction of his arguments, there has been no intellectual leadership since the war to compare with that before the war. Even in the 1920s and 1930s, however, and this is crucial, the leaders of the modern Scottish literary movements were not major public figures. They led only a small army. If writers with the public reputation of John Buchan had supported nationalism an entirely different situation would have been created.

I shall bring evidence on these points in the course of the chapter.

In considering why this change has taken place I shall argue that it has to do with two visions of modernity. In the inter-war period nationalism could be looked on as a reaction against and a move beyond the Victorianism which may have been even more suffocating in Scotland than in England. With the coming of the Spanish Civil War the left-right split became more important. After 1945 a man was marked as being for or against socialism and, as the Labour government progressed, or at least got older, he was marked as being for or against *real* socialism. As an attractive position for the young intellectual nationalism was almost non-existent.

It may be asked why a political scientist studying nationalism should concern himself with a literary movement. I shall argue that the writers and their public combined constituted only the merest handful of the population. It is not even the case that they tried to produce a consistent ideology for the movement. I certainly do not believe that one can explain the rise of support for the SNP as a result of the thinking of these intellectuals. On the other hand there is no doubt that they were valued by leading nationalists and, even for those who did not need them, they were a symbol that Scottish literature could have an honoured place. One may look at modern Scottish literature both as a symptom of an awakened Scotland and also as a force that encouraged some Scotsmen to work in the political field. Quite a few nationalist politicians have said specifically that they came to politics through the influence of works of art. This in itself is reason enough for taking the literary movement seriously.

The creed of the literary nationalist

One of the central beliefs in the creed of the nationalist writer of the 1920s and 1930s was that, with the movement of the Court to London with James VI, a serious, if not impossible, barrier was put in the way of Scots as a literary medium. The Court was the centre of patronage and, even more, of interest and activity. Then as now poets and dramatists did not easily make a living from their art. As a matter of economic necessity it was essential to find a patron and most of the patrons had gone to London. But it was not simply money that was the problem. Without the centre of government Edinburgh became a provincial backwater and the rest of Scotland became even more remote from the sort of events which could make great literature.

More than this, the distinctive languages, Scots (sometimes called Lallans) and Gaelic, were assigned the status of dialects, the mark of

91

the yokel or of the barbarian. Whether or not this is an accurate account overall, it is certainly true that the Scots language soon began to pass out of use for official, literary or polite purposes. David Hume and Adam Smith both remark on the necessity to lose the Scottish accent and the Edinburgh bourgeoisie employed teachers of elocution in order to acquire an English accent. Cockburn's *Memorials* refer to the demise of the Scottish tongue as do Sir Walter Scott and R. L. Stevenson.[4] In short, it was not just the twentieth century nationalists who felt that the loss of the language would have social and perhaps political consequences.

There are several histories of Scottish literature but in any case a detailed discussion would not be appropriate here.[5] It is sufficient to trace in some of the more important points. The end of the eighteenth century and the beginning of the nineteenth concern us most. At that period in Scotland various major writers were active, of whom Scott and Burns were the most important. Their greatness did, however, have certain drawbacks. The first was that they were so totally dominant. Anyone writing after them had the greatest difficulty in being taken seriously. Much of Scottish literary life operated on the basis of being an admiration society for one or other and especially, of course, for Burns. For this or for other reasons, there was a gap in serious writing in the middle years of the nineteenth century with the exception of Carlyle.[6] The other major problem was that the vision that Scott and Burns had of Scotland dominated later thinking about the country. Their picture of Scotland was of a rural society either among the lowland peasants or among other strata of Scottish society, for example in the Highlands. While this was applicable in their day, by the last quarter of the century the central belt of Scotland had come to house most of the population and industrial communities had been formed. Not until MacDiarmid was there any real recognition of this industrial society and, with the exception of perhaps Davidson, no writer tried to write about industrial urban life until after 1945.[7] Even MacDiarmid had very little contact with it.

If we are to understand Scotland's vision of herself in the nineteenth century it must be seen through the eyes of Scott and Burns. One of the most important features of Scott's vision was the emphasis he placed on aristocracy, the ordering of society and the place of the Crown. It is wholly in character that Scott was largely responsible for the visit of George IV to Edinburgh in 1822 and that the citizens of Edinburgh, under this spell and the spell of prosperity and the winning of the European wars, should have given their king such a welcome.[8] The feature which is remembered about this visit was the use of Highland dress and an exuberant and theatrical Scottishness of a certain type. To understand this even better one has to recall the influence of Macpherson's *Ossian* and the belief that in the Highlands there existed a race of noble savages romantically living in a landscape which was only now coming to be highly valued for its wildness.[9] Only a generation before this travellers in those parts were repelled by the isolation and un-cultivated nature of the area.[10] For the world, and for the bourgeoisie of the larger Scottish towns, Scotland became a romantic, rural, tragic and largely imaginary place. An interesting result of Scott's writing was that Scottish people started to travel very widely to visit some of the historic sights. By the 1820s and 1830s many of these places were visited regularly.

It was not surprising that when George IV's niece Queen Victoria paid her first visit to Scotland in 1842 she, and Prince Albert, who was even more obsessed by the Romantic vision, conceived a passion for Scotland and a castle, Balmoral, was built, which epitomises the attitude of the middle and upper classes to the Scotland of those days. Victoria's diary is a remarkable revelation of a monarch's ignorance about her kingdom, in spite of having travelled through it.[11] In the tradition of the 1822 visit she was met by the gentry and chiefs and a charade of traditional Scottish life was prepared for her amusement. She travelled from country house to castle where the estate staffs and farm servants would be called out and drilled to appear as a Highland guard. Pipers piped, dancers danced, deer were slaughtered, quaint customs and even quainter people were observed and the Queen and Albert were charmed. It was indeed as well that they were charmed because the effort must have wellnigh ruined some of those who provided the entertainment. The royals enjoyed it so much that they came again and again. Balmoral Castle was rebuilt to become a regular summer home and all over Scotland gentry who could often ill afford them, built miniature Balmorals.

It was clear that Victoria's influence was very great among the highest strata of Scottish society. The Scottish influence was visible at the Court where some Scottish servants were retained and some acts of 'stage Scottishness' were performed. More important than this was the royal example for the mass of the middle classes. The Queen's fondness for Scotland was known and widely commented upon in the newspapers and finally in Victoria's diaries. They show that the Queen accepted the vision of Scotland which was purveyed to her by those who surrounded her. For her the fact that the glens were empty and the cottages ruined was not a sign of a once-living culture which had been snuffed out. It was a positive incarnation of primitive solitude and romantic melancholy. This vision was widely communicated to the British reading public since the various parts of the *Journal* sold widely. The cult of Scottishness which had been established at the beginning of the nineteenth century by Scott was helped on very considerably and made steadfastly respectable by the Queen.

This was the background to the Victorian cult of 'Scottishness'. It had little to do with the important changes taking place in Scottish life at that time and it was certainly not relevant to the way the majority of Scots lived. Instead it expressed an interest in quaintness and odd forms of speech which was another Victorian obsession.[12] This move from the romantic Highlands to more domestic scenes is the background to the growth of the Kailyard School.[13]

It is important not to see the Kailyard as a unified movement.[14] It had, however, certain central characteristics. The first was that the setting was almost invariably small town or small village. When we remember that these novelists were at their peak at the end of the nineteenth century we realise that they were writing about a Scotland of days gone by. The whole movement looked back to a Scotland which, it was believed, had existed—a rural *Gemeinschaft* where there was security (the overarching British empire), where people knew their place and, on the whole, were nice to each other. There was suffering and personal tragedy, there were stories of pain courageously borne, there was the hope of the life to come when sorrows would be wiped away. Such a vision may seem unpleasant to us but in fact it was a success not just in Scotland but all over Britain.

In order to understand the success of these novels and short stories one must recognise two things. First, there had been a radical change in the social and economic life of the whole of Britain. The industrial revolution had changed the life style of the majority of the population: in the sort of work they did, and, in a hundred detailed ways, down to the sorts of food they ate, their relations with other people and the artefacts they used.[15] The pace of the change was, moreover, rapid and people were well aware that the alterations in their life styles were fundamental. With this in mind it is not surprising that they should look back on the old days with affection and regret, remembering the good points and forgetting less happy aspects. At the same time one must bear in mind that this was a time of great confidence for the British. There were fluctuations in trade but, all in all, Victorians were confident about the expanding place of Britain in the world. The novels and stories of that time give an overwhelming impression of stability. Their authors sometimes express regret about the days that are past but there is no suggestion of a retreat into this bucolic society from the reality of the modern world. There is little suggestion that the life of the metropolis or the industrial town is a devouring monster carrying the seeds of its own destruction.

The second point has to do with the place of the Church in Scottish life. From the fifteenth century until the eighteenth the hold of Calvinism and Puritanism through the established Church was pervasive. The Church was able to depress most artistic activity including poetry and drama. With the eighteenth century, however, came the Enlightenment and a distinct softening in the attitude of some sections of the Church. The 'Moderate' party eventually triumphed and it was no longer considered inherently sinful to read or write secular literature. For certain churchmen this meant an appreciation of the best literature and art of the time.[16] As the nineteenth century wore on, however, the literary quality of Scottish writers deteriorated and what was left was gentility, but without the other, greater qualities. The whole atmosphere of novels which became immensely successful towards the end of the nineteenth century is one in which the Church still exists as a social institution and a guarantor of morality.[17] What has fled from it is the spiritual vision and fervour of the reformers. The evangelical revival was in full flood but this was an aspect that did not come through perhaps because the people who were writing the stories were not in that camp in the Church. What is important for our argument is that the ethos of the Kailyard writings was one in which Christianity was recognised as a social institution but not as a spiritual principle; but it was an *important* social institution and part of it was the somewhat restrictive view of human freedom which has its best known symbol in the practice of Sabbatarianism. It was genteel, it was small-minded, its flights of imagination were on clipped wings. The novels and short stories were such as might be observed by a minister in the villages and small burghs of Scotland. It does not come as a surprise that several of the most successful of the writers were themselves ministers and the greatest of the entrepreneurs of

95

the school, Sir William Robertson Nicoll, was also a former Free Church minister.[18]

It was against this type of literature and view of life that the poets of the Scottish literary renaissance revolted. They disliked virtually everything about it. For our purposes it is most important to recognise that they disliked the portrayal of Scotland as a quaint 'pawky' province of North Britain. If there was one thing that the Kailyarders did not do it was to question political authority or even to mention politics as a serious theme. For their opponents this was the centre of the whole affair. They reacted against the almost total Kailyard domination of Scottish literature by raising these awkward questions.

The evidence is fairly clear that nationalism came before the move to literary nationalism on the part of two of the most important of the modern poets, Hugh MacDiarmid and Lewis Spence. In both cases their early work is in English.[19] It is only after 1918 that the attempt to recreate the literary language begins. MacDiarmid says specifically that the experiences of the war contributed to the change.[20] Britain was supposed to be fighting for the rights of small nations and it was difficult to see why the small nations within the United Kingdom should not have their claims heard. MacDiarmid claims to have been a nationalist since boyhood and Spence's interest in self-government for Scotland also seems to go back to the time before he started to write in Scots.[21] What is important for both is that they were interested in the re-creation of Scots as a literary language and both were active nationalists.

Writing in Scots had never ceased completely. In the nineteenth century, however, it was almost entirely in the language of one or other of the Scots dialects.[22] There are one or two exceptions and it is important to say that Burns and Stevenson both used words and forms which did not necessarily come from the same dialect.[23] Spence and MacDiarmid, however, were different in that they wanted to write in a *literary* language which would be definitely Scots. Both felt that the dialects could not express the complex thoughts and high sentiments which were now necessary for the poetry of a modern nation. Poetry in the dialects was too much associated with the Kailyard to be of any use. Spence tried to go back to Middle Scots, the language of the so-called 'Scottish Chaucerians', but MacDiarmid, apparently influenced by Norwegian *Landsmaal*, put together words from all the Scottish dialects to produce what he hoped would be a new literary language. The reasons why these men and others became involved in this was that they were nationalists and they believed that the nation should have a literature that expressed its ideals and could educate the people for their place as Scots in the world of nations.

There is no doubt about the nationalist credentials of Spence and MacDiarmid. MacDiarmid was one of the first members of the Scottish Home Rule Association when it was re-founded by R. E. Muirhead in 1918 and he was a prolific propagandist for nationalism through the medium of articles in local newspapers.[24] Spence was the central figure in the Scots National Movement, one of the four organisations joining together to make up the National Party of Scotland in 1928. It is fair to say that the early nationalist movement of these days was partly led by literary men and intellectuals. This is not, however, the main point here. Here the central consideration is that MacDiarmid especially introduced a new movement in Scottish literature which was to have very wide implications for Scottish letters and intellectual life generally.

In the years after 1918 there was a strong feeling in the intellectual world that the days of Britain's greatness were over. For many this also meant that European culture as a whole was in its dying stages. This is a view to which MacDiarmid subscribed but it was a view fairly widely held at this time. MacDiarmid saw England as one of Spengler's 'exhausted civilisations' and believed, also with Spengler, that the new way might be shown by one of the smaller nations.[25] Scotland was an obvious candidate for this role. It was extremely important that Scotland should have a vigorous intellectual and literary life. This was the critical difference between MacDiarmid and most of the others. The tradition of vernacular or dialect verse might be quite vigorous. Indeed, it was not just the nationalists who were active in the cause of Scottish literature at this time. The Burns Federation, about the same time, began to act as a pressure group on the Scottish Education Department in favour of the teaching of Scottish literature in the schools. The Vernacular Circle in the London Burns club and other Burns clubs were interested in the dialect poets other than Burns. As William Power put it: 'The main and immediate purpose of the vernacular movement is to ensure that every Scottish child shall be placed in possession of a key to the national treasure house of vernacular literature.'[26] But, for MacDiarmid, this was still a backward-looking movement. He placed himself foursquare in the modern movement. For him the same currents that were moving in contemporary literature elsewhere in the world had to be expressed in Scots. His work in poetry and prose is full of references to current thought in European literature.[27]

In his stance as a nationalist, MacDiarmid was firmly in a tradition in Scottish literature. This was a tradition which had often gone underground and might be little known but only elementary research is necessary to find it. Burns wrote 'Scots Wha Hae', perhaps the best known of all the Scots patriotic songs. In other writings he was much more explicitly nationalist, in 'Such a parcel of rogues in a nation',[28] for example, or in passages in his corres-pondence. Similarly, Allan Ramsay was openly against the Union.[29] MacDiarmid's importance is not just that he was a nationalist but that he was also a 'modern'. It is very important to be clear about what this meant to him.

Some aspects of MacDiarmid's modernism have already been noticed, for example, that it was an attempt to break out of the traditional moulds of Scottish writing. In a critique of Edwin Muir, MacDiarmid praises his knowledge of European literature and says of himself: 'I wanted to escape from the provincialism of Scottish literature.'[30] Secondly, MacDiarmid brought a whole new set of subjects into his poetry. I have already mentioned his nationalism and it was fairly unusual to do this in Britain at the beginning of the twentieth century but, in addition, some of his longer poems contain long discussions of Marxist ideas and even of science.[31] What this does to the quality of the poetry is debatable but these were certainly subjects more modern than most poets were prepared to deal with. Thirdly, MacDiarmid was and is a left wing socialist. Indeed, he thinks of himself as a Communist and since 1956 has once more been a party member. Throughout his life he has been associated with the radical and progressive train in politics. There is an interesting contrast here with Lewis Grassic Gibbon (Leslie Mitchell), who has roughly the same stature in the realm of the Scottish novel as MacDiarmid has in poetry. Lewis Grassic Gibbon was also a Communist. In the third part of his great trilogy he makes this point quite clear but at the same time one of his themes is the link between modern Scots and their prehistoric ancestors.[32] His implication, moreover, is that this earlier time was better. MacDiarmid comments: 'I do not share his belief in any such Golden Age. Any Golden Age humanity might have lies in the future and must be worked for.'[33] MacDiarmid works for a better state of society in which the power of intellect applied to new social and physical science will bring men on to a new plane of being.

The empty hand of my brother man,
The humanity no culture has reached, the mob.
Intelligentsia, our impossible and imperative job![34]

And again:

> He canna Scotland see wha yet
> Canna see the Infinite
> And Scotland in true scale to it.[35]

A further important general point about MacDiarmid should be
appreciated in order to understand his impact on Scottish literature
and nationalism. His early training was as a journalist and in the
1920s he both reported for a local newspaper in Montrose, the
Montrose Review, and worked in the field of public relations. This
experience was important in the future reception of his work.
MacDiarmid was an indefatigable publicist. He was certainly aware
of his own qualities as a poet and never missed an opportunity to
point them out but, in addition, he seldom missed opportunities to
publicise the work of his fellow intellectuals in the Scottish
movement. Thus apart from any claim which MacDiarmid has to
being a poet of European stature, he has been a major influence
simply because he continually worked to bring the modern Scottish
movement, which was a nationalist movement, to the attention of his
audience. They might not have read his poems, or the work of
William Souter,[36] or Fion McColla,[37] or Maurice Lindsay,[38] but it
was much more likely that they would have read his reviews or essays
under many different pseudonyms in every sort of publication from
literary quarterly to local weekly. What MacDiarmid did was to
build up the atmosphere of great things happening in Scottish
literature. Many people, whose reading of the actual poetry or novel
was very limited, were prepared to believe that writing was going on
in Scotland which was fresh, iconoclastic, cosmopolitan and
committed.

It would not be too much to say that MacDiarmid was the
mainstay of the literary renaissance. He certainly raised the issue of
nationalism and its importance for culture and life in Scotland.
There were others who were Scottish writers but who did not agree
with him.

The two Scottish writers who were best known for their disagreement with MacDiarmid in both literary and political matters are
Edwin Muir[39] and Lewis Grassic Gibbon. Both of them were major

figures in Scottish or even European letters and stand well ahead of most of MacDiarmid's followers. Both of them started with a certain sympathy for the nationalist point of view both in terms of art and politics but both of them left it for reasons which are extremely instructive for the future course of literary nationalism and nationalism in general.

The first reason has to do with the language issue. Quite simply, Muir recognised that the Scottish writer laboured under an enormous handicap. If he was to get some kind of admission to a large English-speaking public he had to write in a language which he had not been brought up to speak. He had to learn it. He could not use the rhythms of speech and many of the idioms natural to him. He recognised that the reasons for this were largely political and that the situation was applicable to all Scottish people and not just to those who tried to write. They carried within themselves 'the broken image of the lost Kingdom'.

Muir's definitive statement of his position comes in *Scott and Scotland*,[40] which must stand as one of the most perceptive criticisms of the entire corpus of Sir Walter Scott's work. What did Scotland give to Scott? What was the cultural and social basis on which he could found his writing? Muir answers that it gave Scott a legend of heroic deeds, something on which his genius could found great romances but:[41]

> it could not give him a complete framework of living experience on which to nourish his powers and exercise them; in other words, it could not give him a basis for the profound criticism of life of which there is no doubt that he was capable.

As far as the issue of language is concerned, Muir concluded that there is no possibility of going back to Middle Scots or creating a language out of the dialects. The use of the dialects was what brought the curse of provincialism and he was in absolute agreement with MacDiarmid in rejecting it. Scottish writers had to recognise that they must write in English even though it was not wholly natural to them. The Irish, after all, had done it with enormous success by incorporating their own characteristics and the Scots must do the same.

This was an extremely influential essay. Published in 1936, it came at a time when the nationalist movement was beginning to flag under the competing interest of the crisis in Europe. It also came at a time when MacDiarmid himself was starting once more to write in English.[42] In any case Muir was rightly an enormously respected commentator and it was difficult for the younger writers to pay quite the same respect to MacDiarmid's position after this essay appeared. Several poets went on writing in Lallans and still do but it no longer holds the centre of the stage for the literary nationalists. For the bulk of nationalist activists and supporters, literature became less important although articles by MacDiarmid and others appeared in their periodicals such as the *Scots Independent* and, even more, in the *Free Man*. MacDiarmid's immediate influence on the movement declined after he was expelled from the NPS in 1933. The first reason for this expulsion was that he was simply too uncompromising a personality to be contained in a young movement which was going through a bad patch. The second was that he was an outspoken adherent of the Douglas Social Credit Proposals which the party examined and rejected about this time. Perhaps most important of all was the fact that he announced and kept on announcing that he was a Communist and in his poetry and prose kept up a regular stream of criticism of the capitalist order whether it was English or Scottish. We shall see that in 1933 the leaders of the NPS were trying to engineer a fusion with a more conservative self-government movement, the Scottish Party. A person like MacDiarmid would be difficult to have around.

I said that there were two reasons why Muir and Lewis Grassic Gibbon denied the nationalist position. The second has to do with the point just raised about MacDiarmid. Somehow MacDiarmid managed to remain both a nationalist and a socialist. The trend among intellectuals in the 1930s in the whole of Europe was to form up along a left-right spectrum and the vast majority of the younger ones chose the left. For both Muir and Gibbon this was more important than nationalism. In his essay on Glasgow in *Scottish Scene* Gibbon is quite explicit about this:[43]

If it came, as it may come, to some fantastic choice of a free and independent Scotland, a centre of culture, a bright flame of artistic and scientific achievement, or providing elementary decencies of food and shelter to the submerged proletariat of Glasgow and Scotland, I at least would have no doubt as to on which side of the battle I would range myself. For the cleansing of that horror, if cleanse it they could, I would welcome the English sovereignty over Scotland until the end of time. I would welcome the end of Braid Scots and Gaelic, our culture, our history, our nationhood under the heels of a Chinese army of occupation if it could cleanse the Glasgow slums.

MacDiarmid characteristically comments: 'I on the other hand would sacrifice a million people any day for one immortal lyric. I am a scientific socialist.'[44] The fact was, however, that the issue of nationalism became much less important for the younger writers by comparison with their attitudes to socialism. This is not to say that there were not poets who were also interested in the national community of Scotland. Those who became known after 1945 tended to align themselves with the Communist Party or with the left of the Labour Party but they were also interested in national questions as the poetry read at the 1948 John Maclean meeting shows quite incontrovertibly. But somehow the issue of the Scottish nation did not take off as a central artistic concern as it had in the inter-war years. Poets and novelists might not be nationalists but if they were not they had to present arguments against that case. It is true that Muir and Gibbon were in the first rank of writers but, on the national issue, they were in a minority among their contemporaries.

Any review of Scottish literature in the twentieth century must mention Neil Gunn. He is remarkable for having produced novels of a consistently high quality[45] but what is less well known is that he was a senior figure in the inter-war nationalist movement.[46] We shall discuss this in Chapter 13. The sole point which is to be made here is that Gunn's novels, in their sensitive, lyrical treatment of Highland life were widely read and appreciated in a way which was not possible for MacDiarmid's difficult poetry or even the more accessible work of Muir or Souter. The theme which recurs in Gunn's novels is of the community which is breached and torn but which, once again, establishes itself. Gunn's work is, in a way, the antithesis of MacDiarmid's professed aim to portray a modern Scotland. His settings are almost always of a society that is gone. On the other hand the quality of his writing commands attention. His themes of community and of the recurring heroic character who both embodies and re-establishes the values of that community sum up very well the noblest aims of the nationalist whose concern is the re-creation of Scotland.

Before leaving the inter-war period something must be said about the position of Gaelic. It is an original Scottish language and is thus a candidate for the attention of the nationalists as a Scottish characteristic distinguishing them from the English. This indeed, is a point made by MacDiarmid in a context where he seems to downgrade Scots or Lallans to a tongue which could hold the line for Scottish individuality until a Gaelic commonwealth could be brought in. Thus, a major figure in the development of intellectual nationalism in Scotland recommends the same sort of position for Gaelic as was hoped for Erse in Ireland. It is not too much to say that MacDiarmid took up the same cry, 'No language, no People'. It is almost possible to say that the whole logic of MacDiarmid's case took him in this direction. It must also be pointed out, however, that he did not express these sentiments for very long and he never attempted to write in Gaelic. In Chapters 12 and 13 we shall study the development of the political side of the movement and, at the very beginning we shall see the deep involvement of individuals for whom Gaelic links were very important. By the end of the 1920s, however, the importance of this aspect of Scottish nationalism was only as a marginal programme for the parity of Gaelic in the Gaelic-speaking areas and as a hobby for a few of the activists. There is no evidence that Gaelic literature in the twentieth century had any impact on the advance of nationalism despite the fact that some distinguished Gaelic writers like Derick Thomson have been nationalists.

After the end of the war there were signs that the literary nationalists were coming into their inheritance. By this time there was no doubt about MacDiarmid's stature and he was accompanied by several other poets who wrote entirely or partly in Lallans. They came together at meetings such as the John Maclean Memorial meeting in 1948 and at many poetry readings. Their poetry was published in several magazines.[47] There was, indeed, a feeling in the 1960s that they represented a kind of establishment in Scottish poetry and some of the younger poets reacted against this.[48] One might have expected that in this way they would have an increased influence on thinking in Scotland. If anything the reverse seems to have been the case.

One feature of the post-war scene was like the 1920s and 1930s. Although there was a great deal of lip service paid to the quality of MacDiarmid's writing, not many people read it. Scottish school children will have read his work but it is still more common to be examined on his English contemporaries, Eliot, Auden, Spender and MacNeice. Therefore, if the school of MacDiarmid became the

103

poetic establishment it was not an establishment which ruled over a large empire. But there is more to it. The battles of the 1920s and 1930s about the use of Scots and the importance of literature for the new nation were fought and over. Many of the younger poets, especially towards the end of the 1950s, became involved in other things. The issues then were those of 'commitment' and those poets and other Scottish writers who were aware of politics took up more or less the same stands as their politically aware colleagues in England. The impetus of the *New Left Review* and the radical movement was simply too strong to be avoided. Nationalism did not have a place. For many of the others, unlike the young poets in the 1930s, politics was not interesting. In common with the majority of the British people, and perhaps the majority of European people, the predominant political attitude of the 1960s was cynicism.

One reason for this situation was the international climate. Another was the climate in Scotland. Whereas the early days of the SNP had seen literary figures like R. B. Cunninghame Graham and Compton Mackenzie in important positions, the small, defensive post-war SNP was in no sense an attractive environment for them. It seemed to outsiders like a tiny body of purists intent on navel gazing. In terms of popular appeal it had been overtaken by the Covenant. Although poets like Hamish Henderson might attend the Convention Assemblies and sign the Covenant, this was too much of an establishment and bourgeois organisation to be a spiritual home for writers. Thus, the paths of the poets and the nationalists of whatever kind diverged. A third point which must never be forgotten is that a great deal of the public attention to literary nationalism and the language question is due to the propagandist activities of MacDiarmid as a literary journalist. As he grew older he was no longer able to engage in this sort of work at the same rate. The controversy, which had almost been created by him, to a very large extent quietened down.

It is a notable feature of the nationalist movement in Scotland today that it has little overt support from the intellectuals. Their work has often been set in a Scottish setting and has dealt with situations which were peculiarly Scottish.[49] They have tended to deal with these themes in terms of the isolated individual or of a class situation[50] and it is difficult to understand what they have done in terms of its relevance to the Scottish community as a whole. Certainly none of them has been identified with the cause of nationalism or even with a particular concern for Scotland in the way that MacDiarmid, Gunn and McColla were nationalists before the war or even as Muir and Gibbon wrote about Scotland from a non-nationalist point of view.

The rank and file of SNP voters and workers, in turn, do not support the intellectuals. One may argue that the reason for this is that we are now dealing with a mass party and the masses are seldom interested in poetry. The aims of a mass movement are not likely to have much to do with the world of ideals. One can, however, look at the matter in rather a different way. Despite the obvious quality of the modern writers, they seem to have ignored the questions of national identity which have come to be an interest of the Scottish people. The support the Covenant Movement had was widespread. As I have shown in other sections of this book there was, after the war, an upsurge of interest in things Scottish, quite apart from political questions. The young writers seemed to ignore it. In this field and in others Scotland became a leaderless nation.

7 Youth and Nationalism

When commentators woke up after the shock of the Hamilton by-election one point often made was of the youth of Nationalist workers. In this chapter I shall discuss why youth in particular might have been attracted to this political cause. In previous chapters the growth of Scottish consciousness in the nation as a whole has been tackled. We now move to that critically important section of the political population: the young voters.

The chapter is divided into two sections. In the first I shall discuss an aspect of experience which might have encouraged the growth of nationalism but, I shall argue, did not: this was the teaching of Scottish history. Much more important has been the rise of the folk song movement. This provided a set of Scottish symbols which could be manipulated by Nationalists in order to attract the young voters and even those below voting age. I do not argue that these were the only, or even the major, reasons for the support which the SNP has had from young Scots men and women. On the contrary, the general discontent with traditional politics which communicated itself most powerfully to those who had not the habit of voting was undoubtedly the most important ground for this development. On the other hand the folk song movement gave them a direction in which to press their efforts.

The teaching of history and the growth of nationalism

Nationalists have always believed that the history and traditions of the nation are central for the development of national feeling. They introduce the people and especially the young to the heroes and the great deeds which have forged the community and through this an identity is established. People are taught to know who they are and what is expected of them. We should, therefore, look at the teaching of history in Scottish schools to see whether this provided a basis for the growth in national feeling. It is generally believed that the Nationalist vote is a young vote. A sudden surge in the popularity of Scottish history or a new determination to teach it might have created a generation of Nationalist youth.

There has undoubtedly been an increase in the teaching of Scottish history since 1945. I shall argue, however, that this was not a cause of the rise in the Nationalist vote but rather a result of the same changes that were taking place in Scotland and in Britain as a whole. In order to explain this I shall discuss first the nature of the history that was taught; secondly the structure of the history profession at school and university level; and finally the way in which history has been treated in the schools.

If we read the books used to teach Scottish history from the end of the nineteenth century, we are struck by several features.[1] The first is the enormous importance of Scott's *Tales of a Grandfather*.[2] This is, in effect, a history of Scotland from the times of the primitive tribes down to 1820, told in the form of stories to a boy. If we then turn to even such a serious historical study as P. Hume Brown's *History of Scotland*, we find that many of Scott's *Tales* are repeated without criticism.[3] This is more evidently true of the one-volume edition which was produced for schools.[4] The major difference between the earlier author and the later is that Hume Brown introduces more social and economic history. Especially at the beginning Scott's account tends to be a recital of one battle after another. Much later authors also adopt Scott's approach and interpretation.

The central interpretation of Scott, followed by virtually every historian until Agnes Muir Mackenzie, was what has been called the 'Whig interpretation of history'.[5] In the history of Scotland this essentially meant that the Union of 1707 with England was seen as the crown of the historical process. It was this which finally brought prosperity and happiness to a 'poor though courageous country'. Brown says, 'The consenting testimony of a later time has approved the far-sighted wisdom of this policy.'[6] Andrew Lang, quoting Defoe is more metaphysical: 'It [the Union] was merely formed by the nature of things',[7] and Thomas Wright described the Union as 'an immense benefit to Scotland'.[8]

The picture of Scotland which was painted was of a poor, quarrelsome, uncivilised country with a disreputable nobility and a few romantic figures. Following in Scott's footsteps, a great deal of attention was lavished on Prince Charles Edward Stuart and the 1745 rising. There was often nostalgia for the independence which Scotland had cast aside but hard-headed common sense dictated the view that all had been for the best. In fact, Scott displayed more nostalgia for that independence and for the old customs than was the case in the succeeding histories.

This account of Scottish customs was, therefore, presented to the young in school and university. It is important to notice, however, that very little history of any kind was in fact taught in Scottish schools and universities before 1945.

The teaching of history in schools depended very much on the teaching of history in the universities since it was there that the school teachers were trained. Before the second half of the nineteenth century, history was not taught as a separate subject in Scottish universities. Some history was taught by Professors of Law and incidentally by those in other departments but separate history teaching came only after the report of a Royal Commission in 1876. After this an interest in the teaching of Scottish history developed quickly. The first Chair of History in Scotland was founded in Glasgow in 1894 and the first Chair of Scottish History was established in Edinburgh in 1901 with Glasgow following in 1903. The establishment of the Glasgow Chair was the direct result of public agitation. The Professor of History, Medley, opposed it and he was supported by the Glasgow School Board but funds were raised by a large exhibition of Scottish history in 1911 in Kelvingrove. Lenman's comment on the exhibition is interesting:[9]

> The incoherence of the exhibition from the rattlesnake pit to the bogus Highland village 'An Clachan' and Prince Charles's inevitable walking stick, reflected a basic dilemma of the movement. The new Chair was meant to be different not just by being Scottish but also be embodying a new approach to historical reality emphasising folk values. The term 'folk' implies participation in a tradition but agreement on what constituted the Scottish tradition was far to seek. Supporters of the Chair ranged from supporters of modern Scottish economic history to inhabitants of the Celtic twilight never-never world which was waxing potent around Glasgow.

These problems were to dog the teaching of Scottish history for a long time. As Medley's attitude had shown, it was considered a parochial interest and prominent historians did not encourage their brightest students to go into this field. Partly this was due to the emotions which overlaid the subject. It was controversial and the rigour of scholarship too easily gave way to partisanship. More than this, the study of all things Scottish was considered to be too reminiscent of the Kailyard. Historians saw Scotland as a backward and rather sordid place overshadowed by the more civilised and cosmopolitan England. In any case, academic historians, along with their colleagues in other disciplines, looked to Oxford and Cambridge for their intellectual leaders. The greater number of job opportunities in English universities, either in Oxbridge or elsewhere, meant that there was an emphasis on English or European history. Not many outside Scotland would be interested in a competence in Scottish history where, in any case, history 'ceased' with the Jacobites.

Thus it came about that there was, until the end of the 1950s, little university leadership in the teaching of history. Historians of Scotland were not highly regarded by their colleagues. In the schools the situation was similar. Ever since the nineteenth century Scottish history had been taught to the younger children, indeed by the 1872 Act there was a financial inducement to teachers to teach some history including Scottish history. The intellectual level at which this was carried out was low as can be deduced from the title of one of the most popular texts: the Multum in Parvo *History of Scotland for School Children.* [10] It is still true that most teaching of Scottish history takes place in the primary school. At the secondary level there was hardly any call for history teaching. Before 1939 history was not a subject in the Scottish Certificate of Education which gave qualifications for university entrance. In the whole of Scotland there were only about eleven places for specialist history teachers. The subject was taught but usually by English teachers and not at a very high level. The amount of Scottish history which was taught was minimal and Scottish school children knew more about the Norman Conquest, the Wars of the Roses and other pre-Union English topics than about the development of their own country. In general there was little incentive for students to take up a history course with teaching in mind.

After 1945 the situation changed. First, history became a subject for both the Higher and Lower grades of the Scottish Leaving Certificate. It was still true that very little Scottish history was taught as one can see by looking at the papers themselves. In 1948, for example, out of twenty-eight questions in the Higher paper there were only four on Scottish history and this was a fairly regular proportion up to the early 1960s. In the Lower paper in 1948, for example, it was only five out of thirty.

In the universities of this time, however, things were changing a little. One sign of the times was the revival of the *Scottish Historical Review*. This was established in 1904 at a time when interest in Scottish things and Scottish history was to the fore as we have seen in the foundation of the Chairs and lectureships of Scottish history. In 1928 it was discontinued. In 1947, however, it was started again and has appeared quarterly ever since.

This revival of interest was part of the general interest in Scottish things arising from war-time discussions of reconstruction. Perhaps the activities of the nationalists and what was to become the Scottish Convention also contributed. Another reason was that the study of history itself was beginning to change. Formerly the emphasis was very much on politico-military history. Now a greater interest in economic and social history was being established. Whereas after the eighteenth century Scottish history was of little interest to an historian who concentrated on treaties, battles and court intrigues and Parliaments, for the economic and social historian Scotland was as interesting as anywhere else. Several scholars now began to work in this field and to turn out work which was on a par with work being done elsewhere in the country. It was history about Scotland but it did not bear the professional stigma which Scottish history up to then had had. Either for these reasons or for others a new spirit also came into the teaching of Scottish political history albeit in a more traditional way. Where before work like Hume Brown's or Mackie's had been rather in the tradition of *Tales of a Grandfather*, the *Edinburgh History of Scotland* established, by the end of the 1960s and beginning of the 1970s, a kind of 'bench mark' history.[11] Up to that time many aspects of Scottish history had been inadequately covered or had been done in an oldfashioned way. Each volume of the *Edinburgh History* was written by a scholar of repute and was treated in a way fully within the canons of modern practice. Along with the *Edinburgh History* came a series of monographs which again added to the building-up of information and the ability to work systematically in the field. Works such as *Morvern Transformed* were the fruit of meticulous searches through archives and other evidences and owed nothing to the 'myths' of Scottish history.[12]

Thus, almost for the first time, the increasing number of history teachers in Scottish schools could feel that they could teach Scottish history in a way that was modern and scientific. They could approach the subject with confidence since a great deal of the old feeling of the second-rate position of Scottish history was gone.

One final feature of university life affected the situation. With the general expansion of universities in the 1960s all history departments benefited. Scottish history benefited too and the core of competent academic research workers was expanded.

All this did not, however, mean that there were dramatic changes in the teaching of Scottish history in schools. There were several developments. One of them was the introduction in 1962 of a completely Scottish section into the Lower Leaving Certificate paper. In 1963 the Higher paper followed suit. This meant that candidates could choose to prepare themselves more in Scottish history than ever before. In 1970 the structure of the Ordinary paper (very roughly the equivalent of the old Lower) was again changed and in 1971 the Higher paper was made similar. In this case there was both a 'Traditional' and an 'Alternative' paper in which the aim was to study a 'patch' of history; for example, the American Rebellion or the Russian Revolution, instead of the previous system where a period was chosen, for example, 1425 to 1600. The result of both these changes was that the opportunity existed for teachers to concentrate much more on Scottish history.

They did not take it. If one were to argue that the development of nationalism among young Scots was the result of an increase in the amount of information given them about Scottish history, one would have to find an increase in the numbers doing Scottish history. The Scottish 'period' introduced in 1962 and the Scottish 'patch' of 1871 to the present are not options chosen markedly more than any others. There are a number of reasons for this. The first is that the majority of specialist history teachers did degree courses which did not include much Scottish history, if any. For the older ones this is obviously going to be true but it is the case even for those who graduated in the 1960s. It would therefore require a major effort on their part to prepare courses in Scottish history. Even if they were willing to do this there is a further obstacle. School history books must make a profit for their publishers. If one has a text dealing with the history of Britain or Europe or even America and Africa one can go to the much larger market in England. A text book on Scottish history can be sold only in Scotland. Publishers are usually less than

111

keen on such a proposition although the situation is changing now. There is, therefore, a serious limitation in the choice of texts which could be used by a teacher presenting Scottish history although some publishers are now remedying this. The easy way out is to choose another topic within the history papers.

One must conclude that the revival of the Scottish consciousness of young people has not come through the teaching of history. We should also notice that the increase in the number of Scottish questions in the Scottish Certificate of Education papers does not seem to have come as the result of a ground swell among the history teachers. They were too conservative for this. After each diet of examinations a meeting is organised by the teachers' union: the Educational Institute of Scotland and others, at which the papers are analysed. Some of those attending these meetings have pressed for more Scottish content but their important allies were among the inspectors at St Andrew's House.

If one is to regard any school subject as encouraging an interest in politics and in Scottish nationalism in particular one might be better advised to look at the development of Modern Studies. This is an amalgam of modern history, geography, economics and political science and was introduced in 1959. About 11,000 Scottish pupils were presented for the Ordinary or Higher grade in this subject in 1975 as compared with 15,000 in history but it is extremely widely taught to less able pupils who would never take the examination. The course is heavily biased towards the study of Scottish problems including economic problems. There is a great deal of attention paid to project work which inevitably brings the pupil into contact with local Scottish situations. There is, of course, no way of demonstrating that exposure to Modern Studies courses has led to the growth of nationalism among young people but it is not fanciful to imagine that it might make them more aware of political and economic questions and that this might be interpreted in Scottish terms.

The folk song movement

Any assessment of the growth of Scottish nationalism must discuss the folk song movement. Other nationalist movements have based themselves partly on the folk traditions so that the link between the two subjects is well within the field of nationalist studies. I have placed the discussion at this point because its role in nurturing a growth of Scottish consciousness among young people is peculiarly important. I shall argue that the singing of folk songs helped in the development of, in Smelser's terms, a general belief about the condition of Scotland and, after this, that folk songs were used as a weapon consciously by the Nationalist leaders to organise support for the SNP.

In the previous section the contribution of a change in history and other teaching was assessed and was judged to be not strong. If we want to explain the recruitment of large numbers of young Scots to the Nationalists in the late 1960s we must go to extra-curricular activities.

Scotland is a country with a wide range of good folk songs. In the eighteenth century a great deal of interest had been taken in folk songs by such writers as Allan Ramsay.[13] The best known collection of this time is, of course, the *Ministrelsy of the Scottish Border*[14] but there were many collectors such as Childe[15] and Gavin Greig[16] who saved the dying tradition from disappearing altogether. For such people, enthusiasts and scholars as they were, folk song was an antiquarian interest. In the years after the First World War, when the modern nationalist movement started, this was certainly not a living tradition for more than a handful of people. The move from a rural to an urban way of life ensured that the old songs would cease to be sung. The vast majority of Scotsmen did not even know that such a tradition remained alive.

There were, however, several ways in which folk singing in Scotland never quite died out. First, although there was a special tradition of Scottish music hall songs, many of the artists sang songs which were linked to folk music. It might be a debased form but the link still existed. Perhaps this was specially clear in the north-east of Scotland where there was a close connection between the town and the surrounding countryside. Performers like Harry Gordon used the ideas and music of the bothy ballad and the 'cornkister' songs made up by nineteenth century itinerant workers to describe conditions on the farms. Even more important in the rural and small town society of the east coast from Buchan to Fife were the concert parties which sang the bothy ballads and many other songs in that idiom. Many of those which are most famous today were written in the twentieth century but are firmly in a humorous Scottish tradition. When the folk song revival came along in the 1950s it was recognisably close to this type of music.

The original folk song had been 'prettied up' for the eighteenth and nineteenth century drawing rooms. Even today these versions are sung and in the age before radio they were extremely popular. They were sung in urban settings in the knowledge that these were folk songs and in the belief that what was being sung was the true version. At the same time such writers as Lady Nairne wrote Jacobite songs in the nineteenth century at a time when it was romantic and quite safe to be a Jacobite.[17] Immediately they appeared they had a strong nostalgic popular approach and still do.

Much more important than these was the Burns cult which has already been mentioned. Burns himself was knowledgeable about folk songs and some of his finest lyrics are adaptations of old songs. The immense popularity of Burns meant that at least one type of Scottish folk song was well known to Scottish people in virtually all stations of life.

Finally it should not be forgotten that singing folk songs was part of life in the Scottish youth hostels and in climbing huts at least since the 1930s. For another group of young people the folk song revival introduced something not totally new.

For all these reasons Scotland had a musical life even in the twentieth century which had some relation to the folk tradition. Although individual nationalists might have been aware of this tradition before 1939 one cannot seriously claim that this was an important interest in the nationalist canon. This in itself is quite interesting because folk songs and practices have had an honoured place in other nationalist movements. How did it come about that folk music was to play such a dramatic part in the Nationalist revival?

The central figure in the Scottish folk song revival is Hamish Henderson. In order to understand the relation between folk music and nationalism it is necessary to know something about him. Henderson established his interest in the subject as a young man in the years before 1939 but during the war and immediately afterwards his main interest was writing poetry. He did not, however, see poetry as the preserve of an intellectual *coterie*. Poetry should be for the people. He came easily to writing soldiers' songs which became very popular in North Africa and Italy. Henderson wrote several which were well known including the famous 'D-Day Dodgers'.[18]

After the war Henderson helped organise the 1948 John Maclean Memorial Meeting in the St Andrew's Halls, Glasgow, under the auspices of the Communist Party and the Scottish-USSR Friendship Society. He wrote 'The John Maclean March' to be sung at this meeting and it has subsequently become famous. Maclean, as we saw, was a supporter of the idea of a Scottish Workers Republic and in writing the march and a great deal of his subsequent poetry Henderson was aligning himself with socialism and with some form of independence for Scotland. This meeting was important in the post-war literary nationalist movement. There were present at it many of the major Scottish literary figures such as McDiarmid, Sorley McLean and Sidney Goodsir Smith, virtually all of whom had nationalist sympathies though hardly any were SNP members. Thus we have the picture of Henderson as a man of the left interested in folk music but interested also in writing poetry and songs that would be sung by ordinary people, soldiers in the 51st Highland Division and welders on the Clyde. He saw the folk tradition as a living one which could be added to and made relevant to present-day conditions. Henderson expresses both these points of view with other major figures in the folk song world outside Scotland, for example Ewan MacColl and A. L. Lloyd, two of the foremost folk song collectors.

In 1950 Alan Lomax, the American folk song collector, came to Britain in part at least to gather material for the Scottish volume of a sound collection, the *Columbia World of Folk and Primitive Song*.[19] He financed Henderson to go ahead of him on a reconnaissance trip and, in this way, Henderson was able to start a major collection. After the trip he took premises near the University of Edinburgh and started to edit and analyse his tapes. In such a location he was accessible to students and an immediate interest grew up. The Scottish folk song revival was on its way.

In 1952 Henderson organised the second 'People's Festival' at the same time as the Edinburgh Festival in honour of Hugh MacDiarmid's sixtieth birthday. The idea was that the 'official' Festival did not cater for the working man and his culture. Some of the traditional singers discovered in the 1950 tour were brought together and were heard by a wider audience than before. Among those who were present were two left-wing Glasgow school teachers: Maurice Blytheman and Norman Buchan. Blytheman was a poet and writer who himself had contributed to the corpus of political songs. He set up one of the first folk song clubs in the country at Allan Glen's School in Glasgow in 1952 and was soon followed by Buchan at Rutherglen Academy. Thus in the early 1950s Scottish schoolchildren were being introduced to folk songs in a more or less systematic way. This beginning by the enthusiasts was soon to blossom into something very important.

In 1952 the folk song revival was still several years off. Apart from

115

the school clubs of Blytheman and Buchan there was very little general interest except for the activities of the Bo'ness Rebels Literary Society which in 1951 first published the *Rebels Ceilidh Song Book.*[20] This and a stable mate, *Patriot Songs for Camp and Ceilidh*[21] were reprinted many times. It was extremely important in spreading knowledge of simple folk songs and of the political songs which were almost invariably sung alongside them in all but the purest of traditional circles. As the preface to the 1951 edition said:[22]

> This book is Labour, it is Nationalist, it is Tory in the original
> sense of the word—it is a Rebel Song Book uniting all the
> varieties of Scottish Rebels to the realisation that what's wrong
> with the world is wrong here and now in Scotland.

This was a theme which was to characterise the whole movement in Scotland.

As yet, however, it had to get off the ground. This happened in two ways. First, the young people who listened to Henderson's tapes soon began to sing the songs and there was soon a fairly large group who met in ceilidhs in each other's houses. This had an effect on the traditional singers themselves who, for a long time, had been alone in having any interest in the songs. Suddenly they realised that their work was valued and they began to come a little more into the open. Those who might otherwise have rejected the old songs began to recognise their merits. In a relatively short time, due almost entirely to Henderson's efforts, traditional singing had a new lease of life in Scotland.

This was, however, only one of the two sources of the Scottish revival. The other was the re-establishment of American folk song on a commercial scale. In the mid-1950s such songs as 'On Top of Old Smoky' and 'Zena Zena' became so popular that they were listed in the Hit Parade. Here at last were songs which got away from the traditional Hollywood icing sugar. Other songs were written by people like Pete Seeger and Woody Guthrie and were soon brought across to Europe. By 1956 or 1957 the skiffle groups had arrived. Teenagers could make their own music for the first time for a very long time. Much of the music that they made was in this American folk style. Skiffle encouraged others to recognise that they could make music from their own countries and soon folk singing in Scotland was accepted by a much wider audience. At first, even in Scotland, it was the American songs that predominated but soon they were squeezed out. In general terms this meant that against all previous trends Scottish teenagers listened to and sang Scottish songs. They were traditional but, in a sense, they were also modern because they were not the sort of songs sung by gentlemen in kilts and velvet jackets or ladies in long dresses. They spoke about a Scotland which was rough and ready and they were mixed with political songs. In a short time many clubs had grown up all over the country. The people who had come to listen to Hamish Henderson's tapes very soon joined the traditional singers as they went round the clubs. With the growth of so many clubs it was possible to go professional or at least semi-professional. The setting-up of Scottish Television also helped. STV was looking for cheap artists and folk singers were cheap. Various programmes were produced around such groups as the Reivers and the Joe Gordon Folk Four. A new atmosphere came into the Scottish folk scene. It became professionalised and commercialised. There were still the traditional singers and the enthusiasts who sang at the clubs and in the pubs but the arrival of the groups who made a living from appearances meant that their performances would be planned for a mass audience who might not be able to take the subtleties of traditional music. It also meant that the professionals were less keen to experiment with new material. Thus folk music rather quietly became part of show business in Scotland but this also meant that it went out to a much wider audience, which, though not particularly knowledgeable, was very large indeed. It was to this wider audience that some of the commercial groups were to start singing the covertly or openly nationalist songs in the early 1970s.

This brings us to a discussion of the political tradition in folk song. I have already pointed out that folk song was linked in the United States and in Britain with left-wing politics. In America the work songs and Negro spirituals had been encouraged by people associated with the Communist Party such as Paul Robeson. In this country we have seen that Hamish Henderson was a socialist. The person who did most to develop the modern nationalist folk song was Maurice Blytheman. From 1936 to 1951 Blytheman was a member of the Communist Party. He was associated with Henderson in the 1948 John Maclean Rally and in 1949 along with two others published a collection of poems among which was 'Til the citie o' John Maclean'.[23] Both these men were thus in the same left-wing nationalist tradition. Blytheman was active in various ways, including the founding of the first school folk club already mentioned. It was

117

at such clubs and their successors outside the schools that the political songs were sung mixed up with traditional folk song.

The first wave of these political songs came in 1950 when, on Christmas Day, the stone of Scone, the ancient crowning stone of Scotland which had been brought to London by Edward I and placed in Westminster Abbey, was removed from the Abbey by four young Scots. The whole incident was a romp which was hugely enjoyed by the vast majority of Scots and probably by other people too. A large number of songs were written about the incident, of which 'The Wee Magic Stane', written by John McEvoy, was probably the best known.

The Wee Magic Stane
(Tune: The Ould Orange Flute)

O, the Dean o' Westminster wis a powerful man,
He held aa' the strings o' the State in his hand,
But wi' aa' this great business it flustered him nane,
Till some rogues ran away wi' his wee magic stane.

Chorus: Wi' a toora, li oora, li oora, li ay.

Noo the Stane had great powers that could dae such a thing,
But without it, it seemed, we'd be wantin' a King,
So he caa'd in the polis an' gave this decree:
'Go an' hunt oot the Stane an' return it tae me.'

So the polis went beetle'n' up tae the North,
They huntit the Clyde an' they huntit the Forth,
But the wild folk up yonder just kiddit them aa',
For they didnae believe it wis magic at aa'.

Noo the Provost o' Glesca', Sir Victor by name,
Wis awfy pit oot when he heard o' the Stane,
So he offered the statues that staun, in the Square,
That the High Church's masons might mak' a few mair.

When the Dean o' Westminster wi' this wis acquaint,
He sent for Sir Victor an' made him a Saint,
'Now it's no use you sending your statues down heah,'
Said the Dean, 'but you've given me a right good idear.'

So he quarried a stane o' the verra same stuff,
An' he got it dressed up till it looked like enough,
Then he sent for the Press an' announced that the Stane,
Had been found an' returned tae Westminster again.

118

When the reivers fund oot what Westminster had done,
They went aboot diggin' up stanes by the ton,
An' for each wan they feenished they entered the claim
That this wis the true an' original Stane.

Noo the cream o' the joke still remains tae be telt,
For the bloke that wis turnin' them aff on the belt,
At the peak o' production wis so sorely pressed,
That the real yin got bunged in alang wi' the rest.

So if ever ye come on a Stane wi' a ring,
Juist sit yuirsel doon an' proclaim yuirsel King,
For there's nane wuid be able tae challenge yuir claim
That ye'd croont yuirself King on the Destiny Stane.

The major sentiment of this song is irreverence for authority. On top of this there is a certain feeling that the Scots have had a joke at the expense of the rest and it was, of course, well known that those who stole the stone were nationalists and took it for nationalist motives.

This nationalism was much more explicit in the next wave of songs. These had to do with the controversy about the new Queen's titles. There was a strong sentiment in Scotland that this should be Elizabeth I and not II. The best known song of this group was written by Blytheman and had an even more radical message which was clearly nationalist.

The Scottish Breakaway
(Tune: The Sash)

O, Scotland hasnae' got a King,
An' she hasnae' got a Queen,
For ye canny hae, the saicint Liz,
When the first yin's never been.

Chorus: Nae Liz the Twa, nae Lillibet the Wan,
Nae Liz will ever dae:
For we'll mak' oor land republican
In a Scottish Breakaway.

Her man's cried the Duke o' Edinbury,
He's wan o' yon kiltie Greeks.
'Here, but dinnae blaw ma kilts awa,
For it's Lizzie weirs the breeks.'

He's a handsome man, an' he looks like Don Juan,
He's beloved by the weaker sex,
But it disnae really matter a damn,
'Cos it's Lizzie signs the cheques.

Now her sister Meg's got a bonnie pair o' legs,
But she didnae want a German or a Greek.
Paer auld Peter wis her choice, but he didnae suit the boys,
So they selt him up the creek.

Here but Meg wis fly, an' she beat them by an' by,
Wi' Tony Hyphenated-Armstrong, ding! dong!
But behind the pomp and play, the question o' the day
Wis who the hell did Suzy Wong? yum! yum!

Sae here's tae the Lion, tae the bonny Rampant Lion
An' a lang streetch tae its paw.
Gie a Hampden Roar, an' we're oot the door
—An' ta-ta tae Chairlie's maw!

After the Coronation there were several incidents where pillar boxes bearing the EIIR monogram were blown up. Blytheman wrote celebrating these events, again in a nationalist vein.

Sky-High Joe
(Tune: Ricky doo dum day)

O, Sky-High Joe is on the go,
    Some gelignite tae buy,
So he gangs tae the Carron Iron Works,
    For tae get a guid supply.

Chorus: Ricky doo dum day, doo dum day,
        Ricky, dicky doo dum day.

'Ah want it for a special job,
    Ah want the real MacKay,
Are ye shair yuir gelignite ignites?'
    The Foreman says: 'Och, ay!'

So Joe says: 'Quick, ah'll tak a stick,'
    An' he's intae Embro toon,
An' he's cotch a tram at the GPO,
    An' the Castle's glow'rin doon.

When Joe alights wi' the gelignite,
  He looks oot for the cops,
He bides his time till he hears the chime,
  Then he nips up tae the box.

When the Pillar Box sees Sky-High Joe,
  It blenches deidly pale:
'Staun' back, staun' back, wi' yuir hair sae black,
  Ah dinnae want your air-mail.'

But when ye're postin Valentines,
  Wi' a yaird o' fizzin' fuse,
Ye hinnae ony time tae be polite,
  Ye've an' awfy lot tae lose.

So he disnae hesitate or wait,
  Or staun' an' sing 'The Sash',
He staps its gob wi' his special job,
  Then he jouks like a razor flash.

A meenit later aff it went,
  Wi' a flashin' an' a thump,
An' noo' they're cairtin the bits awa,
  Tae the Corporation Dump.

The bottom bit wis staunin' there,
  Aa' ragged-edged an' sherp,
But the lid wis in St Peter's hauns,
  —He wis playin it like a herp.

They say that on the folliean day,
  Pit there tae get thir rag,
Upon the mound o' rubble,
  Wis a wee bit Scottish flag.

The moral o' this story shows,
  Ye canny go too far,
For when Lizzie got her Valentine,
  She scratched her EIIR.

The next batch of political songs did not have a nationalist theme
specifically but they *were* written in Glasgow dialect. They were
centred on the anti-Polaris demonstrations of 1962 onwards. The
CND marchers had always been accompanied by singing. Most of
the songs were adaptations of American protest songs. When the

American nuclear submarine sailed into the Holy Loch in 1961, however, a whole new set of songs began to be written in Scotland. The best known of these was undoubtedly 'Ding Dong Dollar'.

Ding Dong Dollar

Chorus: O, ye canny spend a dollar when ye're deid
O, ye canny spend a dollar when ye're deid
Singing Ding Ding Dollar, everybody holler;
Ye canny spend a dollar when ye're deid.

Now when the Yankees they drappt anchor at Dunoon,
Sure they got a civic welcome frae' the toon,
As they cam up the measured mile
Bonnie Mary o' Argyll
Wis wearin' spangled drawers ablow her goon.

O, the Clyde is sure tae prosper noo' they're here,
For they's chargin' wan an' tenpence for a beer,
Ay, an' when they want a taxi,
They shove it up their jersey
An' charge them thirty bob tae Sandbank Pier.

An' the publicans will aa' be daein' swell,
For it's juist the thing that's shair tae ring the bell,
O, the dollars they will jingle,
They'll be no' a lassie single,
Even though they mebbe blaw us aa' tae hell.

But the Glesca Moderator didnae' mind,
In fact, he thinks the Yanks are awfy kind,
For if it's heaven that ye're goin',
It's a quicker wey than rowin'
An' there's shair tae be naebody left behind.

Blytheman did not write this song although he was the centre of the group known as the Anti-Polaris Singers. Using this he developed a singing campaign. Wherever the campaign went the Anti-Polaris Singers went too. They roared out simple, catchy songs to tunes that were already well known and did not have to be learnt. The aim was to keep up morale but also to educate their followers and anyone else in the reasons for the demonstration. They learnt that there was no point in using the original music of folk songs because it was too complex. They even learnt that non-Scottish songs might be best if the tune was well known and simple. Everything was subordinated to the aim of getting the message across. In doing so every device of AGITPROP was skilfully used.

The SNP itself made no official pronouncements about the American submarines. There were, however, several prominent Nationalists who were active in the demonstration. One of them was Billy Wolfe, later to become Chairman of the Party, and another was Winnie Ewing who won the spectacular by-election victory in Hamilton in 1967. Both Blytheman and these SNP party members learned the techniques of the singing campaign during these Polaris demonstrations.

By this time the folk revival was in full swing and many of the young people who went to the folk clubs also supported CND. The songs sung at the Holy Loch therefore gained a wide currency and with them the more specifically nationalist ones. Most of the songs were, after all, Scottish and by this very fact young people saw Scottishness as a modern alternative to the glossy picture of London or America. It is not surprising then, that when the Nationalist wave started to roll they should use folk song, ceilidhs and singalongs as a method of attracting young people. For this the members who had worked with CND were largely responsible. More than this, Blytheman and his colleagues, although not members of the SNP, started to produce the same sort of campaign songs as they had produced for the Anti-Polaris marchers. Some examples will make the point.

Swing to the SNP
(Tune: I shall not be moved)

Chorus: All together—Swing to the SNP (twice)
          Make up your minds and make up for those wasted years,
          Swing to the SNP.

The times they are changing, Swing to the SNP (twice)
Make up your minds and make up for those wasted years,
Swing to the SNP (etc.)

Watch your sons and daughters, Swing to the SNP (twice)
Make up your minds and make up for those wasted years
Swing to the SNP (etc.)

Labour is out-dated, Swing to the SNP
The Tories antiquated, Swing to the SNP

Make up your minds and make up for those wasted years
Swing to the SNP (etc.)

O Swing now
(Tune: Pay me my money down)

Chorus: O Swing now, O Swing now, Swing to the SNP
        Time now to change your vote—Swing to the SNP

There's changes here in Hamilton, Swing to the SNP
We've got the big boys on the run, Swing to the SNP (etc.)

The Tories haven't got a chance, Swing to the SNP
The Twist is still their favourite dance, Swing to the SNP (etc.)

They've had their turn and been on top, Swing to the SNP
But now we've got them on the hop, Swing to the SNP (etc.)

Now don't believe the Labour lies, Swing to the SNP
They're just Tories in disguise, Swing to the SNP (etc.)

So you see you really have no choice, Swing to the SNP
Show them Scotland's got a voice, Swing to the SNP (etc.)

Harold Wilson's double-dyed, Swing to the SNP
He's tryin' all the tricks the Tories tried,
                        Swing to the SNP (etc.)

Shout
(Tune: Michael row the boat ashore)

Chorus: Shout to the man in Number 10—Independence!
        Scotland will be free again—Independence!

River Tweed is a great divide—Independence!
Take your stand on the Scottish side—Independence (etc.)

Good for the brown man, black man too—Independence!
Good for me and it's good for you—Independence! (etc.)

Now Wallace did not die in vain—Independence!
Neither did great John Maclean—Independence! (etc.)

These are very simple songs devised to be shouted over a loud speaker and learned fast. For these reasons they do not use Scottish music but much simpler music which may be better known. The basic themes are the appeal to youth as the group who are going to

124

lead Scotland, including their elders, into independence. Another theme is the idea of swinging to the new course and the idea of wrongs to be righted.

By 1970 and 1974 these songs had become part of every SNP campaign at national or local level. At the same time the folk revival had very much declined from its original peak around 1967 when there were well over a hundred clubs all over Scotland. What remained were a few clubs interested in traditional folk music and still popular with individual Nationalists. Quite apart from these were a number of commercial groups like the Corries, the Lomond Folk Four and the Gaberlunzie who sang simplified versions of folk songs and many of the newly written political songs. Many of these groups circulate almost exclusively on a circuit made up of SNP functions: dances, ceilidhs and discos. The legacy of the movement for the SNP was an enormously powerful propaganda technique which was to put them in the forefront of every campaign. Part of the legacy is one song which was written by Ronald Williamson, a member of The Corries group which has become an informal national anthem.

O Flower of Scotland

O Flower of Scotland
When will we see your like again
That fought and died for
Your wee bit hill and glen

Chorus: And stood against him
        Proud Edward's army
        And sent him homewards tae think again

The hills are bare now
And autumn leaves lie thick and still
Oh land that is lost now
Which those so dearly held

These days are past now
And in the past they must remain
But we can still rise now
And be a nation again.

Although it was written only in 1969 its wide currency is shown by the fact that it is sung at international football matches where Scotland is playing and, more than this, on the day of the 1976

125

Scotland-England match its words were printed in Scottish news-papers, including the *Glasgow Herald* which has traditionally taken up a strong anti-nationalist stand. It takes only a moment's reading to realise that the song is distinctly nationalist in sentiment.

Conclusion

Many people who became Nationalists before the war or before 1960 were also interested in traditional Scottish folk music. In the present SNP a great deal of music is used which has its roots in folk music but is certainly not traditional. On the contrary, it has been consciously manipulated to secure political ends. The development in the relation of folk music to the party illustrates strikingly the change that has taken place in the party. It is not a party which looks back to the values of a peasant culture in any serious way. It has its romantics and the vast majority of the party have a romanticised notion of the history and rural traditions of Scotland. In this it is not very different from the vast majority of people of every country. One would expect nationalists to pay more attention to their history and there is a great deal of singing about the history of Scotland. On the other hand there is not the attention to the folk tradition that there was in previous years. For the vast majority of Nationalists the songs they sing at ceilidhs and other gatherings are sung for entertainment rather than to express a deep feeling for Scottish history. They do establish a sense of Scottish identity but it is of a modern identity and not one linked to a past golden age.

It must be said, however, that the folk song revival probably helped to draw the attention of Scottish people to some of the aspects of a Scottish tradition, and in this way it probably contributed to the increased sense of Scottish consciousness.

8 The Role of the Church, the Army and Football

In several nationalist movements the Church has played a central role. In contemporary Basque nationalism the clergy have been leaders of popular feeling.[1] Welsh nationalism has been associated with the non-conformist chapels[2] and the Roman Catholic Church in Ireland was a major rallying point for Irish sentiment. To what extent can it be said that the Churches in Scotland were peculiarly important in experiencing the strains in Scottish society and expressing them? My answer is that the Church of Scotland has been aware of the economic problems and has expressed a Scottish point of view but the Church has not led opinion on the issue. Rather the Church has followed opinion and there is doubt whether the pronouncements of the Church have had much importance.

The Church of Scotland is the dominating religious body in the country. The most recent survey is now seventeen years out of date but the proportions are unlikely to have changed much.[3] In this it was estimated that 37·6 per cent of the Scottish adult population were members of the Church of Scotland: a much higher proportion than the proportion of English adults who were members of the Church of England. This dominance of the Church of Scotland reflects its historical position as, for many years, the only body which could be considered representative of Scottish opinion. The Presbyterian form of government imposes a certain equality among its members and the institution of the Eldership means that the laity are well represented. In the seventeenth century when, for practical purposes, the Scottish Parliament did not meet, the Church, through its General Assembly, carried out many of the functions of a

127

parliament. After the Union of 1707 it was again almost the only body to gather together people from all over Scotland to discuss religious and other questions. The estate of the burgesses still continued to meet as the Convention of Royal Burghs but it did not have the same prestige as the Church and most of the nobility turned their attentions to London. Until the middle of the nineteenth century other denominations were of no real account. After the Union the Church of Scotland was, as we have seen, one of the protected institutions. Without this agreement it is difficult to see how the Scots would have accepted the Treaty since the Presbyterian and Calvinist Church of Scotland was utterly opposed to the imposition of bishops and to the latitudinarian theology of the Church of England.

There can be no doubt that the Church of Scotland of this time was wholly convinced of its theological superiority. The Church of John Knox, and especially of Andrew Melville, was argumentative, narrow and intolerant. As the eighteenth century progressed the 'Moderate' party came into the ascendancy. This was a more tolerant and worldly group roughly equivalent to the 'Broad Church' party south of the border. With the nineteenth century came the evangelical revival and in many ways the harsh and uncompromising quality of the original Calvinists was re-established. It would be unwise to ignore the fact that, during this period, the Church of Scotland built up a special relationship with the monarchy. Queen Victoria was not simply a formal member of the Church of Scotland but took an active interest in it. In her regular visits to Balmoral she made communion at the parish church and used several Scottish churchmen as her confidants. She wrote to the Marchioness of Ely, 'I would never give way about the Scotch Church which is the real and true stronghold of Protestantism.'[4] This relationship between the church and the monarchy is today buttressed by many devices. The Queen's Commissioner (and in 1960 and 1969 the Queen herself) always attends the General Assembly. Again, at the time of the Queen's annual residence at Balmoral, six Church of Scotland ministers take it in turn to spend a few days there. Thus a fair proportion of the clergy of this Church have had direct contact with the sovereign.

How shall we sum up the position of the Church of Scotland? It is a distinctively Scottish institution with some reason to argue that it speaks for the Scottish people. At the same time it is firmly attached to various aspects of the Establishment including the monarchy. It should also be remembered, however, that members and ministers are often irritated by the dominance of the Church of England in many affairs. One aspect of this is the fact that the Church of England appears to have much more broadcasting time. Another is the Anglican domination of the chaplaincy system in the armed forces.

We know the Church of Scotland expresses Scottish feeling. Should we expect it to be associated with nationalism? The Church of Scotland is a traditional institution which expresses the past consciousness of a nation but which nationalists consider too compromised by its past links and too backward looking for the modern society which they want to create.

Two nineteenth century events affect the relation between the Church of Scotland and Scottish nationalism. In 1843 the Church split in half at the 'Disruption'. The details of the argument need not concern us but it is worth remembering that one strand of it was about the power of the Church to make its own decisions about who were to be its ministers. Those who left, the Free Church of Scotland, were not willing to tolerate external interference. The healing of this great split was to absorb the attentions of the Church until 1929. There was very little energy to spare for the serious consideration of Scotland's position in Great Britain. It would be fair to say that the Church of Scotland simply followed the Conservative line which desired that the British arrangement of Scottish business would continue. For whatever reason, the Church of Scotland was not prominent in the agitation for Home Rule either before or after the First World War. On the contrary, most of its clergy and leaders appear to have become associated with the anti-Home Rule position. This arose principally because the Gladstonian Liberals who were the party of 'Home Rule All Round' also became associated with the idea of Church Disestablishment. Disestablishment was sternly opposed on the grounds that the Church of Scotland was the Church of the majority of Scots unlike the situation in Wales or Ireland. The Church opposed the Liberals for this reason and also because there was a great deal of sympathy among Scottish Presbyterians for the Protestant cause in Ireland. Many Protestants feared the arrival of the largely Catholic immigrants from Ireland. It was felt that this might be the first stage of a Roman take over and the party which seemed to sympathise with the Irish hardly encouraged strong Protestants to vote for it. Thus it seems that largely because the Liberals were the party of sympathy for

Ireland and for disestablishment the Church of Scotland also opposed the Liberals as a party of Scottish Home Rule.[5]

As far as the Roman Catholic Church was concerned they naturally supported the Liberals in the nineteenth century. It was the party associated with Home Rule for Ireland. On the other hand there is no evidence that this also made them sympathetic to Home Rule for Scotland. There is no reference to it in the Catholic papers between the wars or afterwards. Indeed, whereas the Church of Scotland did stand for a peculiarly Scottish approach to affairs albeit not a nationalist one, the Catholic Church in Scotland did not seem to see itself as, in any way, peculiarly Scottish. The universalistic tradition of the Catholic Church was clearly against this. Mixed with this tradition may also have been the fear that an independent Scotland would be a more intransigently Protestant Scotland. The experience of Ulster would alienate Catholics from this solution.[6]

If we are to identify support for the SNP we would not expect to find it in strength among Catholics. We would expect Scottish sentiment to exist in the Church of Scotland since this institution bears much of the tradition of Scotland but the Church itself is too intertwined with the existing order in which it has a privileged position, to be a very active supporter of nationalism.

The Church of Scotland has certainly been one institution if not *the* primary institution which has expressed the Scottishness of Scottish society. It has consistently been determined that Scottish life styles should be maintained in a way which has not been raised by other institutions. Thus it is easy to look through the deliverances of the General Assembly of the Church and to come upon deliverances concerning the keeping of the Sabbath, the changes of Catholicism and the virtues of Calvinist theology. On a more secular level the Church through its Church and Nation Committee has concerned itself with the material life of Scotland. From 1920 onwards there has been detailed discussion about the state of the Scottish economy and society. It was not until after the war, however, that the subject of Home Rule was raised. From 1948 onwards the Church of Scotland has pronounced continuously in favour of a Scottish Parliament to deal with Scottish affairs. Its Annual General Assembly has had regular reports from the Church and Nation Committee supporting the idea of Home Rule and pressing the government to take steps in this direction.

The first step came in 1948 when, commenting on the White Paper on Scottish Affairs[7] the Committee commented:[8]

The White Paper . . . manifests no real awareness of the
Scottish determination—which is no longer limited to any party
but is nationwide—to have Scottish affairs dealt with in Scotland
by a representative assembly functioning within the British
framework.

After considering this report the General Assembly resolved as
follows:[9]

> The General Assembly, conscious of growing dissatisfaction
> throughout the country with the Government's conduct of
> Scottish affairs and convinced of the necessity for a large measure
> of devolution of legislative power, greatly deplore the refusal of
> His Majesty's government to institute an enquiry into the issues
> involved and urge upon the Secretary of State for Scotland to
> take every possible step to have the whole situation further
> investigated.

In 1949 and again in 1950 similar deliverances were made. We
should, in particular, note that of 1950:

> The General Assembly, impressed by the fact that more than
> one million people have signed the Scottish National Covenant
> by the Third National Assembly in Edinburgh, renew their
> appeal to His Majesty's government to appoint a Royal
> Commission to investigate all the issues involved in the proposed
> measure of devolution.

This deliverance specifically mentions the Scottish National
Assembly and it seems quite clear that the whole position of the
Church has been taken in response to the work of these Assemblies.
In Chapter 13 we shall see that many Presbyteries sent representatives
to these meetings and several clergymen were prominent in its work.
It seems clear from the timing, therefore, that this was not a case of
the Church leading the nation but the Church following an existing
lead. The importance of the Assemblies for the thinking of these
churchmen comes out in the deliverances of the Church and Nation
Committee in 1949. 'Few responsible people would desire to see
Scotland once again a separate state. Her interests, her culture and
prosperity are too inextricably bound up with that of England,
Wales and Northern Ireland.' The Scottish Convention which ran
these Assemblies broke away from the Scottish National Party in
1942 partly on the issue of Home Rule as against the full programme
of independence adopted by the SNP.

In 1951 the Stone of Scone, the ancient Crowning Stone of Scotland, was, as we have seen, removed from the Coronation Chair in Westminster Abbey. It had been taken to London by Edward I of England after subduing the northern kingdom. Its presence in England had always rankled among the Scots. The Church and Nation Committee was rather guarded in its comments.

1) The Stone has been generally accepted and long cherished as a Scottish possession. . . . 2) The original . . . transportation of the Stone to London intended as a symbol of the subjection of Scotland to the English Crown was unjust. . . . 3) These facts cannot be considered as in any way justifying or condoning its forcible and secret removal from the Abbey by unauthorised persons. . . . 4) While this is true, however, it must be recognised that those who carried out the removal of the Stone were activated only by motives of patriotism and not by a desire for personal gain. . . . 5) . . . It would seem that the Stone should most properly be in the custody of the Church of Scotland.

Again the Church showed its Scottish feeling but again it reacted to events rather than leading the nation.

In 1951, 1952 and 1953 there were again comments by the General Assembly on the need to consider devolution and when, in 1955, it commented on the report of the Royal Commission on Scottish Affairs[10] the deliverance welcomed the document.

The General Assembly regret, however, that the Commission did not regard as falling within its remit any consideration of the larger cultural and national issues which seem to call for a much greater measure of devolution than is recommended in the report.

There followed a period where the issue of a Scottish Assembly was not raised in a deliverance of the General Assembly. In 1960 a well-known Nationalist, Miss Wendy Wood, petitioned the General Assembly that, since the last Scots Parliament of 1707 had been adjourned and not dissolved, it ought now to be recalled. The Church was unwilling to pronounce on the legal status of the situation but it reaffirmed its support for Home Rule. Once more there is a gap interspersed with references to the need for more Scottish control of Scottish affairs.

At length, commenting on the winning of Hamilton by the SNP, the deliverance of the Church and Nation Committee in 1968 read:

The Committee takes the view that this development is not a passing phenomenon which can be alleviated by minor measures of further devolution or dispelled by an improvement in economic conditions. The growing concern for recognition of Scotland's nationhood and for greater control by Scots over their national affairs arises from causes which cannot be so easily remedied or removed.

The Church's idea of how the situation could be remedied came out clearly in the Church and Nation Committee's deliverances in 1974 commenting on the proposals of the Kilbrandon Commission.[11] It criticised them since, 'Such powers (as were proposed) do not amount to an effective form of self government since no provision is made for direct Scottish control of finance and economic affairs.' The General Assembly agreed and in 1976 its own deliverances were unequivocal.

While welcoming Her Majesty's Government's firm binding commitment set forth in the White Paper entitled 'Our changing democracy' . . . [we]
i) regret that the powers proposed to be devolved to the Assembly are inadequate to enable the Assembly to deal with Scottish problems.
ii) reaffirm many deliverances of previous General Assemblies and again call for an effective form of self-government for Scotland under the Crown within the framework of the United Kingdom, such self-government to be exercised through an assembly with adequate financial and economic powers . . .
iii) urge that the Scottish assembly be granted control of a reasonable proportion of the revenues from North Sea Oil in order a) to provide economic development in Scotland b) to protect, preserve and safeguard the countryside.

The Church's position

There can be no doubt that the Church of Scotland is unequivocally for a very considerable measure of devolution to Scotland. There can also be no doubt that this stance was taken thirty years ago and has been consistently held ever since. It is not possible to dismiss the content of these deliverances as something of peripheral concern to the majority of churchmen and women which could be forced through by a few hotheads. If this were so then 'saner elements' seem to have taken thirty years to realise what the 'hot heads' have committed them to. Again the Church and Nation Committee's report is one which is scrutinised by the General Assembly at some of its best attended sessions. The content of its reports are on matters of general interest and are well covered by the press. It is unlikely that such well considered matters would throw up a deliverance which was not representative of Church thinking. Finally, it should be said that the Church's attitude to devolution grows out of a general concern for Scottish society. The deliverances of the Church and Nation Committee have, at least since the end of the First World War, been concerned with economic state of Scotland and now they range very widely over all aspects of Scottish life. The Church has also been regularly concerned about the destruction of Scottish national life even where it has not considered Home Rule. Thus in 1960 the Church and Nation Committee commented on the condition of Scotland.

> The sense of hopeful nationhood, of a country with tradition, characteristics and opportunities strong enough to hold its own young people in their country and with a future bright enough to attract them, seems to be losing its force in an ominous way.

We should also bear in mind the fact that the Church cannot be said to lead the Scottish people on this issue. In the pronouncements just listed they have reacted to events: the Scottish National Covenant, the Hamilton by-election and the Kilbrandon Commission, rather than leading the country as they did in the seventeenth century. Ministers have made pronouncements from their pulpits but the fact of the matter is that the Church's opinions are important only for a tiny minority of Scots. With the drop in church attendance and general secularisation the Church of Scotland is now a peripheral organisation in Scottish life. While a large proportion of Scots are members, their membership is purely nominal. We cannot explain the rise of nationalism on religious grounds.

Before closing this chapter let me turn briefly to two other institutions which express Scottishness very strongly. One is football and the other, the Scottish regiments in the British army. I do not believe that either was important in the development of political nationalism but, in a sense, it is surprising that this is so since they are, both of them among the few areas of institutionalised Scottishness that one is likely to meet in the course of ordinary life. They are examples of the way in which these traditional institutions might be difficult to use for the new political developments.

The Army

One of the most striking features of the British army for a layman is the sight of a Highland regiment. The wearing of the kilt and the use of bagpipes means that there is a very distinct personality. One may go further than this to say that in so far as kilts are worn by the civilian population this is a practice which was spread by army experience. There is an extremely strong feeling of regimental pride and a myth, based in fact, of the courage and dash of these units. There is also an affection for them among Scots which was shown very clearly when the government tried to disband one of them: the Argyll and Sutherland Highlanders.[12]

Given this, one might expect that, when a large proportion of Scottish men were in intimate contact with these Scottish institutions during the two world wars, this would have brought some feeling of heightened nationality. There is no evidence that this happened. Although the Scots National League was founded immediately after the First World War those instrumental in setting it up do not seem to have been ex-soldiers. After the Second World War it was not until 1947 that the first Convention met. If experience with the Scottish regiments made men more nationalist it does not seem to have had this effect immediately.

There are one or two explanations of why this happened. The simplest is, of course, that a large number of Scotsmen were in units other than the Scottish regiments. Apart from the Navy and Air Force, recruits were placed in other army regiments, in the Royal Engineers or the Royal Artillery and so on. It is not true, therefore that the majority of Scottish combatants would have gone to Scottish units. Secondly, it is worth remembering that men were not necessarily assigned to regiments according to their place of origin. Large numbers of Scotsmen were placed in infantry regiments with an English territorial affiliation and, in the same way, Scottish regiments contained many Englishmen. On the other hand the spirit of these regiments was so strong that it very often affected the Englishmen. Writing about the First World War Cuddeford says:[13]

As I have already remarked as large a percentage of the men in the Scots Guards were Englishmen but, while in the regiment, they seemed to come to look on themselves as 'nationalised' Scotsmen. Many of them even picked up a Scottish accent and they always addressed one another as 'Jock'. The most extraordinary thing was that, in the rows with the Grenadiers by far the most patriotic Scotsmen amongst us were our Cockneys. These nationalised Scotsmen were usually the aggressors too, and in their altercations with the Grenadiers the most weird mixture of dialect would be heard.

Although this passage shows the power of regimental feeling it also suggests why experiences of this sort did not lead to the development of nationalism at the 1919 or 1945 elections. What counted in the army was regimental feeling or feeling for the unit rather than feeling for Scotland. It was regimental pride that was instilled rather than pride in Scotland as such and, whereas soldiers fought in the pubs at night, they did not choose Englishmen specifically as their enemies. There are some well-known rivalries among Scottish regiments. The way in which military loyalties are built up from the smaller unit is noted by Nisbet:[14]

So too in the direct experience of war and military organisation many millions of men learned even more certainly during the two World Wars the contrast between life charged with moral means and life that is morally empty. Military society is closely associative. . . . One of the most noticeable capacities of military life is to inspire in the individual soldier a feeling for the warmth of comradeship. Something of that spirit which, during an earlier age of European history, unfolded itself in a great profusion of fellowships and associations, reaching all spheres of social life, permeates the soldier's consciousness. There is an almost medieval hierarchy in military society with the individual identity passing through the concentric rings of platoon, company and regiment and into the field army itself. His identification with each of these units, especially the smaller ones can become intense and morally exhilarating.

Perhaps most obviously, it should be said that we are talking about a situation in which men often did not know from hour to hour whether they would be alive the next day. In these circumstances loyalties were likely to be to the immediate unit in which one's safety depended. Finally it is worth remembering that it was a British Army with all the wealth of British symbolism overlapping

Scottish symbolism that provided the setting. Although there might be rivalries the need to beat the enemy was seen as by far the most important job.

Football

Scotland's passion for football is a very large subject. Many foreign observers have commented that it seems to play a larger role for Scottish people than is true for the English. It would, of course, be very difficult to prove this but it is less difficult to observe that the mood of England-Scotland international matches has changed very considerably over the last ten years. Two things here appeared which were almost unknown before. The first is that a very large proportion of the Scottish supporters carried Scottish flags; mostly the yellow and red Lion Rampant. It was always true that the Scots would wear tartan rosettes or tam-o'-shanter bonnets and some went in for more exotic displays. The flags, or at least the scale on which they are displayed, are new. The other thing is much more striking. At the beginning of international matches National Anthems are played. In the annual Scotland-England matches there is, of course only one anthem to be played, 'God Save the Queen'. Up to the mid-1960s this was treated by the crowd with reverence and most spectators would have sung it. From about 1966 onwards some spectators began to whistle or boo the national anthem. At the last few internationals it has been impossible to hear the band let alone to sing the tune. The sign for the band to play has also been the sign for a pandemonium of whistles, cat-calls and jeers to break out. In the last few years the custom has grown to sing a song which has come to fill the gap as a kind of popular national song: 'The Flower of Scotland'. This has been referred to in Chapter 7 and I noted that the words are nationalist in sentiment. By 1976 this song had become so much a part of the International that the words were printed on the day of the match in the *Daily Record*, the paper with the largest circulation in Scotland, and the *Glasgow Herald*. It should also be said that the same disrespect for 'God Save the Queen' is shown at the Scotland-England rugby international and that it is not only the terraces that join in but also the older, more sedate and more middle class stands.

These developments have to be noted in a book on nationalism in Scotland because of their striking public effect. It is not true that the competition on the football field has helped to launch the political nationalist movement. There have, after all, been Scotland-England matches since 1872,[15] and it was not until the political movement was on its way that these displays took place. The sequence of events suggests that it was the political developments and events like the winning of the Hamilton by-election which led to them rather than the competition in sports leading to nationalism.

For all this there are two reasons why it is important to be aware of the sort of national feeling which one sees at football matches. Even though the nationalist wave preceded the new type of display, it is possible that an incident at a football match could precipitate more nationalist feeling. There is no way of proving that this has happened so far. The other point which makes football interesting is the way in which it exemplifies the attitudes of many Scottish people to England. The match between Scotland and England is very much a David and Goliath affair in that England has ten times the population resources from which to draw her team and this situation is recognised by the Scottish supporters. Secondly, there is a feeling that Scotland is in other ways inferior to England and must demonstrate her superiority. This comes out most vividly on the occasions when, in every second year, Scotland play in London at Wembley. The experience of going from a grimy industrial town in the Clyde valley to a prosperous confident metropolis is fairly traumatic especially if it has been preceded by a night's hard drinking on the train. The resentment and anger of the Scottish supporters often spills into high spirits on the way to or from the match. Many writers have commented on this including some of the most gifted football journalists in Scotland.[16]

The situation may be summed up by saying that football was one of the institutions which maintained for Scots the feeling of rivalry with England. When Mrs Ewing won Hamilton it was one of the elements in the situation which caught the attention of a great many ordinary Scotsmen. Probably they were not very serious but the fact was that football kept the feeling of Scottishness alive. The interests of this feeling are brought out by Alan Sharpe: 'For a time before, throughout and after [the match] I have the feeling that my personal worth is bound up with Scotland's success or failure.'[17] This was not the feeling which got the nationalist movement going, it was traditional rivalry which had become institutionalised within a British framework,[18] but, once the SNP was on the way, one can easily see football as an element in the conduciveness of the situation.

9 The Scottish Press

One important issue in social science is the extent to which the mass media can affect public opinion. Can it be said that the Press and television in Scotland contributed to the Nationalist wave? I shall argue that the press to some extent set the agenda for Scottish politics and that, once the strength of the Nationalist vote had been recognised as a result of the Hamilton by-election and other events, the Press contributed by leading a public recognition that nationalism was a serious political movement.

Let us first be clear about what the Scottish Press is. There are two mass circulation papers. The *Daily Record* is owned by the London IPC group and has a circulation of about 660,808. It is printed in Glasgow. In general approach it follows its English sister paper the *Daily Mirror* and it thus supports the Labour Party. For a long time the *Record* fought a battle for circulation with the *Scottish Daily Express*. Lord Beaverbrook took the *Express* to Glasgow in 1928. At one time it was the most widely read paper in Scotland but at 345,500 its circulation is now below that of the *Record* and, in 1974, it ceased to be printed in Glasgow. A new office was opened in Glasgow but the printing moved to Manchester. In Aberdeen the morning and evening papers: the *Press and Journal* and the *Evening Express* are owned by Kemsley Newspapers and the Dundee *Courier and Advertiser* and the *Evening Telegraph* are owned by D. C. Thomson. There are two 'quality' newspapers. The *Glasgow Herald* is owned by a Scottish firm, Outrams. By far the best known Scottish 'quality' is the *Scotsman* published in Edinburgh and owned, since 1956, by the Thomson organisation which also owns *The Times*. Perhaps the first point to be made is that most of those papers are owned by non-Scottish organisations. Only the *Glasgow Herald* and the *Courier* of those mentioned are home owned. This is not a new situation for most of them. The non-Scottish take overs were, most of them, effected well before 1935. This may be one of the reasons why, until comparatively recently, the amount of specifically Scottish news carried was low. By Scottish news I mean news about Scotland as a whole as opposed to news about Britain as a whole or news about some local event within the circulation area of the paper. What is true of the *Glasgow Herald* is almost certainly true at least of the *Scotsman*. As we shall see the *Scotsman* initially led the field in the space given to Scottish politics. We may say therefore, that the newspapers may have contributed to the new interest in Scottish politics and therefore in nationalism by giving it considerable coverage.

One of the main complaints by minor parties and minority groups in general is that the mass media prevent the spread of their beliefs simply by not printing news about them. To put their point in more modern language, the Press is one of the main 'agenda setting' agencies in politics. What is not dealt with there does not, by and large, become an issue and events which have hitherto been unimportant achieve some currency through the Press. A discussion of nationalism in Scotland must include a reference to the ways in which the mass media have dealt with the subject.

There is one complication which ought to be cleared out of the way before this discussion begins. It is difficult to distinguish between a newspaper treatment which is based on a genuine point of view on a subject and one which is taken up to encourage the circulation. When the history of the SNP is reviewed, we shall see that the *Daily Record* publicised the activities of the early NPS in the late 1920s. The editor, David Anderson, was a friend of the nationalist publicist, Wendy Wood, and was sympathetic to the idea of Home Rule but, at the same time, he was faced with the arrival of the *Scottish Daily Express* and had to find issues which would sell his paper. By the same token, Beaverbrook also reported these events and showed sympathy to the nationalists in private contacts.[1] It is difficult to distinguish the initial motives which led to these actions but, to a large extent, it is not important. An article written to increase circulation could encourage nationalism among voters. A paper which started to publish for reasons of its own economy was persuaded to believe in its own articles.

One striking feature of the Scottish Press even before the latest developments was that most of them were at pains to identify themselves as Scottish papers. The *Record* specifically entitled itself 'Scotland's Newspaper' and the *Express* has always had the prefix 'Scottish' to its name. When it ceased to be printed in Glasgow in 1974 it ran a considerable poster campaign to identify itself with Scotland but this was, of course, long after nationalism came on the scene.

Although there has been a Scottish consciousness in Scottish newspapers for some time and although, as I have suggested, the Scottish content has increased since 1945, the Press generally treated nationalism as a joke or was actively hostile. The *Glasgow Herald* was, perhaps, the most notable paper which stood four square against nationalism. It has always been closely associated with the Glasgow business community who feared separation because it would mean the closing of the English or the imperial market. When the Nationalists started to make their gains in the late 1960s it was uncompromisingly against them and, although a Conservative paper, it criticised Edward Heath's 'Declaration of Perth' very bitterly in a leaflet published on the day before the Conservative leader's devolution plans were made public. The *Courier* in Dundee has also taken this stance but it does not have the circulation and status of the *Glasgow Herald* and, unlike the *Herald*, it has maintained its anti-devolution stance.

Both the *Record* and the *Express* have shown great sympathy for the SNP. When Mrs Ewing won the Hamilton by-election both papers carried columns by her. Along with less sympathetic papers they were quick to criticise the Nationalists when things went wrong after 1969 but they have consistently supported devolution and have argued for more powers to be given to the Scottish Assembly than appeared in the government's 1976 Bill. In particular they have recommended fiscal powers and some control over oil revenues.

Of all the newspapers it is the *Scotsman* which has had the longest record since the war of supporting devolution. Even before 1939 it had continuously followed this line. Thus on 4 October 1932:

We are convinced therefore that the wise policy is not to meet Scottish nationalism with unsympathetic opposition still less with foolish and shallow ridicule but to try to understand its aims and guide it into the safest channels . . . this question is likely to be settled by clear evidence that the Scottish people as a whole desire a separate parliament. Such a popular demand could not be and should not be resisted.

A major development in the history of the *Scotsman* was when it was taken over by Lord Thomson of Fleet (as he was to become) in 1956. Up to then it had been Scottish owned but had been a rather dull newspaper. Thomson, a successful Canadian newspaper proprietor, wanted the paper to be a commercial success. He appears to have exercised little or no editorial direction but his general line was that the paper was to be a Scottish paper. Magnusson reports him as saying to Dunnet, the new editor he imported from *The Record*:[2]

It is the voice of Scotland. It is conservative in that we believe in private enterprise. But that does not mean it agrees with everything the Conservatives do. In matters directly affecting Scotland the paper takes the line that it thinks is best for Scotland.

From the mid-1960s the *Scotsman* gave serious consideration to the question of a Scottish Parliament and, in 1968, it published a series of articles which were later published as a pamphlet.[3] In them the paper recommended a federal solution for the devolution problem and it has stood by this ever since. In addition it has greatly increased its reporting of the activities of the Nationalists and their policies on the question of Scottish government. It employs an able young columnist, Neal Ascherson, whose work appears in the paper very often. In short, the paper which has the highest prestige among the Scottish middle classes has, for a long time, taken a clear pro-devolution line and has even shown considerable sympathy towards the Nationalists.

This is not the end of the story as far as Scottish newspapers are concerned. In 1974 Sir Hugh Fraser, the chairman of Outram, the company which owned the *Glasgow Herald*, became a member of the SNP. His father had been, when he occupied the same position, a prominent Conservative. Sir Hugh's Conservatism had been lower in key but this was a fairly momentous change by any standard. Members of the *Herald* staff are emphatic that no pressure was applied to change the policies of the paper but it was fairly clear that the *Herald* could no longer continue what had been at times a rather abusive campaign against the Nationalists. It is difficult to portray Nationalists as dangerous or naïve or both when one's chairman has just become a Nationalist. A new editor, Ian Lindsay Smith, introduced a policy much more sympathetic to devolution to the extent that, when the latest government failed in its attempt to get its Scotland and Wales Bill through the Commons the first leader in the *Herald* read: 'If the cause [of devolution] is allowed to die then the future political unity of this island will be in jeopardy.'[4] The paper had come a long way in a few years. Another striking indication that things had changed came in the week beginning 4 April 1977 when the *Herald* began a week-long series of articles in the important position opposite the leader page discussing the implications of independence in many sectors of Scottish life. The *Scotsman* was to follow with a similar series. Nationalism was certainly now on the Scottish agenda.

A final paragraph should be devoted to the influence of television. As one would expect of an organisation controlled from London the BBC was not remarkable for the depth or extent of the Scottish coverage. The coming of independent television in 1956 did, however change the situation. For the first time there were programmes with a large Scottish content. Announcers had Scottish rather than 'BBC' accents and the amount of Scottish material shown on Scottish Television (STV) was more than on the BBC. In 1958 it was 15 per cent which may still not have been very much. Some of this Scottish material may have appeared for rather unfortunate reasons. Basically STV wanted to do things cheaply and it was cheaper to hire Scottish entertainers. Many of them may have been of low quality but they were Scottish.

In the years which followed, the differences between the BBC and STV may not have been so striking in Scottish content but it seems fairly unambiguous that the BBC was partly spurred to present more Scottish programmes by the presence of the commercial company.

10 The SNP Vote: Some Relations and Conclusions

In Chapters 4 to 9 it has been argued that political, economic, cultural and other processes since the beginning of this century have largely awakened a new awareness of Scotland. The material used has been largely historical. In this short chapter I shall explore some survey material in order to see whether it provides any evidence for the deductions which were drawn from historical processes. In particular I shall look at some of the major social groups mentioned in the previous chapters to ask whether the events in the last thirty or forty years have had any effects on them.

Survey material was not collected specifically for this book. I am, therefore, forced to look for data in other studies. The obvious disadvantages of this process are that questions which are central to my interests are often omitted and, where they are asked, this is often done in such a way that the data is not available in precisely the way I would want it. In particular, data may be collected in one part of the whole area which I would like to cover. In this chapter I shall use data collected by the Opinion Research Centre,[1] the British Election Survey[2] and the Strathclyde Area Survey.[3] The first two estimate distribution over Scotland as a whole while the third refers only to the Glasgow area. Despite the limited geographical referent of the Glasgow data, the questions asked are more extensive and consequently use will be made of them. In addition the Glasgow data are panel data interviewing the same group of respondents each year for three years.

In Chapter 5 it was suggested that the economic decline of Scotland had nurtured an awareness of economic problems in Scotland as peculiarly *Scottish* economic problems. Normally those most affected by a recession or by economic problems generally are employees who are likely to be laid off or sacked. Unemployment is a characteristic of manual working class rather than middle class life. If it is the working class who are most affected is there evidence that they are most attracted to nationalism? Alternatively, since they enjoyed improving conditions in the 1950s as I have shown, is there evidence that a sense of relative deprivation encouraged them to support the SNP in the harsher years of the 1960s?

In Chapter 7 I discussed some reasons why young people might be attracted to nationalism. Is there survey evidence to show that young people have indeed supported the SNP in proportions greater than their elders?

In Chapter 8 I suggested that the role of the Church had been an equivocal one. Is there evidence to show that adherents of the Church of Scotland, the traditional people's Church with all its historical associations with Scottish nationhood, are more attracted to political nationalism?

The overall argument of Part 2 is that there has been an all round increase in Scottish identification. Having dealt with the effect of sectional identification: class, age, religion, I shall turn to see whether there is evidence of a general rise in Scottish identification and whether this identification has become political.

Nationalism and social class

When the Scottish economy was discussed it was suggested that the rise in SNP votes was related to the economic downturn of the 1960s. In the 1950s the Scottish economy had progressed more or less in parallel with the rest of Britain but in the 1960s the traditional industries began to contract very clearly and this had a vivid effect on the level of unemployment. I have already suggested that manual workers are most likely to be affected by this and therefore one might expect them to be moved to protest: that they would move first to the Nationalists. There are, however, at least two complications. One is that the Nationalist vote started to rise in the early 1960s and data are only available from about 1974. The other complication is that those who are poorest are the least likely to be involved in any form of revolt. Several writers have shown that it is those with experience of better things who are most likely to revolt.[4]

There is another possibility. It is that the context of Scottish politics has changed in such a way that class has a diminishing role in relation to voting behaviour. People may vote according to their perception of the economic situation and the possibility of unemployment but the unit which they identify with as the one likely to suffer is not class but nation.

The traditional account of British politics has been of a system dominated by class. This tradition has clearly been broken by the SNP in that it has support from every stratum in Scottish society. This point comes out clearly from Table 10.1.

Table 10.1   Social class and the vote, June 1975

	Social Class			
	AB	C1	C2	DE
Conservative	56	40	23	22
Labour	14	23	39	48
Liberal	10	6	6	6
SNP	20	30	32	23
Other	—	1	—	1
	100	100	100	100

These data are taken from a survey carried out by the Opinion Research Centre for the *Scotsman* during June 1975. The population is ranked from those in high status non-manual occupations, category AB, to unskilled manual occupations, category DE. What do we learn from it?

It is clear that both Conservative and Labour are still class parties. The Conservative vote rises with the status of the respondents and the Labour vote drops. It is very noticeable that the Nationalist vote does not behave in this way. The two middle categories are most likely to support the SNP while people of very high status and those of the lowest status are less likely to do so. One interpretation of this is that the SNP is a party of the lower middle class and indeed it might be thought that these are the groups (C1 and C2) most likely to experience problems. They are most likely to be affected by cross pressures in that they may have friends who support other parties and they are also the ones who would be affected by recessions and would be more able to understand their situation than those who were also forced to do the least skilled work. A subsequent ORC poll shows, however, that the situation has changed somewhat (see Table 10.2).

Table 10.2   Social class and the vote, December 1975

| | Social Class | | | |
	AB	C1	C2	DE
Conservative	47	40	20	20
Labour	20	21	32	36
Liberal	11	7	4	3
SNP	22	32	43	40
Other	—	—	—	1
	100	100	100	100

From this it seems that there has been a definite move among the unskilled workers towards the Nationalists. It is also notable that in *every* social category there has been a move to the Nationalists. One might take it that, in so far as the Nationalists are on the way to being the major party in Scotland, the class nature of Scottish politics is beginning to disappear. Thus, Butler and Stokes's 'decline in the class alignment' takes the form of turning to a party whose base may be national identification rather than class identification. We shall explore this further when we look at specifically ethnic identification and the vote.

Relative deprivation

The fact that categories C1 and C2 were formerly those that identified most with the Nationalists leads us to return to the relative deprivation hypothesis.

Before starting a discussion on this point it is very necessary to repeat Runciman's warning that relative deprivation is an ambiguous concept.[5] Does it refer to political or economic or, perhaps, cultural or status deprivation? To some extent this Gordian Knot is cut through by the fact that there are very little data, in any case, and virtually all of them relate to a sense of economic discrimination. It is important to underline the fact that the concept of relative deprivation refers to a perception on the part of an individual rather than an 'objective' economic, or any other, situation. Thus it may be that government expenditure might be higher in Scotland or the emigration rate might be coming down. Both of these factors would be irrelevant to the 'relative deprivation' explanation because this is concerned with perception of a situation, not directly with the situation itself.

From the Kilbrandon Commission itself we have evidence that such a sense of deprivation does exist in Scotland:[6] in reply to the questions, 'Compared with other parts of Britain, would you describe (region) as well-off financially?' and also, 'Compared with other parts of Britain, would you describe (region) as providing lots of opportunities for young people?'

Table 10.3   Regional attributes

Region	% believing that the region was well-off financially	% believing that the region provided lots of opportunities for young people
North	19	31
Yorkshire	55	62
North West	48	65
West Midlands	67	72
East Midlands	62	73
East Anglia	34	42
South East	76	60
Greater London	74	80
South	51	44
South West	·25	21
Wales	24	29
Scotland	22	34

As can be seen from Table 10.3 the Scots respondents contained very small proportions who thought their part of Britain was doing particularly well in relation to other parts of the country. These measures are some indication of the existence of a feeling of relative economic deprivation.

In the 1975 survey in Glasgow the following question was asked:

'Compared with the rest of Britain would you describe Scotland as well-off financially or not particularly well-off?' Table 10.4 shows the relationship between the answer to this question and the respondents' political affiliation. It is clear that there is some effect from the relatively gloomy view of Scotland's prospects. Seven percentage points separate the Nationalist percentage among those who compare Scotland badly with the rest of Britain. It is possible that one factor in voting Nationalist is the perception of this situation. This variable, however, does not alone explain why a large proportion of people who view Scotland in this light vote Nationalist.

Table 10.4 Voting and Scotland's prosperity

	Well-off	Not well-off
Conservative	32·6	22·4
Labour	40·3	45·9
Liberal	4·7	2·2
SNP	22·5	29·5
	100·1	100·0

In a more extensive examination Brooks got more ambiguous results.[7] He found a relation between a perception of political deprivation and support for the Nationalist party. (This deprivation variable was measured in terms of a feeling that Scotland's representation in Westminster ought to be increased.) On the other hand, his findings on the effect of perceived economic or social deprivation were mixed. Such feelings were high but, of the five measures he used, only two were positively related to Nationalist voting: a perception that jobs were easier to get in England and a perception that luxury items were more widely enjoyed in England. Especially in the second case the relationship was weak.

From Brooks's data and from the Glasgow data we conclude that the feeling of relative deprivation may have some effect but we must try to put these data in relationship to the effect of other variables.

Age

There are many sources which can be used to demonstrate the youth of the SNP support. I shall repeat the ORC data for the sake of consistency (see Table 10.5).

149

Table 10.5   Age and the vote, June 1975

| | Age | | | |
	18-24	25-44	45-64	65+
Conservative	19	25	31	44
Labour	27	32	40	40
Liberal	6	8	5	5
SNP	47	35	24	11
Other	1	—	—	—
	100	100	100	100

The SNP proportion falls with increasing age. It is interesting that, for the other two major parties, the vote increases with the increase in age. If we compare these results with similar results in the December survey we see an increase in support from the older group (see Table 10.6).

Table 10.6   Age and the vote, December 1975

| | % in each age range voting SNP | | | |
	18-24	25-44	45-64	65+
SNP	49	45	32	24

Religion

I have tried to demonstrate that the Church of Scotland has a peculiar place in Scottish society. At the same time there was no evidence that it had led opinion formation for devolution or independence.

Religion is one of the most important variables for the explanation of party support. In Germany, Holland and Australia religion has been a major issue which has polarised the political system at one time or another. As far as Britain is concerned there was a traditional relationship between non-conformism and Liberal voting and to some extent this still obtains.[8] The modern data have sometimes been collected in an imprecise fashion but when, as in the case of the study in Dundee by Bochel and Denver,[9] the questions were worded more carefully, the picture has somewhat changed. Both these authors and the authors of *Political Change in Britain* found that there was some residual effect of religion but that there were cleavages by class within the denominations.[10] While membership of the Church of Scotland might have some relationship with Conservative voting, the class of the Church of Scotland member would also have an effect over and above his or her religious identification.

Such appears to be the conventional account of the diminished place of religion in British politics. In this study, however, we are looking at a political situation in Scotland where the effect of religion might be different from that in the country as a whole. There is only one piece of evidence on this relation which is easily available through commercial polls. This is to be found in a study of young voters done by the ORC for the *Scotsman* in May 1976 (see Table 10.7).

Table 10.7   Religion and the vote (1)

	None	Church of Scotland	Other Protestant	Roman Catholic
Conservative	15	18	38	12
Labour	34	19	19	45
Liberal	5	10	13	4
SNP	45	52	25	39
Other	1	1	5	—
	100	100	100	100

It is striking that those identifying with the Church of Scotland are most likely to vote Nationalist. Those who identify with other Protestant Churches number only sixteen and, if we exclude these data because of the small numbers, the Catholics are the least likely to vote Nationalist.

The Glasgow survey also collected data on religion. One should recall that this city and its surroundings have one of the few sizeable Catholic populations in Scotland. If we are to test for the effect of religion, therefore, Glasgow is a good place to do it. We must make clear what is meant by 'religion' in this context. What it does not mean is that the 'Protestants' and 'Catholics' described here are regular church-goers and believers in the particular doctrine of the Churches. Rather it points to the fact that, in the west of Scotland there are two distinct communities which, in most cases, are organised virtually along the consociational lines described by Lipjhart.[11] They are educated in separate schools, they support different football teams and, until recently, there was little inter-marriage. Until 1939 at any rate it was very difficult for a Catholic to get a job in an establishment run by Protestants and vice versa. On top of this, most Glaswegians over forty have memories if not direct experience of the bitter gang fighting that used to take place on a basis of religious identification, though hardly on one of religious practice.

There are also political implications. Many Scots who identify themselves as Protestants hold sympathies with the Protestant cause in Ireland and there are still many Orange Lodges in towns like Glasgow, Paisley and Greenock. Their members in the past voted solidly Conservative since this was the party of Unionism. The Catholics, almost all of them descended from Irish immigrants, look on the Labour Party as their natural home both because their ancestors were poor working class immigrants and because Labour was not identified with the bitter opposition to an independent Ireland which characterised the Conservatives.

Table 10.8   The influence of religion on voting

	Church of Scotland	Other Protestant	Roman Catholic
1970 election			
Conservative	41·6	57·1	11·0
Labour	47·6	37·5	84·7
Liberal	0·7	0·0	0·6
SNP	10·0	5·4	3·7
	99·9	100·0	100·0
1974 (Feb.) election			
Conservative	38·2	31·1	11·0
Labour	34·1	37·8	79·3
Liberal	3·7	6·7	2·8
SNP	24·0	24·4	6·9
	100·0	100·0	100·0

Table 10.8   *The influence of religion on voting* (continued)

	Church of Scotland	Other Protestant	Roman Catholic
1974 (Oct.) election			
Conservative	34·1	40·0	12·5
Labour	35·8	33·3	78·9
Liberal	3·4	10·0	0·7
SNP	26·7	16·7	7·9
	100·0	100·0	100·0

The findings shown in Table 10.8 throw light on the distribution of the Nationalist vote over Scotland as a whole. Although they have won two seats in the industrial Clyde valley at by-elections (Hamilton 1967 and Govan 1973), that part of the country has not been good for them in general. An explanation is suggested by the figures in Table 10.8. Clydeside has a much higher proportion of Catholics than has the rest of Scotland. It is they who are the backbone of the Labour vote and, up to 1974 anyway, that backbone did not bend under the weight of the Nationalist attack. The situation among the Protestants is quite different.

This point is the most important one in terms of the effect of religion on politics in Scotland as a whole. Scotland is overwhelmingly a Protestant country. The last reliable figures showed 72 per cent Protestants and only 20 per cent Catholics.[12] The significance of the data shown in Table 10.8 is that in areas where there is a large Catholic population, the Nationalist proportion of the vote is likely to be lower than elsewhere. We would expect a relatively low SNP proportion of the vote in places like Glasgow and other parts of the industrial south-west where there is a large Catholic, originally Irish immigrant, population, around 33 per cent according to the Glasgow survey.

One must conclude that religion has an effect on the Nationalist vote but, since the religious division is limited to one part of the country, this is not an important factor in explaining the rise of the SNP in Scotland as a whole. It is clear from Table 10.8 that the Church of Scotland voters were much more likely than the Catholics to vote Nationalist and secondly that, while the Protestants moved to the SNP the Catholics moved much more slowly.

The fact that the relation between religion and political affiliation is based upon the community rather than religious practice is brought out if we look at the relationship controlled by whether or not the respondent goes to church (see Table 10.9).

Table 10.9   Religion and the Vote (2)

| | % of respondents voting Nationalist | |
	Church of Scotland	Roman Catholic
Non-churchgoers	31	23
Churchgoers	23	20

In other words, it is clear that among practising members of the Church of Scotland or the Roman Catholic Church there is virtually no difference in the proportions voting Nationalist. Whereas among non-churchgoers the difference is almost three times as great. Religious belief itself is not the effective factor.

Scottish identification

Up to now we have been dealing with groups within Scottish society. Their character and activities do not provide much help in explaining the increase in Nationalist support. They do not represent cleavage lines which would cause a strain resulting in national consciousness. It may be, however, that the group to be represented by the SNP is not some group in Scottish society but the Scots as a group in British society. If the Nationalists have mobilised this Scottish identification, this might account for the rise of the party.

First we must ask, how strong is this Scottish identification? There is information which shows that it is very strong. Budge and Urwin's study *Scottish Political Behaviour* reports a study in Glasgow in which the respondents were asked to say how much they had in common with different social groups. Fifty-six per cent of them said that they had more in common with a Scotsman of a different class from their own as compared with an Englishman of the same class. Only 19 per cent said they had more in common with an Englishman of the same class.[13] This is rather striking illustration of the power of ethnic rather than class identification. There is widespread and consistent evidence that a considerable majority of people living in Scotland consider themselves to be Scottish rather than British. Other data were reported in the *Glasgow Herald* from a series of polls held in medium sized towns in the west of Scotland around Glasgow. Between 75 per cent and 78 per cent identified themselves as Scottish rather than British.

It is, of course, possible to query whether Scottish identification is any more important than the feelings which English people have towards the regions of England they belong to. This is a task which was undertaken in Research Study No. 7 for the Commission on the Constitution. The investigators asked, 'What do you think of as *your* region of the country—what would you call it?' and then some questions later, they were asked, 'If someone called you a . . . (Regional name), would you accept it as reasonable or would you want to correct them?' The investigators report:[14]

> In comparison with this picture of regional definition in England, it is perhaps surprising to find that Scotland and Wales, which are separate countries with traditional boundaries are only a little more clearly defined by those who live in them . . . In Scotland only 45 per cent defined their region as Scotland, a further 15 per cent identified a small region with Scotland.

It is not surprising at all. The idea of Scotland as a region is certainly not common to Scotsmen and there is a great deal of doubt whether most respondents knew what they were being asked.

We have to take it that there is a strong sense of Scottish identification and that there is a great deal of evidence to show that when people are given a choice between a Scottish and a British identification, there is a consistent majority in favour of the Scottish one.

Table 10.10   National identification and the vote

	British	Scottish
1970 election		
Conservative	33·8	27·6
Labour	60·7	61·4
Liberal	1·0	0·9
SNP	4·5	10·1
	100·0	100·0

Table 10.10 National identification and the vote (continued)

	British	Scottish
1974 (Feb.) election		
Conservative	31·5	18·3
Labour	53·9	53·7
Liberal	4·8	4·8
SNP	9·7	24·3
	99·9	100·1
1974 (Oct.) election		
Conservative	27·4	23·1
Labour	56·5	39·1
Liberal	3·5	2·3
SNP	12·6	35·5
	100·0	100·0

Table 10.10, based on the Glasgow data, shows quite clearly that feeling oneself to be Scottish has a considerable effect on propensity to vote Nationalist. Even more interesting is the developmental feature of the table. Where for the 1970 election the increment in Nationalist voting given by Scottish identification was only some six per cent, this increment has gradually risen until, at the general election in October 1974, it represented an increment of 23 per cent. What is also notable is the distinct effect this has had among Labour voters who considered themselves to be Scottish. There has been a clear fall in this percentage and it is difficult to see any other explanation than that these voters voted Nationalist. The Conservatives among the Scots identifiers also declined in proportion when one compares the 1970 results with those of the February 1974 election. In the October 1974 election the Conservative proportion of this group had increased again but it had not gone back to the 1970 level.

It seems consistent with the evidence, then, that the sense of Scottishness is coming to have a political connotation.

The debate on devolution

Scottish support for self-government goes back some way in modern history as we have seen. A Bill to introduce a type of federal Parliament passed its second reading in the House of Commons in 1913 with the virtually unanimous support of the Scottish members. After the war had killed this plan, there was another indication of majority support for a Scottish Parliament when straw polls were carried out by the *Daily Record* and the *Scottish Daily Express* in 1932. There was more solid evidence after the Second World War when at least one million Scottish electors signed the Scottish Covenant (see below, Chapter 13).

If there has been fairly consistent support for some sort of devolution of powers to a Scottish legislature, there have until recently been few votes for complete independence. Since the beginning of the 1970s, however, this policy has been placed firmly on the agenda of British politics.

It is important to outline the options that are open. They consist of proposals which have been made at one time or another by the political parties and are ranked in order of their departure from the existing situation. The first option is for the retention of the status quo with no more devolution. The second is for some kind of Assembly which would have limited powers relating only to Scottish domestic affairs and even then not covering all Scottish domestic affairs. The third option would be for an Assembly which would cover all of this and in addition would have considerable economic powers including possibly some powers over the oil revenues. Finally, there is complete independence. Some complicating factors overlie this simple hierarchy including the question of the responsibility of the Scottish legislature to the Westminster Parliament, and the questions have been phrased in different ways.

The question used by the Kilbrandon Commission research in 1970 was:

For running $\dfrac{\text{(the region)}}{\text{(Scotland as a whole)}}$ which of these five alternatives would you prefer overall?

i   Leave things as they are at present.

ii Keep things much the same as they are now but make sure that the needs of $\dfrac{\text{(the region)}}{\text{(Scotland)}}$ are better understood by the government.

iii Keep the present system but allow more decisions to be made in $\dfrac{\text{(the region)}}{\text{(Scotland)}}$

iv Have a new system of governing $\frac{\text{(the region)}}{\text{(Scotland)}}$ so that as many decisions as possible are made in the area.

v Let $\frac{\text{(the region)}}{\text{(Scotland)}}$ take over complete responsibility for running things in $\frac{\text{(the region)}}{\text{(Scotland)}}$

The results shown in Table 10.11 were obtained and the report deduces from them that Scotland was really very little different from other regions in the extent to which it opted for the fifth alternative although it had the highest percentage under such a choice.

Table 10.11 Percentage supporting differing degrees of Devolution in each region

| | Alternatives | | | | |
	i	ii	iii	iv	v
North	11	27	26	20	16
Yorkshire	16	23	24	20	16
North West	8	19	30	24	15
West Midlands	15	23	26	18	17
East Midlands	12	23	26	21	18
East Anglia	16	24	17	21	20
South East	14	29	21	20	16
Greater London	16	24	24	19	14
South	11	23	20	25	21
South West	20	28	20	17	12
Wales	15	27	21	23	13
Scotland	6	19	26	24	23

The problem is that the political situation in Scotland and Wales was quite different from that of other areas. In Scotland and Wales there were organisations dedicated to making the countries independent and there was a fair chance that Scottish respondents would interpret the fifth option in this way. To ask English people whether they would like a regional government to take over complete responsibility for running affairs in the region is quite different. There is not the presumption of a Declaration of Independence from Westminster. It is likely that a very large proportion of the people who answered 'yes' to this had in mind some kind of powerful local government.

With all its faults it is interesting that about a quarter of the Scottish respondents to this questionnaire answered in favour of the strongest option which was probably seen by them as opting for complete independence.

In subsequent research by other organisations the remarkable thing is that this proportion remains fairly steady. This point is made quite clear by Table 10.12 in which the results of the Kilbrandon survey are put together with the series of ORC surveys published in the *Scotsman*. This shows that support for complete independence has remained fairly consistent over the years.

Table 10.12   Support for Kilbrandon alternatives 1970-5

	Kilbrandon July/Aug. 1970	May 1974	Dec. 1975
Leave things as they are at present.	% 6	% 14	% 11
Keep things much the same as they are now but make sure that the needs of Scotland are better understood by the government.	19	20	16
Keep the present system but allow more decisions to be made in Scotland.	26	24	27
Have a new system of governing Scotland so that as many decisions as possible are made in the area.	24	23	19
Let Scotland take over complete responsibility for running things in Scotland.	23	18	24
Don't know	1	1	3
	99	100	100

If we put this together with another question containing devolution options which the ORC devised when the different party proposals began to crystallise in 1974 we get more or less the same result (see Table 10.13).

Part Two

Table 10.13 Support for devolution option April 1974-December 1975

	April 1974	Sept. 1974	June 1975	Dec. 1975
	%	%	%	%
Keep the present system.	21	21	21	14
Have a Scottish Assembly, not directly elected, but made up of the representatives of the new regional councils, which would handle some Scottish affairs and would be responsible to Parliament at Westminster.	19	14	11	14
Have a directly elected Scottish Assembly which would handle some Scottish affairs and would be responsible to Parliament at Westminster.	24	17	19	19
Have a Scottish Parliament which would handle most Scottish affairs, including many economic affairs, leaving Westminster responsible for defence, foreign affairs and international economic policy.	16	24	26	28
Make Scotland completely independent of the rest of Britain with a Scottish Parliament which would handle all Scottish affairs.	17	20	19	21
Don't know	3	4	5	5
	100	100	101	101

It is interesting that, over the admittedly short run from April 1974 to 1975, there has been a gradual increase in the proportion of people who chose the option of a Scottish Parliament to which would devolve most powers including those over the Scottish economy.

160

More important, since at least 1970, there has been a core of about 20 per cent of the Scottish people who would choose complete independence. The first poll in the series, done for the Kilbrandon Commission, was conducted in July-August 1970 just after the general election and at a time when the fortunes of the SNP were low. Yet after this, when the SNP was doing better and indeed even at the time when, in early 1976, two polls found it to have the highest proportion of votes in Scotland, the proportion of the population opting for complete independence does not change much.

The implication seems to be that there is not much of a relation between voting for the SNP and agreeing with its main policy. This argument certainly has a great deal of weight but the situation needs to be examined rather more carefully. In Table 10.14 we show the percentages of people from each party who chose the various devolution options among the Glasgow 1975 respondents.

Table 10.14   Support for devolution by party support

	Parties			
	Con.	Lab.	Lib.	SNP
	%	%	%	%
Keep the present system.	30	26	20	6
Have a Scottish Assembly, not directly elected, but made up of the representatives of the new regional councils, which would handle some Scottish affairs and would be responsible to Parliament at Westminster.	13	11	19	3
Have a directly elected Scottish Assembly which would handle some Scottish affairs and would be responsible to Parliament at Westminster.	24	22	19	10
Have a Scottish Parliament which would handle most Scottish affairs, including many economic affairs, leaving Westminster responsible for defence, foreign policy and international economic policy.	24	27	30	27

161

Table 10.14   Support for devolution by party support (continued)

| | Parties | | | |
	Con.	Lab.	Lib.	SNP
	%	%	%	%
Make Scotland completely independent of the rest of Britain with a Scottish Parliament which would handle all Scottish affairs.	4	9	9	55
Don't know	5	5	3	—
	100	101	100	101

There has been a fair number of people in the past who were in favour of independence but did not vote SNP. In the more recent surveys these people seem to have become concentrated more and more in the SNP. From this point of view it appears that the SNP has become more and more characterised by the support of those who agree with the main policy of the party. Finally, the data from the Glasgow Area Survey show a clear relation between the devolution option selected and party choice.

Table 10.15   Party support by support for devolution option

	Status Quo	Weak Assembly	Strong Assembly	Scottish Parliament	Independence
Conservative	36·2	27·5	34·8	18·8	7·8
Labour	55·1	64·7	47·1	42·4	29·1
Liberal	1·4	3·9	3·4	3·1	0·0
SNP	7·2	3·9	14·7	35·8	63·1
	99·9	100·0	100·0	100·1	100·0

We are justified in saying that the choice of devolution option seems to be related to voting for the SNP. This is borne out both by the Glasgow data and by the material in the ORC and some other opinion polls. As Butler and Stokes have shown, issue voting is not a common feature of British politics.[15] Perhaps Pomper's comments in relation to the United States are significant, 'Confused voters reflect confused parties; clarity among the voters follows from clear-headed parties.'[16]

All this is not to argue that all or even most SNP voters are issue voters on the issues of independence or devolution. Mixed up with the question of independence is the issue of 'putting Scotland first'. In other words a vote for the SNP is a vote for Scotland. In terms of the various approaches which I described, this is a 'group' explanation of the vote. One suspects that in the minds of most voters the issue of independence and the issue of Scotland are mixed up together. This comes out very clearly if we look at some data from the Glasgow Study. Respondents were asked why they voted as they did. The results are shown in Table 10.16.

Table 10.16 Reasons for supporting parties

	Conservative	Labour	SNP
Always voted for party	27	24	3
Dislike other parties	31	12	22
Put country on feet	14	6	2
Do more for Scotland	1	—	45
For working men	1	41	1
Deserve a chance	—	1	21
I agree with policy	17	10	4
Other	9	6	2
	100	100	100

First it becomes clear that, in every party, very few mention their agreement with a particular policy of the party. We have to remember that respondents were not asked about their support for a particular policy and it is quite feasible that a large number of Nationalist supporters who did not mention it as their first reason for voting Nationalist might have been in favour of complete independence for Scotland. What these data bring out is that the idea is not as salient as are some others. In exactly the same way we do not get Labour supporters mentioning support for, let us say, nationalisation of industry. Instead we find that Labour supporters are such because they see this as the party of the working man. In other words, in the eyes of the largest group of their supporters, Labour is seen as a specifically class party. In the same way it is significant that the SNP is seen as the party for Scotland. What is important and is different from the previous situation is that Scotland is seen as the political entity which is worthy of electoral support.

How are we to sum up the findings about the relation between the demand for some form of self-government in Scotland and support for the Scottish National Party? If we look at the data over time, support for the issue of Scottish independence does not rise and fall with support for the Scottish National Party. What has changed is the proportion of people supporting far-reaching devolution options short of independence. The SNP has successfully made this an issue. In doing so the political debate has been defined in Scotland and all parties have undoubtedly taken their supporters with them. Devolution and even independence have become respectable. What is even more important is that the political significance of being Scottish has become more important. It is the result of the general modernisation of Scottish consciousness.

The nature of this modernisation comes out of more data which was collected in the Glasgow survey. Respondents were asked, 'If you had to choose between these two alternatives, which do you think is the more important: to preserve Scottish traditions or to improve the standard of living for people in Scotland?'

Table 10.17   Attitudes to Scotland

	Keep traditions	Improve living standards
Conservative	9	91
Labour	2	98
SNP	4	96

It is quite clear that the Nationalists are no different from the other parties in their desire to create a modern Scotland. There is no question, for the majority of their supporters, that the SNP is not a party for the re-creating of a kind of 'folk society'. These data confirm quite starkly the fact that the basis of the support for nationalism comes from a deep worry on the part of Scots about their living standards.

Finally, in this attempt to examine survey data for evidence to support hypotheses suggested by more impressionistic data let us look at some rather different material. I suggested at the beginning that part of the explanation for the move to Scottish nationalism lay in the general feeling of distrust for the established political system which could be observed all over Europe and in North America. Can it be demonstrated that SNP supporters are any more distrustful or in any way more alienated than the supporters of other parties?

In the Glasgow survey respondents were asked, 'How much do you trust the government in Westminster to do what is right? Do you trust it just about always, most of the time, only some of the time or almost never?'

Table 10.18   Attitudes to government

	Conservative	Labour	SNP
Trust always	2	7	2
Trust most of time	24	24	10
Trust some of time	51	58	55
Trust never	23	11	33
	100	100	100

This is a question which is always difficult to deal with in view of the confusion between the government in general and the specific party in power. It is difficult to get respondents to think of government in general. It must be said, therefore, that the question was asked during a time of Labour government and one would expect that the Labour supporters would display more trust in their leaders than would the Conservative or Nationalist voters. To some extent this comes out in Table 10.18 but not too much of a 'party effect' is visible. What is remarkable is that none of the parties seem to contain large proportions of supporters who trust the government. In each case the modal category is that which trusts the government some of the time. Looking at the results for Nationalist supporters it becomes clear that they are the respondents least likely to trust the government and this would fit with our original hypothesis. In a recent article Miller also brings some evidence from the British Election Survey of 1974 which also seems to demonstrate the importance of distrust in government for raising the Nationalist vote.[17]

Conclusion

The data given in this section have brought out some of the comments made in the earlier chapters concerning different aspects of Scottish life. The starting point of the argument was that the SNP vote was related to a general feeling of alienation with politics. This relationship has just been illustrated from survey data. On the other hand it was argued that, while this might explain a movement from the major parties it would not explain why the SNP itself had benefited. These survey data have shown that a connection between national feeling and Nationalist voting can be demonstrated. It can also be shown that this is related to the decline in class alignment. It is clear that various other characteristics of Scottish life have also contributed, among them the Protestant community and the younger age group. In the earlier chapters I have shown that these groups had particular reasons for identifying with Scotland.

Part Three

Part Three

The Beginnings
of the Modern
Movement

The purpose of this part of the study is to analyse the events leading to the founding and development of the SNP. In it we shall relate the story of the transition from a small, hopeless fringe organisation to a modern mass party.

In terms of Smelser's approach we may look at these chapters as the study of political mobilisation.[1] Under what circumstances was it possible for a political party to be organised? What kind of an organisation is it? How effective has it been in mobilising Scottish electors?

In many studies of social movements the importance of organisation is ignored. In a great deal of Marxist writings there seems to be an assumption that the working class will be revolutionary by its very nature. Just as Lenin and others following him have pointed out the crucial role of the party in activating the proletariat, so for the Scottish people it is difficult to understand their turning to the SNP other than by the efforts of the party itself. We shall see that the party was not active in organisation at all times but that once they started to build up their organisation there were real returns for them.

Apart from the changes in political climate, the presence of organisational talent was one of the crucial differences between the 1930s and the 1960s. We can look at the data in a different way. In previous chapters I have described how events in Scotland impressed or failed to impress a new sense of Scottishness on different sorts of people: the young, the business community, the Churches and so forth. In the chapters which follow I shall be interested in the impact they had on Scottish people as voters and as potential members of a political movement.

The major emphasis of these chapters will be historical but there are several themes which will be repeated. I shall refer to these now and at the end review their importance in view of the data that have been gathered.

One of these themes concerns the type of nationalism we have in Scotland. In Chapter 2 I discussed some theoretical work on nationalism and referred to a distinction made by Kohn. This concerned the difference between the sort of nationalism that originated in the countries of the developed west and that which came from eastern Europe. Western nationalism was deeply concerned with parliamentary traditions and the freedom of the individual. The other concentrated on the mystical traditions of the folk and on the values of peasant culture, since these nations were outside the great traditions of the European Enlightenment.

It has become obvious that no such clear distinction can be drawn in relation to Scottish nationalism. A movement such as the Scottish Covenant which did not recommend a greater change than a measure of devolution, used many of the arguments of the 'mystical' school of nationalism. Those who demand sovereign independence for Scotland as a natural right, use economic and administrative arguments. There is no correlation between 'extremism' in the cause of nationalism (complete independence being demanded for Scotland) and the use of particular sorts of arguments.

A second important theme is that of modernisation. Briefly, I shall argue that the nationalists saw themselves as responding to certain new trends in the social and political life of Scotland. This was true at the foundation of the organisations immediately after the First World War: the Scots National League and the Scottish Home Rule Association. It was also true after 1945 and especially in the 1950s when the credibility of the traditionalist Labour Party in Scotland had begun to sag. In other words, the main stream of nationalism in this country was not concerned with a lost Utopia and a return to it. Far from this, the nationalists recognised that the economy and society of Scotland were changing and that something had to be put in the place of the old economic and political institutions if Scotland was to regain its prosperity.

One of the problems the nationalists faced was that there was an alternative movement and party which was also modernising but interpreted events in a different way. At the same time as the nationalist movement was finding its feet in the 1880s the Labour Party or its immediate forerunners were established. It is evident that socialism was more successful. While it is not appropriate to go into much detail about this, it is clear that a number of factors helped to bring this about. First the Labour movement was British-wide in a country where there was a tradition that this should be so. The Conservative and Liberal Parties had both set the pattern. Secondly, from its earliest days the Labour movement had the support of established organisations: the trade unions. The national-ists had no similar bases of support. Finally, the leaders of Labour simply seem to have been more able than those who served nationalism. For all his later fall from grace, Ramsay MacDonald had great political talent. So had Robert Smillie, Emanuel Shinwell and Keir Hardie. It is significant that each of these Scottish Labour leaders were also Home Rulers at one time or another but they were much more effective than anyone on the nationalist side. One reason for this may have been the chance for Labour leaders to work full-time in politics through the trade unions. Even for the most dedicated nationalist, politics had to be a part-time job. Whether for this or for any other reason the quality of leadership in the rival movement appears to have been better.

Whatever the disagreements of the two approaches they were at one in regarding themselves as modern movements. One respected Nationalist, Oliver Brown, who habitually wore the kilt, told the story that, as a young man about to fight a parliamentary by-election, he was called over by R. B. Cunninghame Graham. The President of the National Party of Scotland suggested that wearing the kilt was not the thing for a Nationalist candidate to do. In the early photographs of nationalist rallies there were always a few kilts worn, by Oliver Brown, for example, or J. L. Kinloch, but the vast majority were very soberly clad. For most Scottish people, and for the nationalists, the wearing of the kilt was associated with the grouse moor and the aristocracy. To wear a kilt was, and is, somewhat eccentric and this was precisely the image the nationalists wanted to avoid. Their aim was to present themselves to the electors of Scotland as a serious and viable political party—a party to deal with the modern world.

There is one final theme which can be re-emphasised here. It concerns the pressure of British and world events upon the develop-ment of Scottish nationalism. Some commentators on this subject have written as if the SNP's success was almost entirely due to external events.[2] Certain external factors did affect the success of nationalism. The presence of a vigorous and well-led Labour movement was, as we have seen, of central importance. As we have also seen, from the mid-1930s onwards the international situation was such that the domestic affairs of Scotland seemed very small beer compared with the struggle of the Dictators. After 1945 the opportunities and failures of class politics formed *the* essential conditions for the rise of the SNP. It is impossible to consider the development of the National Party in Scotland other than in the context of British politics as a whole and, indeed, in the context of world politics.

11 The Beginnings of Modern Nationalism

The roots of Scottish nationalism go far back, even into the eighteenth century.[1] The historical evidence shows that the Union of the Parliaments in 1707 was unpopular.[2] There is evidence to show that anti-Unionism was the creed of some of the Jacobites in 1715 and 1745.[3] It has been the conventional viewpoint of historians that this was not so and recently the risings have been represented as the extensions of clan wars.[4] Other evidence seems to show that this is not the whole explanation. It was in the 1880s that patriotic societies were founded which began to press for Scottish rights.[5] In 1886, partly as a result of Irish politics, the Scottish Home Rule Association was set up. Later came the Young Scots, a youth wing of the Scottish Liberals, who were dedicated to Home Rule and who were the spearhead of the attack which forced the Liberal government to support Home Rule for Scotland. So successful was this movement that, as we have seen, a Bill to establish such a system passed its second reading in 1913.

I shall not try to cover the period before 1918. It has already been analysed by Professor Hanham in considerable detail and, in any case, my major interest is the modern movement. I shall, therefore, start with the position at the end of the First World War. In order to look at the various organisations and cross-currents it will, however, be necessary to refer to earlier events.

In 1918, the position of Scottish Home Rule in British politics was determined by pre-war events. Perhaps the most important of them was that immediately before the war it had seemed that self-

173

government was about to be established in Scotland. Largely as a result of what had happened in Ireland the idea of giving some measure of Home Rule to the constituent nations was fairly central in British politics. The interests of the major parties in this topic soon faded. In 1918, however, both the Liberal and the Labour Parties had Scottish Home Rule as a part of their programmes. An organisation pressing for this was not in any way eccentric. One of the two major organisations which later merged in the National Party of Scotland (NPS) was the Scottish Home Rule Association (SHRA) which was in the mainstream of British politics. The other was the Scots National League (SNL). It represented an entirely new and significant element.

The Scottish Home Rule Association

For various reasons the pre-war SHRA (founded in 1886) had collapsed but some of its members were to be active in the post-war organisation.

It should be noticed, however, that the bulk of the membership of the pre-war organisation was quite different from that of the post-war organisation. Before the war the SHRA had been made up of the Scottish Liberal establishment: there were several Liberal peers and virtually all the Liberal MPs. In effect, the name was used to create a new body after the war and this was to be almost wholly based on Labour and trade union support. The man mainly responsible was Roland Eugene Muirhead, the owner of Gryffe Tannery at Bridge-of-Weir. This man devoted all his life and a not inconsiderable fortune to the cause of Scotland. Up to his death in 1964 at the age of ninety-two he was to take a tireless part in the movement. He was a humourless man and no charismatic leader. He was an idealist whose ideals sometimes spilled over into utopianism. To the end of his life he was a socialist as well as a nationalist. With all these qualities working either for or against the future of the movement, Muirhead was absolutely central to the developments in the 1920s and 1930s. Apart from the well-known fact that he was the financial backer of the nationalist movement right through to the 1950s, his importance for the SHRA is peculiarly evident. It was he who called the meetings, he who managed the correspondence. The Association was housed in rooms belonging to his brother's business (a private college) and in 1929, after he left it, the SHRA collapsed.

On 9 September 1918 a meeting was held in the Central Halls, Bath Street, Glasgow. A resolution was passed:[6]

That this meeting, representing all shades of Scottish opinion and industrial activity, being convinced that the present centralised system of government from London is inefficient and inconsistent with national sentiment, resolves to form itself into a committee for the purpose of organising and focusing the Scottish demand for self-government in respect of Scottish affairs.

It was at this meeting that the post-war SHRA was set up. Its policy was 'to secure self-government for Scotland' but this was to be in regard to Scottish affairs only. In order to gain this 'the Association shall work . . . by means of (a) public meetings, (b) press correspondence, (c) the securing of pledges from Parliamentary candidates, (d) distribution of literature, (e) the holding of a National Convention'.

Two important points emerged from this resolution. The SHRA did not see itself as a political party. On the contrary it intended to work through the existing parties by extracting pledges from candidates and by putting pressure on Ministers. It was a pressure group. The second interesting point is the reference to the holding of a National Convention. This was not a wholly new idea and it was to be repeated several times in the history of the movement. The idea was that, as a nation, Scotland required a Parliament and one way of emphasising the massive and serious nature of the demand for a Parliament was to set up a Constituent Assembly.

An important feature of the SHRA already referred to was its political colour. The man who called the 1918 meeting and who was to remain its Secretary was Muirhead, a member of the ILP. The man who was elected President and who retained this position until 1928 was Robert Bontine Cunninghame Graham who was a founder member and President of the Scottish Labour Party in 1888 and had been a well-known radical MP. Others involved were William Gallagher of the Scottish Co-operative Wholesale Society and Robert Smillie of the Scottish Trades Union Congress.

The Association was based both on individual and organisational members. In 1919 and 1920 vigorous efforts were made to recruit town councils. It was felt that if these democratically elected bodies could be persuaded to join this would be an impressive proof of the Scottish desire for Home Rule. Many councils debated the issue but came up against the problem that the law apparently forbade them to use public funds (to meet the affiliation fee) for a political purpose (which the aim of the SHRA was seen to be). The culmination of this process was the debate in Glasgow Corporation where the resolution to join was defeated by fifty-two votes to forty-three. The largest group of organisations which took out organisational membership in the SHRA were 'working class' in character. In 1920, for example, after its first full year of operation, out of 138 organisational members, 47 were co-operative societies, 38 were trade union branches and 24 were ILP branches.[7] There were also some 'national' trade union affiliations such as the Scottish Horse and Motormen's Association, the Scottish Farm Servants' Union, the Scottish Mineworkers' Union and the Scottish Trades Union Congress. This bias was to remain fairly constant throughout its history. It was inevitable that the Liberal Party should be less prominent since it was at this time less prominent in the whole of the country. On the other hand the SHRA became associated quite firmly with the ILP despite its declared objective of putting pressure on all parties for devolution. The Marquis of Graham, a prominent supporter of Home Rule and a Conservative, refused to speak at one of its meetings because he considered it too 'Communistic' and even R. E. Muirhead admitted that some Labour members had left because of the fiery nature of speeches delivered at its meetings by the Clyde Group of MPs and especially by Maxton.[8] In its journal, the *Scottish Home Rule Association Newsletter*, founded in July 1920, it is clear that its speakers and propagandists operated very largely in the context of ILP meetings.

It is important to recognise the relation of the left-right issue to the Home Rule organisations. The relation of the Labour movement to Home Rule had been discussed already but, to give a flavour of the situation, it is worth quoting a resolution passed unanimously by the Scottish Divisional Conference of the ILP in 1925:

> In view of the failure of the Government to pass a Scottish Home Rule Act during the last session of Parliament, we demand that, without delay, power shall be given to the Scottish People to select a Constituent Assembly so that the Scottish Nation may themselves [*sic*] determine upon a scheme of self-government suited to their own needs.

The idea of a Constituent Assembly and, indeed, the whole resolution was precisely the policy of the SHRA. It is not hard to see why there was such a close bond between the organisations. The journal of the ILP in Scotland, *Forward*, was founded in 1906 by R. E. Muirhead and Tom Johnston. Muirhead remained a director of *Forward* until its collapse. For his part, Johnston was a familiar speaker at the SHRA annual rallies at Elderslie, the birthplace of Sir William Wallace.

Another important characteristic of the SHRA is related to this point. It was recruited predominantly in the Glasgow area. Glasgow is, of course, the major Scottish centre of population but even allowing for this, there still seemed a preponderance of Clydeside representatives. At the first AGM on 29 March 1929, for example, the office-bearers were as follows: President, W. Gallagher of the Scottish Co-operative Wholesale Society in Glasgow; Vice-President, Mrs Crossthwaite, Chairman of the Eastwood School Board, near Glasgow; Second Vice-President, Peter Fyfe, Chief Sanitary Inspector of Glasgow; Secretary and Treasurer, R. E. Muirhead, whose family business, as we have mentioned, lay a few miles from Glasgow. Practically the same group was re-elected to the offices year after year. As far as the Executive Committee was concerned, in 1923, nine of the sixteen were from the Glasgow area, six were from elsewhere in the south-west of Scotland and one was from Edinburgh. It is worth while bearing this point in mind in any future discussions of the 'Diffusionist' versus 'Internal Colonialism' theories or any other theory about the rise of nationalism. Table 11.1 shows the rate of increase of the organisation.

Table 11.1   Membership of the SHRA[9]

Year	Individual members	Organisations
1919	327	81
1920	1,150	138
1921	1,680	213
1922	1,888	220
1923	2,165	227
1924	2,325	300
1926	2,952	333
1927	3,148	335

As its name makes clear, the object of the SHRA was to secure self-government for Scotland for those functions of government which were specifically Scottish. On the other hand, the Association's interpretation of this was rather broad and became even broader as time went on. On 22 March 1922, for example, to a large rally, the General Council proposed that Scotland should have 'not less power than the Dominions or the Free State'. The meeting turned down this resolution which was supported by its leaders but it did agree that:[10]

> Scotland has a . . . right of self-government and that whatever agreements may have been entered into by our forefathers, it lies with the people now alive to decide as to the continuance with or without modification or the dissolution of these agreements and the substitution of others.

At all times the SHRA would have included fiscal powers for a future Scottish Parliament. It is also interesting to notice in these early resolutions the use of arguments based on the 'rights of nations' rather than just on administrative or democratic need. The same idea comes through again and again:[11]

> that the Scottish people being a nation in the full sense of the term ought to have means of organising, formulating and giving effect to its national will and that a Scottish Parliament democratically elected and sitting in Scotland is essential for this.

What were the programmes and activities of the SHRA? At the very beginning, a lot of attention was paid, in the *Newsletter* and in Council meetings, to the inadequacy of parliamentary arrangements for Scotland. In the September 1920 edition of the *Newsletter*, for example, there was an article about the lack of discussion of Scottish Estimates and another about the problem of legislation applying to English but not to Scottish conditions. In view of the large numbers of clergymen who were individual members, it is not surprising that some time was spent discussing attacks on the independence of the Scottish Church. There is a great deal of criticism of government neglect of such things as Scottish national monuments or Scottish museums. All these deficiencies showed the need for Home Rule.

To press this object the Association conducted meetings all over Scotland. Being in an established tradition of politics, it had an entrée to many organisations, not all of them left-wing. The *Newsletter* mentions speakers at Burns Clubs and other local societies. The Association also put a great deal of effort into open-air speaking tours in the style of socialist agitators and started the tradition of rallying at Wallace's house in Elderslie, Renfrewshire, to commemorate his death. This remains a major nationalist occasion.

The Association was particularly vigorous in the lobbying of MPs, parliamentary candidates and candidates for local elections. It was, after all, an association formally pledged to political neutrality. It would work through any representative who declared an interest in Home Rule. It cannot be said that there was a great deal of keen parliamentary support. On 9 September 1922 a meeting was called with the Scottish Members of Parliament. Thirty ignored the invitation altogether and only six turned up. On the other hand, Scottish Members were usually found to support Home Rule when they had to answer a question before an election. The SHRA *Newsletter* for December 1922 listed forty-four MPs who answered favourably and similar percentages were to be found at other times in the history of the organisation although after 1924 the proportion fell. As the 1922 meeting showed, however, this was not a keen support. A constant theme in the *Newsletter* was criticism of the Members of Parliament who claimed to be sympathetic but who achieved very little.

The second joint conference of MPs and the SHRA was somewhat more successful with eighteen MPs present.[12] It was also a meeting at which the political bias of the Association became clear: sixteen of the eighteen were Labour Members. It was there that two critical ideas came to be aired fully for the first time: the setting up of a Scottish National Convention and the establishment of a Scottish parliamentary party.

It was proposed by some members of the Association that the Imperial government should call a Convention of the Scottish people to formulate a Home Rule Bill. No government could be persuaded to do this and the initiative passed to the SHRA which called the first National Convention on 15 November 1924. Between these two meetings in 1923 and 1924 there was an important event. One of the Glasgow Labour MPs, George Buchanan, had been successful in the ballot for Private Bills. He agreed to bring in a Home Rule Bill for Scotland and was offered the services of the SHRA in drawing it up. Although he did not altogether agree with the Association's draft, the Association regarded this as the opportunity to achieve Home Rule. The Labour government expressed sympathy but, as we have seen in an earlier chapter, allowed the Bill to be lost in the debate. This brought home to many, including Muirhead, that Home Rule

179

would be achieved only by strong pressure from Scotland. They could not trust a Labour government. Great hopes were raised by Buchanan's Bill, much greater than those raised by the more famous Bill introduced by Barr in 1927. It was after the failure of the 1924 Bill that the ideas of a Convention and of a separate party began to gather support.

The Convention was attended by eight MPs and 116 members of the SHRA. In a rather desultory way it discussed the principles of a Home Rule Bill and remitted the details to the committee. The draft Bill before the Convention envisaged a Joint Council of England and Scotland to look after matters of shared concern such as Foreign Affairs and Defence. On demand of the Parliament of either nation, however, the responsibility for these subjects could be separated. In short, the SHRA, for all its modest title was proposing a scheme of devolution far more radical than any that came up in the early 1970s.

The second session of the Scottish National Convention met on 30 October 1926. The Rev. James Barr, MP, a member of the Association, had been successful in the Private Members' ballot and undertook to introduce the SHRA Bill which became 'Barr's Bill'. Plans were made for an extensive series of meetings and demonstrations all over Scotland to strengthen the resolve of the MPs. Despite this, the Bill was unsuccessful. It received even less parliamentary discussion than Buchanan's Bill and a third meeting of the Convention on 19 November 1927 discussed once again the setting up of a Scottish party.

There were some in the leadership of the SHRA who discussed the idea at a very early stage. As early as February 1921 a leader in the *Newsletter* asks how long it would be credible to work through MPs of the existing parties. It comments, 'Patience is a virtue only when it is not a crime.' At this time, however, the Scottish party was spoken of in terms of an *ad hoc* alliance of MPs from the other parties, who would unite to achieve Scottish Home Rule. By 1925 the foundation of a regular party was widely discussed. In October 1925 the *Newsletter* carried an article canvassing the possibility again. The December issue carried a report of a debate in which R. E. Muirhead, the Secretary, discussed the case for a separate party since the existing parties would not support Home Rule. The theme is taken up again in the *Newsletter* prominently in a long article in August 1926 by Dr R. F. Muirhead, Roland Muirhead's brother. Finally, at the third Convention, R. E. Muirhead declared that he had lost faith in the traditional way of working through the existing parties when Buchanan's Bill had failed in 1924. In February 1925 the Convention passed the following motion by fifty-seven votes to thirty-four:

> That this meeting of the Scottish National Convention believes that the passing into law of the Bill for the better government of Scotland depends on the creation of a National Party and decides forthwith to consider how best to create such a party.

Although the Association's AGM did not endorse such a motion the idea of a separate party was well on the way.

Various factors contributed to this decision but there were two predominant ones. It had become very clear to a significant group in the leadership of the Association that working through other parties was getting them nowhere. The position was nicely illustrated when a meeting of MPs was called to discuss the Bill drafted for the SHRA which became Barr's Bill. The Conservatives refused to send representatives. The Liberal Party claimed to be sympathetic but no representatives were appointed and, while the Parliamentary Labour Party appointed a committee of six to discuss the Bill, they could come to no firm conclusions. Among MPs there was no enthusiasm for a Home Rule measure and even among the membership of the Association there was an ambiguous attitude. The *Falkirk Mail* reported the meeting at which delegates of the first National Convention were chosen.[13]

> The Provost asked the members what suggestions they had to make. After a significant silence Councillor Adam said they might at least send a representative to that particular function.
> Baillie Logan: Hear Hear—an interjection which was followed by loud laughter.
> Councillor Adam: I am very glad to hear the 'Hear Hear'.
> Councillor Dillon: Hear Hear—renewed laughter.
> Provost Muirhead: Is there not a seconder?
> Councillor Dillon: Just a 'Hear Hear'.
> Another member: No, two 'Hear Hears'.
> The subject vanished.

The Glasgow *Evening Times* reported a similar meeting of Cambuslang Parish Council.[14]

> A communication was read on the Scottish Home Rule Demonstration to be held on Glasgow Green on 25 August. The Council was asked to send representatives.

> Chairman: We might allow the matter to lie on the table.
> Councillor Smith: I do not agree. Let us be represented.
> Councillor Malon: In kilts?—laughter
> Agreed that Messrs George and McWhannel attend.

We get the impression that even those organisations which were represented did not take the matter very seriously. In other words, the Association was regarded as worthy but faintly ridiculous. Despite its apparently large paper membership, it could not be said that the majority of the members were single-minded and enthusiastic.

On the other hand a minority *was* enthusiastic and the granting of Dominion status to Ireland seems to have had some impact. It was from this time that a demand for more militant action developed. A manifesto issued on 13 January 1922 congratulates His Majesty's Government on an 'epoch-making settlement of the Irish Question' and comments: 'We have refrained from pressing our claims as actively as we might have done because of our belief in the priority of the claims of Ireland for self-government.'[15] Now that this had been achieved, however, the Association claimed a form of Home Rule for Scotland which would be at least as wide as that granted to Ireland. In short, it seems that the ideas of the leaders of the Association were becoming detached from those of the majority of members. For the latter, Home Rule was a traditional radical posture. They might attend demonstrations and keep up their subscriptions but there was no intention of expending a major effort. This seems to have been true from the level of Cabinet Minister (at the 1924 Wallace Commemoration at Elderslie, Walter Adamson, the Secretary of State for Scotland, was the main speaker) to the ordinary rank-and-file members.

It was these factors which finally convinced R. E. Muirhead, the founder and Secretary, to abandon the original idea of an association and stand as a parliamentary candidate. Since Muirhead was the man who kept the Association together by devoting his time and money to it, it collapsed on his departure. We must now look at the new allies whom Muirhead and his colleagues found.

The Scots National League

These new allies came from an entirely different tradition of nationalism. Where the SHRA was in the tradition of Liberal-Labour radicalism, the Scots National League (SNL) was descended from, if it did not embody, the traditions of Gaelic cultural independence movements. It was clear that a great deal of the inspiration was Irish.

In a striking article, Dr James Hunter outlines the relationship between the Highland Land League and Scottish nationalism.[16] He shows the parallels between the peasant economies of Ireland and the Highlands of Scotland as well as their sufferings from the same sorts of exploitative landlords. He shows the way in which this situation was brought home by the activities of John Murdoch, a Scot who had worked in Ireland in the middle of the nineteenth century and who retired to edit the *Highlander* from Inverness. This paper supported the two causes of land reform and the revival of all things Celtic. Both of these were themes quite familiar in Ireland. Just as Sinn Fein grew out of the activities of the Gaelic League and other cultural societies, so Murdoch was to advocate Scottish self-government for a Scottish (or Gaelic) Scotland. The cultural awakening of the Highlands was to be the basis of a national awakening for Scotland. When the Highland Land League was founded and its MPs elected, they took a strongly Home Rule line.

It was from this background that the link emerged between the Gaelic cultural movement and the demand for self-government. The two key figures were Ruaraidh Erskine and William Gillies.

The Hon. Ruaraidh Erskine of Marr was the second son of the fifth Lord Erskine. He was born in Brighton but learned Gaelic from his nurse who came from Lewis. About the beginning of this century Erskine became extremely interested in Gaelic culture. He founded a number of journals which seem to have had some circulation among the Gaelic-speaking or Gaelic-sympathising intelligentsia. The best known of these is *Guth na Bliadhna* (The Voice of the Year) published partly in Gaelic and partly in English. It was founded in 1904 and ran until 1920.

At the end of the first year of publication the editor sums up *Guth na Bliadhna* as a 'Catholic bilingual periodical'.[17] In other words Erskine does not describe it in political terms but in religious and linguistic ones. He goes on to say that the two causes that are closest to his heart are the spread of the Roman Catholic Church in Scotland and the strengthening of the Gaelic movement. As far as the first cause was concerned, the emphasis came out in the very first article to be published, 'On the progress of the Roman Catholic Church in the Highlands'. Later he says 'Nearly every great evil, religious, political, social and commercial which Alba labours under, owes its existence or its continuance to Protestantism.'[18] Sentiments like these were not likely to find wide support among ordinary Gaels who were overwhelmingly Protestant.

As to the cultural interest, the journal is full of articles about traditional Gaelic institutions, folk customs or history but politics is not entirely absent and Erskine comes out as a distinct anti-imperialist.[19]

The English are making frantic endeavours to enlist the sympathies of the young people of these islands on behalf of their overgrown Empire. But the trend of modern politics is, fortunately, in exactly the opposite direction to that in which the friends of 'expansion' would like us to oblige the minds and consciences of our children to proceed.

The general point that comes out of these three positions—religious, cultural and political—is that Erskine owed a tremendous amount to Ireland. This was his primary inspiration. It was characteristic of Irish thinking at this time, or perhaps a little earlier, that the precise form of self-government was not clearly specified. At the beginning it appears that Erskine was some sort of Federal Home Ruler but he seems to have always believed that whatever decision was to be taken should be taken by the Scottish people and not by leave of the English. By the end of the First World War he was a supporter of complete independence and maintained this position for the rest of his life.

Erskine was the intellectual and propagandist for the movement through the written word. He has his journals as witnesses of his place in history. It is much easier to overlook the great importance of William Gillies in the building-up of this side of Scottish nationalism.[20] Gillies was the first editor of the journal of the SNL, the *Scots Independent*, and he wrote Gaelic plays which, though once popular, appear to be forgotten now. His real importance was as a political organiser. He had become a propagandist for the Highland Land League through his ·friendship with John Murdoch. Gillies spent some time in Ireland and had had close contacts with the nationalist movement there. He was among the few non-Irish to support the 1916 Rising. Returning to Britain to earn his living in London as a businessman, he worked continuously and consciously to infiltrate Gaelic and Highland organisations with his ideas and to distribute political literature. He spoke at countless meetings in Scotland and England and finally, in 1921, he was responsible for the organisation of the first meeting of the London branch of the SNL on 26 February. With its membership drawn from Gaelic-speaking expatriates, its bagpipe recital and Jacobite songs, it was a different animal from the SHRA.

This is the first definite record of a public meeting but there appear to have been activities before this. There is a reference to an earlier 'Scots National League' in 1909.[21] The journal *Liberty* refers to the SNL in its issue for June 1920. The SNL seems to have organised a public demonstration in Arbroath in September 1920 at which the socialist leader, John Maclean, took the chair. This was in opposition to an official celebration which was distinctly less nationalist. In October of the same year, the SNL sent an open letter to all candidates at the Scottish council elections asking them whether, if elected, they would bring forward a resolution that the ancient liberties of Scotland should be restored.

The London centre of the SNL initiated most of this activity. The people concerned, Gillies, Hugh Paterson, Angus Clark and others, were expatriate Highlanders, and the inaugural meeting of the London Branch was attended by representatives of the Highland Land League.[22] Inaugural meetings in Glasgow and Edinburgh were held in February and March 1922 and the first National Congress was held in Edinburgh on 23 June.[23] The League was never a large body. At the most it seems to have had a membership of about 1,000 with perhaps seven branches (Edinburgh, Glasgow, London, Dunfermline, Liverpool, Dalkeith and Hamilton). On the other hand it was active and, when the *Scots Independent* was founded in 1926, it seems to have had a circulation well in excess of the membership.[24]

The object of the SNL was not Home Rule but 'the resumption of Scottish National Independence . . . that Scotsmen acting nationally have the sole right to formulate and finally decide upon what scheme of self-government for Scotland should be adopted'.[25] In short, the tactic by which the League was to secure independence was not to be through pressure group tactics upon Members of Parliament in order to get a Bill which would pass through the normal stages of parliamentary procedure; nor even a Bill for the resumption of full independence. As in the philosophy of Sinn Fein, the future of Scotland was the responsibility of the Scottish people.

If one remembers the radical newness of these ideas, it is not surprising that the founders had not spent much time thinking about tactics. They placed a great deal of emphasis on the political education of the people but the mechanics of victory were not discussed. The belief which they held passionately was that they could not get Scottish independence through English political parties.[26]

> The possible advent of a Labour government . . . would not give Scotland freedom. The English Labour men would predominate and, being Englishmen with a national gift for interfering in what does not concern them, would now and again, as long as the Union lasts, prevent the development of Scottish aspirations.

As time went on, however, it became clearer that some thought would have to be given to tactics. For the SNL, as for the SHRA, the idea of a new political party had to be considered.

The major part in fashioning that new instrument seems to have been taken by T. H. Gibson. The idea of the Scots National League as a party independent of other parties is closely associated with him. In 1924 Gibson was working in Glasgow. He was then a lawyer's clerk but his great business abilities, which were later to be recognised when he was appointed Secretary of the Iron and Steel Federation, were already apparent. At all times he was single-minded and a down-to-earth individual. He had been appointed to the SHRA General Council but resigned on the issue of the Association being too closely linked with the ILP which was not fully committed to Home Rule.[27] Only a party devoted to Scottish independence could win full independence.

The fact that Gibson was in the SHRA while a believer in full independence for Scotland is important. It is true of several who later became prominent in the independence movement including Dr Archie Lamont and the poet Hugh MacDiarmid. For all of these people there was a link between their previous association with the Liberal party or the ILP. The founders of the SNL had no such previous links. They were in the more explicitly and exclusively nationalist tradition but they did not, by any means, have the monopoly of those dedicated to complete independence. This was one factor which made the subsequent fusion of most of the membership of both groups somewhat easier.

Gibson's proposal for a parliamentary party was not unanimously accepted by the SNL. At its conference in Edinburgh in October 1922 it had issued a manifesto against contesting the General Election.[28]

The SNL has an alternative, namely that the men and women
of Scotland work toward the objective of a great Scottish
National Convention in which Scotland's right to complete
national independence should be re-affirmed and re-established,
that the sovereign Scottish people take into their own hands all
the public powers of the country and administer them for and
on behalf of the Scottish Nation.

Erskine seems to have been suspicious of the idea of a political party
preferring to take a Sinn Fein position. The London Branch, or most
of its members, were unfavourable but by this time there were
several branches in Scotland.

With the coming of Gibson, the centre of gravity of the League
seems to have moved to Glasgow and various other characteristics of
the League changed.

At the annual conference on 19 June 1925, it was resolved that:[29]

the policy of the Scots National League is, by means of the
existing electoral activity, to obtain a majority of Scottish
representatives pledged to remain on Scottish soil and to
resume the powers of Government in Scotland and that
National candidates independent of all political parties be put
forward at the next General Election.

In short, a decision was taken that the League should operate in the
parliamentary field. It is worth noticing that it was from the SNL
that the present-day SNP policy of withdrawing from Westminster
came. Once a majority of Scottish representatives in favour of
independence was elected they would come to Edinburgh to convene
a Scottish Parliament. The idea was not new. It had been used by
the Irish and Hungarians and in Scotland it had been recommended
by Lockhart of Carnwarth.[30]

Another change of emphasis was important. The early journals of
the League, *Liberty* and *The Monthly Intelligencer* had virtually no
articles on the economic state of Scotland. The *Scots Independent*,
which appears to be largely Gibson's brainchild was heavily biased
in this direction.[31] The early editors, as we have seen, were William
Gillies and his son Iain but, compared with *Liberty* or its successor,
the *Scottish Standard*, the articles on Gaelic culture and historical
topics were very much reduced. As time goes on the concentration of
economic subjects becomes more and more marked. In short, the
SNL moves from a tradition of nationalism which is rather withdrawn
from the main stream of British politics to one which is rather closer

to it, at least in the sense that it plans to participate in elections. This made co-operation with the Scottish Home Rule Association easier. The reasons for this change are not, of course, far to seek. When both the organisations had been set up immediately after the war, economic conditions were not bad. In the early 1920s the economy of the west of Scotland was in a very serious state and considerations of Scottish culture and Scottish rights on parliamentary time very soon gave way to economic necessity.

It would be stupid to ignore the features which made the SNL very different from the SHRA. The emphasis on Gaelic culture has been mentioned but there were also politically radical elements in the SNL. There are many references to the Irish situation and the atrocities committed by the Black and Tans. Gillies was a republican and even a traditionalist like Erskine seems to have toyed with the idea. In 1920 Gillies wrote in the *Scottish Review*: 'The Scottish Republic is an idea, long live the Scottish Republic that is to be.'[32] There is also the relationship with the great Marxist agitator, John Maclean, who was a nationalist. It is difficult to find evidence that Maclean was a founder member of the SNL as his daughter believes.[33] What is undeniable is that, as we have seen, he was at the Arbroath demonstration in 1920 and that he wrote an article in Erskine's *Scottish Review*.[34] Erskine himself wrote an article on Celtic communism in Maclean's paper, the *Vanguard*.[35]

These relations were somewhat outside the world inhabited by the SHRA. It should not be thought, however, that the League condoned violence in pursuit of its aims.

In *Liberty* for June 1921 William Gillies wrote: Supposing some of the wilder spirits amongst us followed the example of such eminent exponents of law and order as Edward Carson, Birkenhead and other Imperial Stalwarts. Well then they would be exterminated at once.' This was a counsel of prudence rather than of principle. There were several Irish members who might have recommended other means.[36]

It was also important that the SNL was not able to rely on even the moderate sympathy which the SHRA was able to enjoy from institutions in Scottish society. Whereas there were Presbyterian ministers in the SHRA, many League members felt that the Church had betrayed the people both during the clearances and at other times. Thus Gillies echoes Erskine in saying, 'When Scotland was Catholic, Scotland was free. The Catholic Scotsmen kept her so even when the Pontiff of their Church sided with England.'[37]

The Scottish National Movement

One further group should be mentioned. On 1 February 1926, following personal disputes in the Edinburgh Branch of the SNL, the poet Lewis Spence set up the Scottish National Movement (SNM) at a meeting in Edinburgh.

Spence was born in 1874 and lived until 1955 although he dropped out of nationalist politics in the 1930s. He came from a middle class family living in Broughty Ferry, near Dundee, and was sent to school in England and then to the University of Edinburgh. With his education complete he worked as a journalist for the *Scotsman* and then moved to London to the staff of the *British Weekly*. By 1914, however, he had returned to Edinburgh to work as a freelance. Spence had enough financial resources behind him to develop his own interests and he did so in two directions. One was in the occult and the supernatural. His other interest, mentioned in Chapter 6, was, of course, the revival of poetry in Scots. It is not surprising to find from these personal details that Spence, although a very gifted man, was not an outstanding organiser and did not establish vigorous branches. On the other hand, he had the journalist's ability to publicise what organisation there was. He seems to have had an understanding with the editor of the *Edinburgh Evening News* who published frequent reports of the Movement's activities. Spence had two further assets. Apart from himself there were a very few dedicated workers who toiled enormously hard holding open air meetings all over the Lothians and Fife. Secondly, Spence was able to attract the interest of a wealthy backer, Mrs Linton, who virtually financed the whole operation. One might thus sum up the activities of the SNM by saying that it was a small group of people in and around Edinburgh who, because of enthusiasm, some financial backing and the sympathy of some newspapermen, were able to present themselves in the most impressive light possible.

The aims of the SNM (like that of the Scots National League) were the re-establishment of an independent Scottish Parliament and the revival of national culture and history. They were summed up in a pamphlet.[38]

1. The restoration of Scotland to her rightful place in the community of nations and her recognition as an independent state within the British Commonwealth.
2. The re-establishment of an independent national parliament sitting in Scotland.

3. Dissemination of propaganda regarding such questions of importance as the land, agriculture, afforestation and fisheries.

4. The revival of national sentiment, the study of Scottish history, the advancement of Scottish art, literature and music.

5. The preservation and restoration of the Scots language.

This is clearly a more culturally oriented movement than either of the two other organisations. It is also worth noticing that Spence, although a romantic, was not as 'extremist' in his attitude to Scottish independence. He wrote, 'I am bound to say that I believe the idea of complete separatism is much more compatible with sentiment than with reason.'[39] For most of its existence the Movement was not in favour of sending MPs to Westminster.

Various claims were made about membership but virtually all of them seem to have been inflated. Meetings were held in Fife and the Lothians and several branches set up but they had a life of their own and the history of the Movement is marked by bitter personal quarrels.[40] From the Minute Book of the Movement, it appears that the regular practice seems to have been to count as members all those who expressed an interest at meetings. These were the days of large public meetings and it was possible to put together impressive membership figures if one counted those who had accepted a membership card at a meeting without paying a subscription.

It was principally these three bodies along with the Glasgow University Student Nationalist Association, to be described later, which came together to form the National Party of Scotland. The move towards amalgamation started in 1925.

We have already seen that, by this time, there was a group of people within the SHRA who were in favour of complete independence for Scotland and who believed that this could only be achieved by the agency of a national political party. The experience of having Buchanan's Bill rejected had had a very serious effect and the credibility of Labour as a Home Rule party was seriously questioned. Of great importance was the fact that the Muirhead brothers were in this group.

In February 1925 a meeting was held between representatives of the Association and the League. Muirhead wanted to persuade delegates from the League to sit on the SHRA's Council but this was rebuffed.[41] By October they met again, without results, and League representatives refused to attend the Convention organised by the SHRA to discuss the projected legislation prepared for the Association. This was to become Barr's Bill.[42] By March 1927, however, a meeting of three representatives from each side resolved:[43]

that this meeting of citizens calls upon the Government to desist from passing any further legislation dealing with Scottish affairs; further declares its opinion that all legislation in reference to Scotland should be placed in the hands of a Scottish National Parliament and that the administration of all Scottish offices should be placed under the control of that Parliament.

In June the two organisations co-operated at the Bannockburn Rally.

The picture which emerges is of increasing contact among the nationalist organisations. The League and the Movement came around to the idea that an educational and 'Sinn Fein' programme was not enough. An independent parliamentary political party was necessary. For its part, the Association was, as we have seen, disillusioned by the treatment of Buchanan's, and later, Barr's Bill. In the Association, of course, the move to a new party was extremely difficult because of the loyalties the Association already had, mainly to the Labour Party.

Up to the end of 1927 co-operation among the organisations had been on an *ad hoc* basis. On 29 November, however, they were brought together by A. L. Henry of the 'Scottish Nationalist Party Group'. This was a small breakaway from the Association determined to set up the new party. Not much is known about this group but it appears to have played rather a major role at this stage of the situation. It was at this meeting that the resolution already quoted was formulated for the Third National Convention. All at the meeting were agreed on the necessity for a party but many Scots National League members not present at the meeting doubted whether Muirhead and his colleagues would really cut themselves off from 'the English-dominated parties'. Their argument, which became the argument of the National Party of Scotland, was that any British party would have a majority of English members who would not legislate in the interests of Scotland. Only a party completely and primarily dedicated to the aim of Scottish national independence could achieve this. Despite the agreement on principle of certain leaders, there was still hesitation. It seems inevitable that there would have been a National Party sooner or later but the entire process was speeded up by the intervention of a new body.

Part Three

The Glasgow University Student Nationalist Association

In September 1927 the Glasgow University Student Nationalist Association was founded. Its principal members came from the University Labour Club and had in fact been prominent members. They shared with the Clydeside group of MPs the idea that Scotland was more radical than England and could hope to have a socialist government sooner. Unlike the MPs they decided to do something about it. It is worth recalling that the early ILP was largely a Scottish movement and that, by going to Westminster, the parliamentarians easily became detached from the views of their activists. The first proposal was to call the body 'The Glasgow University Students Home Rule Association' but this was rejected because of the need to concentrate on cultural and economic matters as well as the political. On the issue of Home Rule as against independence there was a wide diversity of opinions among the members. The aims printed on the membership cards of the new club bring this out. They are:[44]

  i) securing self-government for Scotland
 ii) advancing the ideals of Scottish culture within and without the University.

These aims also bring out the fact that the club considered itself in some way a cultural organisation too. This comes out in its subsequent choice of rectorial candidates as we shall see and seems to have contributed to the early success of the club. In one of their rectorial magazines we read, 'Art and Science transcend party politics and should receive their due recognition from the University. . . . Party politicians as such add nothing to the thought or social progress of humanity.'[45]

The central figure in the new club was John MacCormick and he was to remain at the centre of the national movement for the next thirty years. His original reasons for founding the Association may have had something to do with a personal dispute with the President of the Labour Club (Gilbert McAllister) when he, MacCormick, was Secretary. Whether or not this is true, there is no doubt that his efforts for the rest of his life were directed to the cause of Scotland. It has sometimes been remarked that student organisations were particularly likely to be nationalist. The fact that student nationalism grew strongly in Glasgow and really nowhere else in Scotland is almost entirely due to MacCormick.

192

MacCormick's great gift was as an orator. Everyone who heard him agrees that he was outstanding, with what appear to have been almost mesmeric powers over huge audiences.

The Glasgow University Union is famous for its weekly political debates. For several years in the 1950s and 1960s it seemed to have permanent possession of the *Observer* Mace[46]—its debates are almost exclusively political. Speakers are grouped in party clubs and parliamentary procedures are observed. In such a small face-to-face setting MacCormick was outstanding. Students were easily swayed by such a highly gifted speaker and his allegiance to nationalism almost guaranteed that it had a good chance of success in the University.

One or two other characteristics of MacCormick should help to explain his future career. Despite his enormous gifts in public speaking, he was a withdrawn man. Through his entire career he formed close friendships with a small group and met them daily to discuss and decide on future policy. As far as the public at large was concerned, he was shy and tended to hold himself back until he knew others well.

MacCormick was a romantic. This may have been linked to his withdrawn quality but throughout his life he created or responded to the large gesture. The candidate he proposed for the Glasgow Rectorial election, R. B. Cunninghame Graham, has been described by Hugh MacDiarmid as 'almost incredibly romantic'. The language and symbolism of MacCormick's speeches, the whole context of the late Covenant Movement with its use of traditional Scottish institutions such as the Church and the Law all showed this romanticism in MacCormick's personality. It was, however, balanced by something else. Where many of the members of the SNL would fit Hoffer's description of 'True Believers'[47] MacCormick had a clearer sense of political reality. When he began his career, he worked for complete independence but he was not averse to going for it in stages. Where other members might have rejected alliances with other groups, MacCormick was always keen to try these. Coming out of the highly political tradition of the Glasgow University Union he was, perhaps, less apt to treat his nationalism as a religion.

It was this man who took a central part in the bringing together of the different nationalist Associations. After the setting up of the Glasgow University Student Nationalist Association, MacCormick contacted Muirhead and quickly became aware of the situation. It was agreed that one way of overcoming the feeling that any of the

193

original organisations was trying to take over the others, would be for this new student body to call the meeting. A preliminary informal meeting was held in the Scottish Home Rule Association offices on 6 January 1928. It consisted only of MacCormick and James Valentine of the GUSNA, the Muirhead brothers from the SHRA, Gibson from the SNL and Henry Balderstone from the SNM. It was agreed:

1) that a Scottish National Party be formed
2) that the GUSNA should call a meeting of the other bodies to propose the forming of such a party
3) that the existing group should stay together to make the arrangements.

Delegates from the various organisations were invited to a meeting on 24 March and each agreed to take the proposal back to their organisation. The meeting actually appears to have taken place on 11 February. A resolution proposed from the chair by MacCormick was adopted.[48]

This meeting, representative of the Scottish Home Rule Association, the Scottish National Movement, the Scots National League and the Glasgow University Student Nationalist Association, is agreed in principle to the formation of an independent Scottish National Party and the merging of the existing bodies in one organisation subject to the approval of the governing committee of each organisation.

Although the representatives of the other bodies had been mandated to take this decision, the SHRA delegates had to take the matter back to their colleagues. It was in this context that, at the close of the meeting, T. H. Gibson proposed that those who were there should, as individuals, set up the new Party:[49]

That this meeting of Scots men and women, having regard to the present deplorable conditions of national life and affairs in Scotland, being conscious of the repeated failure on the part of the present established political parties to fulfil their solemn pledges even to formulate a policy for the better government of Scotland, declares that the survival of Scottish life can only be effected by an independent parliament in Scotland and hereby constitutes itself as a National Party of Scotland.

Thus the party was founded. Both the Scots National League and the Scottish National Movement held their annual conferences on 9 June and voted to amalgamate into the party as did the GUSNA. The Scottish Home Rule Association was much less keen. Muirhead's motion at their annual conference that all members should join the new National Party of Scotland was not agreed but many members left to join the new organisation and at the AGM in September 1929 it was agreed by a large majority to dissolve the Association.

Conclusion

We may say that Scottish nationalism had come to a major turning point in terms of mobilising the Scottish electors. It was to be a long time before these moves were rewarded with many votes but, nevertheless, the moves themselves were significant. In deciding to form a political party the nationalists had taken a step away both from the somewhat remote, residually cultural organisation which was the SNL and it also moved away from the equally closed world of the radical pressure group, the SHRA. From now on it was to be a party mobilising electors in the way in which they can be most effectively mobilised: at elections. From now on the appeal was to be directly to the people.

12 The National Party of Scotland

The development of policy

In 1928, the National Party of Scotland was set on its way. This was the direct predecessor of the SNP. Where the SNL and the SHRA were both associations rather than parties there was no doubt but that this new organisation was founded to fight parliamentary seats. It was the NPS which set the pattern for many of the features and controversies of the present nationalist movement.

Roche and Sachs distinguish between the personalities and functions of the bureaucrat and the enthusiast in social movements.[1] The enthusiast is the man or woman with a clear picture of the aim of the movement and an intolerance of any backsliding. It is the enthusiast who has the type of energy to go out preaching the message but who is also ruthless in excluding those who are not truly converted. The bureaucrat, by contrast, is the man or woman who recognises the organisational values and tries to keep the movement together. He is especially keen to keep up numbers and to prevent potential supporters from being lost to·the movement.

In these terms the NPS was a party of enthusiasts. It was a gathering of people who believed wholly in their cause and at various times it was put at great risk by different interpretations of the dogmas. Being a small but fairly visible movement it was particularly prone to this sort of problem.

It was not a party wholly made up of enthusiasts. There were a few, of whom R. E. Muirhead is the best example, who were

196

conscious of the needs of organisation and who provided stability. The problem was that, although the whole movement would have collapsed without Muirhead, he was not the sort of man to lead a national crusade. He was more suited to sitting in the office ensuring that there was at least some finance, and working incessantly for the movement. We shall see that, as we go through the 1920s and 1930s, there is some sympathy for the movement and on the whole a respectable by-election performance. The problem was that there was no 'bureaucrat' who seemed capable of organising the membership into a large permanent organisation.

This was a party of men with fairly remote contact with the world of politics. This was to become even more true later: in the 1940s and 1950s, for example. At this earlier period there were a few who had experience of politics in the ILP. On the other hand, no major political figures came over. This has remained true up to the present day. In the NPS the members tended to be minor members of the major parties: Muirhead and MacCormick from the ILP, Cunninghame Graham from the Labour Party and so forth. After 1945 members were much more likely to have had no contact with a party at all.

Finally, and perhaps linked to the lack of establishment figures, this was a party which thought of itself as thoroughly modern. This comes out very clearly in the concerns of the party and is well expressed in a letter from Tom Gibson to Neil Gunn: 'We are not a society of lost causes but a modern, practical and—if one likes—a matter-of-fact movement to create an up-to-date and efficient organisation of all things Scottish.'[2] The Celtic dusk was chased away by the modern neon lights of the new party. It might be a movement of enthusiasts but there were also those in the new movement who were determined to be respectable and serious-minded. Again, this characterises the hard core of Scottish Nationalism to this day. Although it makes a revolutionary proposal about the political future it does so in constitutional ways. In this sense it is firmly in the mainstream of British politics. One cannot help being struck through the whole history of Scottish nationalism since 1918 by its 'reasonable' quality. There was another way of looking at that quality of Scottish nationalism and it was referred to by George Scott-Moncrieff:[3]

I remember my disappointment when I first made the journey from Edinburgh to Glasgow to meet the leaders of the SNP.

Glasgow at that time was still firmly bowler-hatted. . . . The grave aspiring politicians donned their bowlers and took me out to coffee in an oppressive, over-oaked coffee room where conversation lapsed in mutual discontent.

Two final points in particular bring out the lack of wild-eyed revolutionary fervour. Although it did not have quite the representation of ministers of religion that were in the old SHRA, there were certainly a few who became prominent. One of the earliest editors of the *Scots Independent* was the Rev. Walter Murray and several others were active at this stage and indeed right down to the present. The other indicator of 'respectability' was the concentration, already mentioned, on the economic arguments for independence. Under Gibson's influence this had been a feature of the League's approach and it continued into the NPS. We can see a progression of concerns in nationalist literature. In the early days of the twentieth century there was an emphasis on legal questions such as the correct use of the royal titles and arms or, in the case of the group around Erskine and Gillies, there was an interest in the historical rights of nations and races. This was followed just before 1914 by economic arguments like the disproportionate contribution by Scotland to the Tax Fund and administrative arguments like the congestion of Parliament. After the war most attention was paid to the bad social conditions of Scotland and the miserliness of government grants to institutions like the Scottish universities. Finally, in the 1920s and 1930s the overwhelming considerations were the collapse or take over of Scottish businesses, unemployment and emigration.

These last themes came out clearly in accounts of speeches by NPS spokesmen and in election addresses. In the 'Speakers' Service' which operated through a series of circulated notes from about November 1931 to February 1933 there is a rich flow of information about the natural resources of Scotland and the way in which they have been underworked or worked out or closed down in favour of 'big business' interests with headquarters in England. This is also the theme of many articles in the *Scots Independent* and in the material placed by the Scottish Secretariat.

The Scottish Secretariat was set up in 1924 as a weapon against 'the wall of silence on all things Scottish'. It operated by placing a large number of articles in local weekly newspapers all over Scotland which were usually short of copy and welcomed well-written pieces. Most of the writing was done by Hugh MacDiarmid either anonymously or under the pseudonym of 'Mount boy'. It was used to spread Home Rule and Scottish propaganda under the name of an apparently neutral body when articles would not have been accepted had they come from an identifiably political source. The whole operation was financed by R. E. Muirhead from 1924 until his death. Up to 1928 it was carried out on behalf of the SHRA and thereafter on behalf of the NPS and SNP although after 1945 Muirhead used the Secretariat to publish independent nationalist pamphlets.

In a similar way the NPS ran a lecture scheme from 1929 to about 1932 whereby speakers on all sorts of Scottish subjects went out to address organisations, sometimes in the open air. Often they were not identified as party speakers and could thus contact a very large audience. In these ways the NPS recognised and used the Fabian tactics of 'permeation'. In the lecture notes, the Scottish Secretariat material, and the lecturing scheme the economic position of Scotland was explored.

In his election address for the East Renfrewshire by-election in 1932 the candidate said, 'Oliver Brown stands for your taxes for your own use, your own remedies for your own problems.' At the St Rollox by-election in 1931 Elma Campbell's address began:

> In view of the widespread dissatisfaction in the English
> controlled political parties and the ever-growing realisation that
> Scotland will never become prosperous and well-governed until
> the people of Scotland take their own affairs into their own
> hands, I appeal with confidence for your support.

Robert Grey, standing for Dunbartonshire in 1932, declared, 'I stand for Scottish Independence on the grounds that Scottish affairs are neglected and mismanaged by the London Parliament.' The remainder of the address is devoted to the decline and closure of Scottish industries and the loss of population.

What all this amounts to is an 'extremist' nationalist organisation making its demand for independence for Scotland rather than Home Rule, on the basis of economic necessity. One would have expected the NPS to be much more 'mystical' in their approach, much more concerned with the natural rights of nations and the influences of the Scottish people. This was a theme but there is no suggestion that the nationalists used the economic approach simply as a tool to get to the voters. In their private correspondence and public statements

199

they genuinely regard this as the major concern. It is taken for granted that Scotland is a nation, a community, but it is because economic forces are destroying the nation that they become nationalists. It is interesting that in the Kilmarnock by-election, when the NPS case is being put forward by a 'Home-Ruler', Sir Alexander McEwen, he is much more likely to use philosophical arguments. In a speech in Kilmarnock on 13 October 1933 he said:[4]

In other words, in the opinion of Mr Lindsay (the National Labour candidate) Scotland is merely a province of England and stands in the same position to England and the Empire as Liverpool does. If you are prepared to accept that doctrine you are prepared to accept anything but you are not fit to call yourselves Scotsmen.

Once again we see that it is this shared feeling for Scotland, implicit or explicit, which links the two approaches.

There can be no doubt that the early NPS stood for a full programme of nationalism in the sense that it was in favour of re-establishing Scotland's sovereign status. On this it was in direct line of descent from the SNL rather than from the SHRA. There was no point, it argued, in giving a Scottish Parliament control only over Scottish 'domestic' affairs. Decisions on foreign affairs or defence or on taxes could have very far-reaching effects on life in Scotland and a Scots government must have control over them.

At the same time the NPS was a party of realists. They were well aware that Scotland existed in an international system of politics and economics. Then as now, in the case of the SNP, their opponents accused them of being separatists but from the beginning they were in favour of a very controlled form of separatism. They assumed that there would be co-operation between the independent governments of the nations in the British Isles and that formalised institutions would be set up to deal with this. Their critics portrayed the NPS policy as 'customs posts at the border' but a glance at official documents or the *Scots Independent* shows that, from the beginning, they assumed that a Customs Union would be negotiated.[5] It was also proposed that a Joint Council should be set up at which representatives of Scotland and England with equal status and voting powers would confer on such things as foreign policy, defence, economic affairs and the empire. Similarly, the independent armed forces of Scotland and England would be under Joint

Executive Councils.[6] The decision of this Joint Council would have to be ratified by the member governments thus ensuring the sovereign status of Scotland. The sheer facts of world politics would, however, make it more than likely that the nations would co-operate closely. From the beginning, therefore, to regard the nationalists as a group in favour of total separation is to misunderstand them and to underrate the realism of their approach.

Another indication of the future relationship which they planned comes out of their attitude to the empire. At the very outset, in a statement prepared for a Policy Committee meeting on 17 November 1928, it was resolved that:[7]

The party, having regard to the large contribution made by Scotland in building up the British Empire, is desirous of increasing the interest of the Scottish nation in the affairs of the Empire to the extent her contribution warrants and, as a Mother Nation, thereby demands complete recognition of her rights as such in that Empire. . . . The Party cannot, in these circumstances agree to acquiesce in any situation that does not permit of a Mother Nation exercising her right to independent status and her right to partnership in that Empire on terms equal to that enjoyed by England.

This is a long step away from the anti-imperialism of the SNL but it is very significant that this proposal, which was accepted, was prepared by Tom Gibson who had been a member of the earlier body. Gibson was a most unyielding opponent of any dilution of party policy to one of Home Rule. At the same time he envisaged intimate co-operation between two equal nations. It was only in the later 1930s that the anti-imperialist group reasserted itself. Finally, at no point was the NPS or the SNP republican. Both saw the future of Scotland as 'independent under the Crown'.

There was another issue on which Gibson was adamant and it became the policy of the party. No one could be a member of the NPS and of another political party. This again was a theme drawn from the tradition of the SNL. There was no possibility of Scottish independence through an English-dominated party. In any case, to work through such a party suggested that Scotland must beg for independence when, in fact, it was rightly hers. This again is a position which has been maintained by the present-day party but it was to cause a great deal of controversy in the years to come. Part of this controversy arose from an argument about whether this was a feature of the constitution. A glance at Clause 4 in the NPS constitution in Appendix A shows that there could be doubt about this even in the early days.

It is very difficult to assess the size of the new party. Records are now in a fragmentary state but, by looking at the *Scots Independent* and papers in the National Library of Scotland and elsewhere some estimate can be made. In 1928 the *Scots Independent* has regular reports from twelve branches and this agrees with the reports to National Council.[8] The branch with the largest recorded membership is Edinburgh Central with 148 but there were several branches in Glasgow, for example, Camlachie, Glasgow Central and Maryhill. Of these only the Camlachie membership is recorded at 102. At a half-yearly conference on 30 November 1928 it was reported that there were 41 branches of which 25 functioned completely in the sense that they had a branch executive and regular monthly meetings. At the 1931 conference 70 branches were reported but again only 25 were fully operational. Finally, in 1932 a National Council Minute shows that there were just over 8,000 members with subscriptions fully paid up.[9]

A glance at Table 12.1 shows that the election record of the NPS was not wholly disastrous. It is true that it started badly but just

Table 12.1   Nationalist election record 1929-35

	NPS Election performance	
1929	Glasgow (Camlachie)	4·9
	Midlothian	4·5
1930	Glasgow (Shettleston)	10·1
1931	Edinburgh East	9·4
	East Renfrewshire	13·1
	West Renfrewshire	11·0
	Inverness	14·0
	Glasgow (St Rollox)	15·8
1932	Dumbarton	13·5
	Montrose	11·7
1933	East Fife	3·6
	Kilmarnock	16·9

Table 12.1   Nationalist election record 1929-35 (continued)

	SNP election performance (after 1934)	
1935	Greenock	3·3
	Kilmarnock	6·2
	Dumbarton	7·8
	E. Renfrewshire	10·4
	West Renfrewshire	11·3
	Inverness	16·1
	Western Isles	28·1

before the merger with the Scottish Party, NPS candidates were saving their deposits. It is quite clear that the NPS was not considered to be totally a fringe party. As Hanham remarks it is interesting that the elections fought tended to be in Scottish urban constituencies.[10] This is wholly consistent with the outlook of the party. From the beginning it was concerned with the future of a modern Scotland and this meant a Scotland which was urban and industrial. At least as important as this is the fact that the party was largely based in Glasgow. The headquarters were there and the major figures in the leadership—MacCormick, Muirhead, Gibson— all lived in or near Glasgow. It is true that there were other elements in the party. The remnants of the old, anti-imperialist group were still there, concentrated mostly in the London branch. Their suspicions of the headquarters' moves to compromise the demand for complete independence led to a great deal of abuse and the expulsions of 1933. It is also true that the NPS never lost its interest in certain aspects of rural life. For the party, as for the rest of Scotland, the symbol of the Highlands was a very important one. There are frequent references to the unfortunate effects of the development of deer forests and the destruction of Highland and other communities through the policies of rapacious (and often alien) landlords.

There is also attention paid to the state of the fishing industry. The British government's anti-Russian policies after 1917 involved an embargo on exports of herring to that country. This hit the Scottish fishing industry very hard indeed. Attention to fishing and farming does not represent a desire for a simpler, Arcadian economy. For a small country such as Scotland, fishing and farming simply are more important than is the case in England. As a clue to the party's general attitude, however, we can do no more than quote from an article in the *Scots Independent* in March 1929. In referring to fears expressed by the Association for the Preservation of Rural Scotland that flooding of a valley would lead to a spoiling of its amenities the leader writer comments:

> To us more bread (or oatcakes) for the living is of greater importance than traditional associations of feudal kings and power for national industries of greater value than sights for jaded townspeople in the holiday season.

It was from this basis that the NPS concentrated on issues like the development of the 'branch factory' syndrome for Scotland, the amalgamation of the Scottish railways and the disaster of emigration. Until the 1930s the *Scots Independent* kept up a series of articles on Scottish history and Scottish culture but, on the whole, the party was built resolutely on an economic base.

The impact of Social Credit

There were, of course, several schools of economic thought operating at this time. The NPS at no point worked out a clear policy largely because few in the party were able to see much beyond the straightforward demand for Scottish independence. The duty of the NPS was to explore ways in which independence could be achieved. The strongest representative of this approach was the group supporting Social Credit.

In the *Scots Independent* of July 1928, among other messages of support and welcome for the new party, is one from Major C. H. Douglas:

> Nationalism is a function of culture, possibly climatic or geographical in origin but ultimately spiritual in its nature. It derives from within as the trees grow from the seed. Internationalism is, in the literal meaning of the word, an impostor, it is something imposed from without. In its modern and most dangerous form it is an effort to impose a culture and a suspect culture by control of economic resources through hidden finance.

Douglas was a Scottish engineer who developed the basic ideas of Social Credit around the time of the First World War. His starting point, or one of them, was the fact that there was poverty in the midst of plenty. Not only was it true that some people were very rich while others starved but the multitudes starved while there were mountains of food available. Grain accumulated in large stores, usable meat and fruit rotted. Food was destroyed rather than distributed to those in need. In the Scotland of the 1920s and 1930s there were plenty of people in need and one can imagine that Social Credit ideas would have an immediate audience.[11]

In fact it is not easy to say exactly how Douglas argued from this point because, although his analysis of the evils of the existing system was telling, he was by no means clear about how he would reform it. For our purposes it is not necessary to go into the theory.

Douglas believed that the centre of the trouble lay in the control of credit by international financiers. It was critically important that a government should exclude this alien political power and that credit should be organised on behalf of the society by the government. One can see at this point why such a doctrine should appeal to nationalists. There were already people who believed that the country was threatened by an external conspiracy. The international financiers fitted just such a role. It was a further implication of the Douglas doctrine that small ventures were economically healthier than the huge units that would need finance on a large and probably international scale. All in all it was an approach that appealed to the lower middle-class tradesmen working on their own, especially when such a person had been put out of business by a failure of credit. It was, for example, in this sort of economic situation that the Social Credit Party rose spectacularly to government in Alberta.[12] With farmers and small businessmen being ruined on every side in the slump conditions in the late 1920s and 1930s Social Credit was very quickly a success. In Scotland there was no charismatic leader like Aberhart with an established radio audience but, none the less, it was an attractive idea.

In order to place the 'Douglas Doctrine' in context it should be remembered first that it was extremely popular for a short time in a certain circle of British intellectuals. It was radical but it was not anti-capitalist. Unlike Marxism there was no threat to tear out the existing order root and branch. There was also no enormous and tedious corpus of literature to be plodded through. It was also important that the cause was taken up by a brilliant journalist, C. M. Orage, in the *New Age*. In many ways the *New Age* was like the *New Statesman*. One of its features was that, along with the Social Credit articles, it had an outstanding literary and artistic section and appears to have been bought by many for this alone. Thus the major journal of Social Credit in Britain had a wide circulation.

Another point that should be borne in mind is that Douglas actively tried to interest governments and parties in Social Credit. I have quoted his message of good wishes to the NPS. In the same way he was prepared to travel to Alberta to meet the ruling Farmers' Party to explain his ideas and their relevance to the economy of the Province.[13]

In Scotland there was a small but active group of Douglasites. For reasons that had to do with intellectual links between the two sets of ideas, the majority of these were, and are, nationalists. The significance for the study of the NPS is that they were nationalists of an uncompromising type. Perhaps because Douglasism promised a fast and complete remedy for a fearful situation, its followers have tended to resemble closely Hoffer's paradigm of the 'true believer'. This characteristic was transferred to their nationalism.

The NPS never adopted Social Credit. At a Council meeting on 10 May 1930[14] the executive undertook to examine the scheme on the motion of the Aberdeen branch and in September a committee was set up to do this under Hugh MacDiarmid, who was and is a follower of the doctrine. Despite this the report to the 1931 party conference declared:

> While they believed that the Social Credit proposals contained a great deal that would be of immense value to Scotland in the future, the time was not ripe for them to recommend that these proposals should be embodied in the policies of the Party.

The 'respectable' and 'main line' approach of the party extended to its understanding of economics and, in a letter to R. E. Muirhead, Tom Gibson declares that the doctrine was confused and unfinished.[15]

When this is all said and done, however, it is still true that Douglasism had an important effect on the party. In the economic sense this is true, or at least it is the case that the NPS and the present party took over elements of the Douglas ideas. Hanham mentions this only in the years after 1945 but it is possible to see the influences in the early 1930s although the National Council once more turned down the Douglas theory on 19 March 1933.[16]

First of all it may be argued that, in the 1930s, about the same time as the Douglasite controversy, there is a strong emphasis in the *Scots Independent* on the benefits of small industry as opposed to large units. In the *Free Man*, an independent Social Credit Scottish nationalist journal, this theme is very often taken up and in the very first number[17] we find an article by John MacCormick himself in which he gives various instances of the disadvantages of size in cities, in business, in the arts and concludes, 'Men worship before the great God Size.'

In this context it is interesting that one of the first campaigns run by the NPS was opposition to the 1929 Local Government (Scotland) Act whereby parish councils were abolished. 'Nothing less is involved than the total destruction of all real local self-government in rural areas and its careful hampering in the towns.'[18] This was a very unpopular Act in Scotland, with the Convention of Royal Burghs and the majority of Scottish MPs opposing it. This was not, of course, a theme exclusive to the Douglasites.

Much more characteristically Douglasite is the question of the control of credit. In a resolution at the 1932 conference the NPS recognised that 'complete self-government must include national control of credit'. This is a policy which has survived to the present day. Another surviving policy, which is also Douglasite and which also originates in the 1930s, is the decision to concentrate on the home market rather than on exports. For Douglas, overproduction was to be avoided and the interdependence of nations opened a door to international capital. Once more this was not an idea taken up exclusively by the nationalists. Indeed, in a statement by the Scottish National Development Council published in September 1932 we read of the need to establish economic self-sufficiency of Scotland.[19] This idea was not shared by all of the business community. The *Glasgow Herald* commented that the only way back to prosperity was to avoid 'violent economic nationalism'.[20] In these three approaches: the belief in smallness, concentration on the home market and the national control of credit, the NPS was close to Social Credit policies and seems to have been influenced by them.

It was not only in the economic field that the followers of these dogmas were important for Scottish nationalism. I have already suggested that they were more fervent in their nationalism than were many other party members. A great deal of this comes over in the weekly paper the *Free Man*. In October 1935 it was renamed *New Scotland* and after many vicissitudes it appears to have been closed down about 1941 but none of the later numbers seems to have survived. This paper was in many ways an important journal. It carried on a tradition of nationalism which was closer to Erskine of

Marr than anything expressed through the *Scots Independent*. In fact, a theme repeated quite often, especially in early numbers, was that of Scotland's 'mission' in the world: 'We believe passionately that Scotland can and ought to play a notable part in world affairs. . . . Only a virile nationalism can create and maintain a vital internationalism.'[21] In general the *Free Man* operated as a radical critic of the NPS and this was particularly important in the months when some party leaders were trying to find an accommodation with the Scottish Party, a Home Rule body.

Another line of thought cultivated by this paper also looked back to Erskine and forward to the debates in the early 1940s. Where the NPS had started to speak about Scotland being a 'mother nation of the Empire' and send loyal addresses to the King from a Bannockburn rally, the *Free Man* was firmly anti-imperialistic and anti-war. A typical article praised the students of Oxford and Glasgow when, in their respective Unions, they refused to fight for King and Country.[22] It bitterly attacked Mussolini's Abyssinian adventure and criticised the action of the British government.

Finally, the *Free Man* kept up the tradition of cultural nationalism. It is true that there was some space given to cultural questions in the *Scots Independent* but it diminished rapidly. In the *Free Man*, by contrast, Hugh MacDiarmid had a weekly causerie, 'At the Sign of the Thistle', and there were frequent articles by creative writers and other intellectuals. Poetry was a regular feature of the paper and some serious attention was given to the language issue. There was, for a considerable time, a regular article in Gaelic and a position was taken editorially on this question.[23]

> Language is not an accident. It is not a trivial external thing which a people adopt or discard to suit the occasion as a man puts on or throws aside an overcoat. On the contrary, it is organic in the whole being of a people. It grows as they grow.

These sentiments, so reminiscent of Herder, find no ready expression in the official publications of the party.

Student nationalism

Social Credit was and is a strand in Scottish nationalism. It has had some permanent results in the party's policy and its journals provided a platform for those who were uncompromising in their desire for independence.

There was another group whom we would expect to be extremists. The Glasgow University Student Nationalist Association, one of the founding organisations of the NPS, was certainly influential in the building of the party but its influence was in the direction of moderation. Its best known activity after the founding of the party was in the rectorial campaign in Glasgow University. In order to understand the development of the movement for the next twenty-five years it will be helpful to say something about this. I shall argue that some of the characteristics of university politics stamped themselves on the mind of one at least of the leading nationalists and that this model of the situation was disastrous for the development of the party.

In the older Scottish universities the rector is elected by the students every three or four years. Traditionally the candidates were well-known politicians but recently they have been chosen from a much wider field. The Scottish parties in the 1920s and 1930s took them with some seriousness in so far as the candidates represented their parties and any setback was to be avoided. In Glasgow the election has been especially political just as the University Union is, as I have already pointed out, the most political of all the Scottish University Unions.

The earliest handbooks of the GUSNA (1928-9 and 1929-30) do not set out the aims of the Association as exclusively political ones. They mention the decline of Scottish culture and the 1928-9 edition says:[24]

> convinced that the 'political' tradition of the Rectorial does nothing but harm to University life and that it is true that a Scotsman of great intellect and international fame should occupy the Rectorial Chair, the Nationalist Students Association has nominated Mr R. B. Cunninghame Graham.

This 'anti-political' theme fitted in with the approach of nationalists outside the University. For them party squabbling was ruining Scotland. Throughout the campaigns the students used a slogan 'We are not a political party; we are a movement!' It also explains the romanticism of the dominating figure in the Association, John MacCormick. I have already suggested that MacCormick was a romantic but with a streak of realism. This comes out clearly in his decision to run a rectorial candidate. Any new political organisation needs the maximum publicity and, if there is to be any hope of success, it is essential to use the elections. The mixture of romanticism and realism comes out in his choice of the candidate.

Cunninghame Graham's photographs show an appearance that owed a great deal to his aristocratic Spanish grandmother. He has become known to some extent through the writings of Tschiffely[25] and, rather less so, through his own stories, whose style owes a great deal to Conrad.[26] Although Cunninghame Graham had a literary and political reputation, his support among Glasgow students did not come because they had all read his short stories. Rather it came from his romantic 'image', the support of many literary figures and from the political ability of a small group of students.

The fact that these students put forward a literary candidate meant that they could claim to be different from the 'standard' political campaigners. It has already been noticed that there was a disillusionment with the parties after 1918 and this was peculiarly true among students. It was also true that other literary figures came up to support the candidate and this was a source of interest. Well-known writers such as Compton Mackenzie, Eric Linklater, Hilaire Belloc and G. K. Chesterton either spoke for the candidate or sent messages of encouragement. This was an astute tactical move.

Most important of all in the campaign was the sheer talent of the student leaders. Head and shoulders above the rest came MacCormick himself. He had several talents which were peculiarly appropriate for his situation. In the small introverted world of University Union politics MacCormick's talent as a speaker was overwhelming. During the campaign the nationalists held daily meetings which were extremely well attended principally to listen to MacCormick. Both in these meetings and in the large set piece debates he was the star. Outside the meetings he was energetic in lobbying students to join the Association and support their candidates.

MacCormick was not the only nationalist who contributed to the campaign. It was he, however, who attracted the others who then made this 1928 election so remarkable. Harold Collier, for example, was a particularly gifted student journalist who produced literature far beyond that of other candidates both in quantity and quality. Thus in the small society of Glasgow University in 1928 the great talents of MacCormick and such people as Collier were critical.

To almost everyone's surprise outside the University, and apparently inside it, Cunninghame Graham almost won; surprise because his opponent was the Conservative Prime Minister, Stanley Baldwin, who was able to call on the talents of the Parliamentary Front Bench and the Conservative Central Office. Baldwin gained 1,044 votes against Cunninghame Graham's 978, while the Liberal, Sir Herbert Samuel and Labour's Rosslyn Mitchell won 396 and 226 votes respectively. An old, little-known literary figure almost beat the sitting Prime Minister; did beat him among the male students. The result was an immediate tonic to the nationalists.

Three years later in 1931 the nationalist candidate, Compton Mackenzie, did win the rectorship thanks to the same combination of external support and internal talent. The team was not identical but MacCormick was, once again, the dominating figure. Two additional factors may have helped. The *Daily Record*, a widely read local newspaper, took a great interest in the election. Although it may not have persuaded the Scottish electors that nationalism was the wave of the future, it seems to have persuaded students that they were doing something important. Within the student community itself one event which may have tipped the scales for Mackenzie was the founding in 1930 of yet another society, the Distributist Club. The person largely responsible was John Bayne who came up to University under the influence of G. K. Chesterton. Chesterton published a newsletter called *G. K.'s Weekly* which had been taken by a master in his school and Bayne was determined to spread this message. The doctrines were not worked out in detail but involved a redistribution of income and a return to a simpler, traditional, agricultural and hopefully Catholic society. When Chesterton was asked to speak to the club he agreed and persuaded them that members should support Compton Mackenzie, a fellow Catholic and NPS member who had been nominated for the rectorship. Many of the Catholic students were members of the Distributist Club and it seems likely that Chesterton's meeting had the effect of bringing them over. There had been real hesitation by the Catholics about Scottish independence. It was felt that it might lead to another Stormont regime with a ruthless Protestant ascendancy. Among the students, however, where Chesterton's ideas of a small self-sufficient society had become fashionable, these fears melted away. The majority of Catholic students seem to have voted for Mackenzie.

Whatever the reasons, Mackenzie won the 1931 Glasgow rectorial beating his Conservative opponent, Sir Robert Horne, a prominent politician and Member for a neighbouring constituency, Glasgow, Hillhead.

It is difficult to know what effect the 1928 near-win and the 1931 victory had on the politics of Scotland. Certainly two leading Unionist politicians had been seriously challenged by political nonentities and it is not fanciful to imagine that this set off the Conservative campaign to combat nationalism. Certainly this was started almost directly after Mackenzie's victory. More important, the experience of University politics seems to have affected the style and attitude of the dominant figure both at Glasgow University and in the NPS, John MacCormick. Where his oratorical powers could command a University Union for the short space of a rectorial campaign, more was needed to build a party. MacCormick never understood this and consistently neglected organisation. We shall see that his speeches were often filled with the romantic imagery which might appeal to undergraduates but would mean nothing to shipyard workers and miners. If Scotland was to be won for the nationalists it was these people who had to be persuaded. It was sufficient for the rectorial campaign that MacCormick should work daily with a small coterie of intimates. A political party, especially one which would attract self-willed and even eccentric people, needed someone with other gifts such as the gift of appearing to be democratic even if the reality was otherwise. MacCormick was a manipulator who manipulated rather too obviously.

MacCormick's contribution

There can be no doubt that MacCormick's personality and methods of operation alienated many of the old nationalists just as, in the late 1930s and early 1940s, some of those coming newly into the party also reacted against him. It is impossible to account for the development of nationalism in Scotland without discussing this man's character. In a small movement in a small country the personality factor was critical. It is less than credible to explain the entire development of the movement in terms of impersonal social or market forces.

In the ILP MacCormick had been within grasping distance of political power. The NPS must have seemed very far removed from it. He had had a taste of success in two rectorials. He had had contact with practising politicians both in the ILP and through the Union debates. These considerations help to explain the fact that he looked around for every means of access to political success. There have been many attempts to belittle him but the fact is that he could easily have rejoined the Labour Party and made a successful career; that he did not bears a tremendous witness to the importance he placed on Scotland. Nevertheless, he was prepared to compromise that ultimate aim in a way that caused great difficulties. Also important was his habit of taking decisions himself or with a small kaffeeklatsch. He made little effort to persuade the rest of the party of the necessity for his compromises.

The key to understanding MacCormick's actions seems to rest on the one hand with the great hostility to, or apathy towards, nationalism in Scotland in general and the sympathy which was shown by a few apparently influential individuals and groups. It is understandable that MacCormick should seek allies where he could get them. It is also understandable that the 'true believers' of the party should regard this with great suspicion. The world of the establishment was almost uniformly hostile. Nationalism was heavily concentrated in the industrial west around Glasgow but the business world in that city was uncompromisingly Unionist.

What is characteristic about this period is that precisely those institutions that were suffering were hostile to nationalism. Business and industry in Scotland were suffering heavily and they recognised the facts of the situation. In January 1929 the *Glasgow Chamber of Commerce Journal* remarked:

> The spirit of self-reliance and self-help will lead us to realise that the international nature of trade and finance does not necessarily mean that our large enterprises must be controlled from London, Liverpool, New York, Montreal or Lorraine.

Yet the Glasgow Chamber was not noted for its political nationalism. This desire by businessmen to make Scotland an economic force again also comes out strongly from the Clydesdale Bank's *Survey of Economic Conditions in Scotland* in 1934. But precisely these business groups feared nationalism because it threatened to frighten away those who controlled foreign markets.

At the other end of the scale, the cultural group which one might have thought of as the most Scottish of all was also anti-nationalist. An Comunn Gaidhealach was, despite its rooting in Gaelic rural culture, firmly in the control of the Unionist gentry. In between these 'extremes' it was hard to find friends in the established Church (although they existed) or among the Catholics (who feared the imposition of a Scottish Stormont, as we have seen).

There were, however, a few friendly figures. While he was leading the rectorial campaigns MacCormick must have been aware of the interest of the *Daily Record and Mail*. Especially during the 1931 contest there was heavy coverage and immediately before the election day back pages of the paper were given over to it. The man behind this policy was the editor, David Anderson. Influencing him were two factors. First, there was his lifelong interest in painting and culture generally. He had been an art student in Paris and had known many of the Scottish colourists and, in particular, J. D. Ferguson. After an early resignation from the paper in 1938 he devoted himself completely to painting and had several successful exhibitions. It was the policy of the *Daily Record* to encourage creative work in Scotland. As early as 1930 a prize was offered for the best Scottish play sent to them. It was wholly in line with this orientation that Anderson should be friendly with Wendy Wood, herself an able water colourist as well as a nationalist. When Miss Wood started her nationalist youth movement the Scottish Watch she was given a regular column in the *Daily Record* for a few months in 1931-2.

The other major reason for Anderson's interest in Home Rule was the arrival of the *Scottish Daily Express* in Glasgow. Anderson saw the danger of the *Express* beating the *Record* in a circulation war and fastened on the slogan of being 'Scotland's newspaper' as opposed to an alien importation. Whether his cultural interests or his business sense was uppermost, there is no doubt that the *Record* started to comment regularly on the question of Home Rule and, moreover, to be extremely sympathetic. It was not just the students' campaign which was reported and editorialised but also the activities of the NPS. Thus the main mass circulation paper in the major city of Scotland considered nationalist activity as news. Its editorial policy was not completely sympathetic. On 17 June 1932 it published a four-column manifesto, 'Scotland and Home Rule'. Following a questionnaire to the NPS on 4 July 1932, it drew attention to public fears that the NPS was a party of extremists who advocated compulsory Gaelic, customs posts at the border and a militaristic youth movement. It published a demand that the leaders of the new party declare their true intention. Were they extremists or would they work for Scotland within the United Kingdom and by means of democratic techniques? The *Record* supported the monarchy and the continuance of the present economic and imperial systems. Within these bounds it was enthusiastic about the future of Scottish Home Rule. Lord Beaverbrook soon took up the subject. On 6

August the front page of the *Scottish Daily Express* carried a letter from him saying that he was strongly in favour of Scottish self-government and that 'it should be the ultimate intention to capture the Unionist party for the Home Rule project'. This was followed by the publication of a straw poll in which it was reported that 4,596 opposed Home Rule and 112,984 supported it.[27]

The significance of this Press war is twofold. First, the 'respectable' papers such as the *Scotsman* and the *Glasgow Herald* gave nationalism very little coverage. There was even less on the radio. The fact that two mass circulation newspapers took it up made the debate more public. Other papers followed the *Record's* lead and some, like the *Edinburgh Evening News*, which had always taken an interest, increased their coverage. From 1931 until 1934 it was difficult to avoid the Home Rule issue if one read a Scottish newspaper.

The second important point was that the *Record* questionnaire and Beaverbrook's letter were couched in terms of the policy of another new party which had recently been established. The Scottish Party sought Home Rule rather than independence. Reading the editorials and articles of the *Record* it is difficult to avoid the conclusion that the *Record*, at least, was trying to steer the NPS nearer to the Scottish Party and a merger of the two organisations. To understand this we must now turn to the Scottish Party itself.

The Scottish Party

The Scottish Self-Government Party had its first public meeting on 21 September 1932. Sir Andrew McEwen put up the principal resolution which sums up the nature of this organisation.[28]

It is agreed that, in view of the ever-increasing burden laid upon Parliament at Westminster with the consequent congestion of business, the good government and industry and social welfare of Scotland demand the setting up of a responsible Parliament in Scotland with full control of all purely Scottish affairs. That it is desired to maintain, unimpaired, Scotland's loyalty to the Crown and Empire. It is further agreed that separation from England could not fail to be other than prejudicial to national interests and commerce and must, therefore, be opposed.

It would be a mistake to deduce from this resolution or from the

215

discussion of some commentators that the new party was simply a rebirth of the Scottish Home Rule Association recently deceased in 1929. This organisation was different and the difference casts an interesting light on the politics of inter-war Scotland.

The Scottish Party was, from the beginning, headed in the direction of Home Rule rather than the re-establishment of Scottish sovereignty but where the SHRA was drawn largely from the ILP, the Scottish Party was overwhelmingly Liberal and Conservative. Its best-known figure was the Duke of Montrose (previously the Marquis of Graham). He had been in and around Scottish Home Rule politics for at least ten years. In the early 1920s he had been President of the International Scottish Home Rule League which seems to have federated several organisations of businessmen and others of a similar social status who were interested in Home Rule. He had had some contacts with the SHRA and even with the NPS. The *Glasgow Herald* reported on 30 October 1928 that he presided over a rally of about 3,000 people called together by the NPS. Montrose was a man who had a longstanding interest in Scottish politics. On the other hand he took the Conservative whip in the House of Lords and this confined the boundaries of his agreement with the nationalists. When John Neil of the Glasgow Student Nationalists wrote to Montrose to ask him to support his own kinsman, Cunninghame Graham, at the 1928 rectorial, Montrose replied that although he supported self-government for Scotland, support for the nationalist candidate would mean going against the leader of his party.[29] His conservatism also showed itself in an exchange with R. E. Muirhead. He had been asked to speak at an SHRA meeting and, having first agreed, he then complained that a well-known Communist was to be on the same platform. In fact, he had confused Gallacher of the Communist Party with Gallagher of the Scottish Co-operative Wholesale Society who was a prominent member of the Association. Montrose's correspondence shows that he was not happy even with the Labour man.[30]

Perhaps the largest contingent of members in the organisation came from the Cathcart Divisional Unionist Association. The Secretary of the Scottish Party, J. Kevan McDowall, had been the Chairman of the Imperial Committee of that Unionist Association and brought several of his colleagues along with him. These men stood on Milner's platform of Imperial Federation. They explained their objects as the greater unity by Imperial Federation of the Commonwealth of Nations of the British Empire and the better government of Scotland, England and Wales by devolution of limited powers to local national legislatures.[31]

Among the most important people in setting up the organisation was the Professor of Scots Law at Glasgow University, Andrew Dewar Gibb. He had been Winston Churchill's aide-de-camp during the First World War and had stood unsuccessfully as a Conservative candidate. In 1930 he had published *Scotland in Eclipse*[32] which was strongly in favour of extensive Home Rule and he was later to produce many books and articles which took a similar line. His papers in the National Library of Scotland reveal a man of great political energy who was the main force behind the new party, approaching McEwen himself and obtaining Montrose as a useful figurehead. The papers also show that he undertook this in consultation with George Malcolm Thomson, who never joined either party but was a considerable influence on Scottish politics.

George Malcolm Thomson was educated at the University of Edinburgh and then went to London to join the Beaverbrook newspapers, where he became Beaverbrook's personal assistant. He wrote several books already referred to which showed his concern for the disastrous economic condition of Scotland and provided some of the best analyses of these conditions.[33] These were widely read and commented upon. What was less well known was the vigorous efforts which Thomson made to start off a group of Unionists who would work for Home Rule. There is no evidence of his influence on Beaverbrook when the latter wrote commending Home Rule in the *Scottish Daily Express*. What is certain and what comes out in his correspondence[34] is that, from 1930 onwards, there was a regular exchange between Thomson and Dewar Gibb in which they speak about gathering a small group of Tory nationalists who, according to the first plan, would first work separately but then, at an election, come to the support of the NPS.[35] It is also certain that Thomson saw the role of the new group as bringing over the Unionists to a Home Rule policy. There are continual references to trips up to Scotland made by Thomson to lobby and cajole. Furthermore, when the Scottish Party was set up, Thomson played a central role in putting the new men, and especially Dewar Gibb, in touch with a friend, Neil Gunn, an NPS member in Inverness, who then played his part as intermediary between the parties.[36]

The other major element in the party was from the Liberal Party. Sir Alexander MacEwen was a solicitor and for six years a respected Provost of Inverness. He had been born in India and spent most of

217

his youth outside Scotland but he had occupied himself with Highland problems, had learnt Gaelic and generally was regarded as a knowledgeable and able spokesman for the northern and rural parts of Scotland. He was a man of energy and political skill. Among other prominent Liberals in the party was Sir D. M. Stevenson, who had been Lord Provost of Glasgow. Lord Dalziel, a former proprietor of the *Daily News* who had flirted with the NPS, is also recorded as being at the meeting, as is Sir Hugh Roberton, the founder of the Glasgow Orpheus Choir.

Two main points can be made at this stage. The first is that the split between the NPS and the Scottish Party was not a matter solely of Home Rule versus independence but, perhaps more importantly, of Labour and radical politics against conservatism and more traditional approaches. Only one member of the Labour party is identifiable in the lists of attenders at Scottish Party meetings. Rosslyn Mitchell was a Glasgow solicitor who later became a Labour MP and was not notably socialistic.

Perhaps more important is the point that this group of 'establishment' figures should have rallied under a Home Rule banner at all. The Liberal Party was formally committed to Scottish Home Rule. It is much more of a surprise that prominent Conservatives should join. In this earlier period an interest in Home Rule clearly seems to have been more widespread as compared with the 1940s and 1950s.

It was the arrival of this new party which seems to have galvanised the establishment of the Scottish Unionists and some Liberals into action. We have seen that the NPS had already had considerable publicity. Although its by-election performance was not striking it could not be ignored. In the years since 1931 the nationalists had not stood in many places but they had not lost all their deposits. They had collected 11 per cent and 14 per cent of the vote in West and East Renfrewshire respectively and 14 per cent in both Inverness and Dumbarton. When the new party appeared to attract much more solid citizens the Unionist establishment took fright. The affair which probably crystallised this was the defection of the Cathcart Unionists in June 1932. Almost immediately they were condemned for their 'narrow foolish nationalism' by the ex-Secretary of State for Scotland, Sir John Gilmour, in a speech to the Stirlingshire Unionists.[37]

On 5 September the Glasgow Conservative Association issued the following statement: 'This committee strongly condemns the divisive, disloyal and unconstitutional procedure adopted by the Secretary and some Members of the Cathcart Unionist Association.'[38] Finally, after various statements and speeches by Unionists and businessmen at the Chamber of Commerce, a manifesto was issued:[39]

That this meeting, representative of all sections of industry, commerce, agriculture, banking and the professions in Scotland, hereby makes declaration of its definite and absolute objection to the setting-up of a national Parliament for Scotland; it is convinced that the interests of Scotland are so interwoven and the ramifications of trade so intricate that Home Rule for Scotland would be altogether contrary to the interests of the country; affirms that England and Scotland, having become indivisibly one, any interference with that unity would be gravely prejudicial to the interests of Scotland; believes that whatever reforms are necessary in the administration of Scottish Affairs can adequately be achieved within the present British constitution; and hereby constitutes itself as a committee to take such steps as may be deemed requisite to oppose any proposals for a Scottish Parliament.

Here was a classic Unionist statement. From its timing it was obviously called forth by the setting-up of the Scottish Party just two months before. Most important of all was the fact that it was signed by 456 Scottish notables including six dukes, three marquises, nine earls, three viscounts, ten lords, fifty-seven knights, two ladies, two Highland chiefs, four senior clergy, seventy-six justices of the peace, eleven professors and thirty-nine gentlemen with military titles. The chief speaker at the meeting was Lord Maclay, a Glasgow shipowner. The petition was nicknamed 'The Ragman's Roll' by the nationalists, recalling the petition of the Scottish nobles supporting Edward I against Robert Bruce. Its existence is a sign of the deep disquiet felt by an important section of Scottish opinion. Nationalism in 1932 was not considered to be a fringe movement.

In view of their several political origins, it is no surprise that the Scottish Party was not monolithic in its attitude to Home Rule. Several of their speakers are recorded as regarding the devolution programme as a stepping stone to much greater powers for a Scottish legislature and even to eventual independence.[40] Dewar Gibb, for all his conservatism, had such an aim. This comes out clearly in the course of a paper which he put up to an informal meeting of NPS and Scottish Party representatives in 1933.[41]

To the National Party of Scotland (I say). If you present to
Scotland your old full programme of independence overnight
you will scare so many people so long (I don't say rightly) that
you are adding enormously and unnecessarily to a difficult task.
To the Scottish Party: if you think that a so-called 'moderate'
scheme which provides for full financial control will prove
ultimately to be any brake on Scottish aspirations, however
wide, you are deceiving yourselves. The germ of full
independence is in the scheme.

It is worth remembering that Dewar Gibb was a prime mover of the
Scottish Party, not a slightly odd hanger-on. On the other hand,
McDowall left the SNP very soon after its foundation because he
believed that it went too far and the Duke of Montrose was, as we
shall see, committed only to Home Rule.

This leads to a further critical point. The new organisation
intended to work by the Fabian tactic of infiltrating the other
parties, principally the Liberals and the Conservatives. It did not see
its primary role as putting up its own candidates though it did not
exclude this. At the East Fife by-election in 1933, for example, it
operated by sending questionnaires to the candidates. By contrast the
NPS was committed to working on its own. Any co-operation would
mean being swamped by the English majority of the other party.
Dual membership was totally excluded. This was an issue which had
been settled in 1928 with the merger of the SHRA and the SNL.

Newspaper reports of the first open meeting put the attendance at
between sixty and eighty. It is doubtful if the Scottish Party ever had
more active supporters than this. It was a party of notables in the
traditional sense: a few lairds, provosts and businessmen. There are
no records of membership cards and no drive to recruit a membership. There is also no record of a constitution and, in a speech to the
NPS National Council in 1933, MacCormick affirmed that none
existed. This fact was to take on a greater significance later but at
this point it is only necessary to identify the traditional and informal
nature of the Scottish Party.

It should not be thought that the Scottish Party showed less
political competence than the NPS. On the contrary, where the
nationalists may have had some experience of politics through the
ILP, the new group consisted of men who were in public life and had
regular contact with the government and political affairs. This was
their attraction to the members of the NPS who began to negotiate

for a merger. They believed that the members of the Scottish Party would give a new 'weight' to nationalism. MacEwen and Montrose exacted a high price for their agreement and generally showed a great deal more political astuteness than the other side. Their victory was to have serious consequences for the later history of the party.

Thus the differences between the NPS and the Scottish Party were threefold. There was a difference of balance on the question of Home Rule as against independence, but it is worth pointing out that there were supporters of each position on both sides. Rather more unequivocally, the Scottish Party was made up of experienced public figures who were mostly conservative in their socio-economic philosophy where the NPS was made up mostly of radicals who had little experience of politics outside the party and certainly not at the level of leadership.

Very soon after its inauguration it became even clearer that the new party was not simply in favour of limited devolution. The more radical elements appear to have captured the day at a conference in October.[42] A policy statement was issued in which a Scottish Parliament was demanded. This Parliament should have power over all affairs for Scotland except those expressly reserved for the UK Parliament. Scottish members should remain at Westminster until a Council of Empire was set up to look after Imperial affairs. Although the statement is vague it revealed a great deal of common ground between the two parties. This also appears to have been hinted at in exchanges of letters between the members where individuals like Dewar Gibb and Robert Hurd aired their view that the Scottish Party should be used as a way of bringing over the fearful to full nationalism.[43] By October 1932 the Scottish Party had gone far beyond the position taken by the *Daily Record*. This is not to argue that all members, the Duke of Montrose for example, were in full agreement with this position but the majority of the party seem to have agreed with it.

It is not surprising that people in both nationalist parties began to have talks about amalgamation. These were informal at first but as early as November 1932 MacCormick reported to a special conference of the NPS that:[44]

The National Council is of the opinion that the new party is working towards the same ultimate objectives as those of the National Party and therefore considers that nationalists should concentrate on attacking their opponents rather than stress the

221

differences of views between those who realise the necessity of
Scotland re-affirming her nationhood.

In view of the setting-up of the Scottish Party it was agreed that
other tactics should be abandoned and an effort made to negotiate
with the newcomers.

Whether or not MacCormick or a Scottish Party representative
made the first move to negotiate, MacCormick was certainly given
authority to negotiate at this conference.[45] The process was made
simpler by the fact that two NPS members were closely in touch with
the leaders of the Scottish Party. The novelist Neil Gunn lived in
Inverness at this time and was a friend of MacEwen through
MacEwen's son Robin, who was an NPS member. There was a
constant three-way correspondence between Gunn, Dewar Gibb and
MacEwen,[46] and others were pulled into it.[47] Although he was
suspicious at first,[48] Gunn became one of the most active negotiators
for amalgamation.[49]

Against the background of these private exchanges the annual
conference of the NPS met on 27 May 1933. A National Council
resolution was put forward which summarised the principal aims of
the party in such a way that they would appeal to the other party.
They were as follows:

1. The establishment of a Parliament in Scotland which shall be
the final authority in all Scottish affairs including taxation and
finance.
2. Scotland shall share with England the rights and
responsibilities they, as Mother Nations, have jointly created
and incurred within the British Empire.
3. The NPS believes that, in a manner representing the will of
her people, Scotland should set up jointly with England
machinery to deal with those responsibilities and, in particular
with such matters as Defence and Foreign Policy and the
creation of a Customs Union.
4. The NPS believes that these principles can be realised only
by an independent political party which has no connection or
alliance with any English controlled party.

The resolution ended:

It may be inadvisable to attempt to define too narrowly the
machinery by which these principles shall be realised.

There were several interesting modifications of the original aims in this resolution. The first point referred to a Scottish Parliament for 'all Scottish affairs' where previous documents had spoken about 'Scottish sovereignty' without any limit. The emphasis on Scotland's role as a Mother Nation, although not new, would clearly be important to the Cathcart Unionist Imperialist members of the Scottish Party and again in the third point, a prominent place is given to the need for joint arrangements where before this would have been a subordinate point to be dealt with after independence was accepted. We may compare this with the old formula of Scotland as an independent member of the group of British nations. Thus, by modification and re-emphasis, the National Council resolution was aimed at the attraction of the Scottish Party. By these changes MacCormick had significantly moved the NPS from a position demanding full independence to something closer to the Home Rule and gradualist position.

The fourth point was one which would cause at least as much trouble. Virtually all Scottish Party members were also prominent members of one of the established parties and apparently saw no contradiction in so remaining. The principle of no contamination with an English party was so important for the NPS that there was absolutely no chance of getting their agreement without a firm commitment on this.

The conference was a shambles. Although the National Council's resolution was passed, there was continual and uninhibited opposition and the vote of 71 to 44 showed that there was a considerable minority. This opposition was not based on simple rejection of the Council's resolution. Mixed in with it was a personality clash between MacCormick and some of the older 'hard line' nationalists. Some, from Edinburgh for example, expressed this in an allegation that he had been profligate with party funds at the recent (and disastrous) East Fife by-election. The main opposition came, significantly, from the London branch. This was composed very largely of ex-members of the SNL. They condemned any moderation of the desire for complete Scottish sovereignty and they condemned MacCormick for his undisclosed understandings with the Scottish Party. More than this, they delivered the condemnation in such a way as to antagonise MacCormick and he was left in an impossible position.

Although he was successful in getting the National Council resolution through, other resolutions were also passed that contradicted it. Immediately after the lunch break a Kelvingrove branch resolution to go back to the original constitution of 1928 was approved by 51 to 47. Since this included the idea of a Scottish Parliament having control over all affairs and not simply Scottish ones, the Council resolution was put again. Again it was passed, this time by 69 to 45, but the resolution that the Executive be empowered to negotiate with the Scottish Party was defeated by 47 to 40. It would be charitable to say that the situation was confused.

MacCormick was committed in his own mind to negotiate with the new party and this could only be done by clarifying the situation. In addition he was, as ever, sensitive to personal criticism and there had been a great deal of it. Thus he demanded and got a reconvention of the conference which had ended in uproar and mutual insults. This took place on 1 July 1933 and was used to expel two of the leading dissidents from London, Clark and McColl, and some others, by 72 votes to 57. The expulsions were triggered off by some articles written by those members of the London branch in the *Free Man*. For MacCormick these articles were so important that he threatened to resign if these authors were not expelled.

With his best known opponents gone MacCormick could begin to negotiate openly again. The cost of his victory was severe. Hanham estimates that about one fifth of the membership left and, from the papers in the National Library of Scotland, this appears to be an accurate guess.[50] The London branch, which had for a long time been the biggest, disappeared for a time and the Edinburgh branch also collapsed with the expulsion of the South-East Area Council. MacCormick had done some branch building around the west of Scotland and owed his narrow victories to this. The weight of membership at this time, and at others was around Glasgow and under MacCormick's influence. It was clear, however, that he did not have things all his own way. The expulsions and the resignations changed the balance of the party to the Home Rule side but not all of these who supported complete separation left. Tom Gibson and his wife Elma Campbell did not; neither did Dr Archie Lamont, a well-known and vociferous 'hard liner'.

The occasion of a great many of the amalgamation talks which followed was the Kilmarnock by-election. Both parties had put up candidates: MacNicol for the NPS and Dewar Gibb for the Scottish Party. As a compromise it was agreed on 5 September 1933 that both sides should withdraw the men they had put up and it was left to the local NPS branch in Kilmarnock to nominate a candidate.

They chose MacEwen and he joined the NPS Kilmarnock branch as Vice-President so that he could stand as their candidate. Considering that the Scottish Party had no organisation in Kilmarnock and generally was unknown, their action in putting up Dewar Gibb seems to have paid off handsomely. There can be no doubt, however, that the parties were not far apart in their policies.

Co-operation yielded a good result at this election but it was arranged only for that specific election and a more formal settlement had to be reached. This was much easier to come by than had been the case before. MacEwen had attracted 16·8 per cent of the vote at the election; the best performance ever put up by a nationalist. There was a considerable impetus towards amalgamation.

The co-operation they experienced in the election generally helped the process of amalgamation but there were specific agreements reached in the course of this. At the meeting on 5 September 1933, for example, the Scottish Party representatives accepted the four points of the NPS May conference subject to the following under-standings:[51]

1. The Scottish parliamentary representatives shall remain at Westminster during the transitional period to allow for machinery being set up to deal with joint and Imperial matters.
2. Both parties oppose tariff barriers between the two countries but they are agreed that the industrial and agricultural interests of Scotland in regard to customs and excise must be safeguarded.
3. Nothing in the Scottish constitution shall deter Scotland from having a separate seat at the League of Nations and at the Imperial Conference.
4. There shall only be such alterations in the Union with England as are necessary to obtain the above.

It can be seen that the exigencies of fighting the campaign had encouraged the Scottish Party to go very far towards the NPS's position. In a letter to the *Free Man* of 4 November 1933 Muirhead replied to criticism by Angus Clark by pointing out that even the Duke of Montrose had declared that Scotland should have no less independence than the Irish Free State.[52] The fact was, however, that Montrose seems to have been the least convinced party to the agreement. Thus, an agreed statement issued by a small meeting of representatives on 22 December 1933 was approved by the NPS National Council but not by a meeting of the Scottish Party. From a memorandum in the Muirhead collection it seems that it was the Duke who had second thoughts although he had been one of the representatives.[53] A further representative joint session met on 24 January 1934 where MacEwen denied the NPS assumption that their constitution should be automatically accepted by the new party. He also demanded that the Scottish Party should have more representation on the Council and among the office-bearers of the amalgamated party than would be indicated by their small size. This Scottish Party tactic of agreeing and then hanging back was effective in forcing MacCormick to accede. The constitution was somewhat modified and all the major figures of the Scottish Party bore office after the amalgamation. The agreements were then put to special conferences of the two parties on 24 February 1934, on the basis of identical resolutions and on the basis of the four points of the NPS conference of May 1933. Finally, a joint meeting was held on 7 April 1934 which sealed the bargain and founded the modern Scottish National Party under that name.

How are we to assess this development? The first question is whether it did the cause of nationalism any good. No party records show a bleeding of NPS members to the Scottish Party after the latter came on the scene. On the contrary, quite a few left when amalgamation was being considered. MacEwen did better at Kilmarnock than any previous nationalist candidate but a glance at Table 12.1 shows that there was no long-term benefit for election performance. Quite a few of the 'knights and notables' who made up the Scottish Party did not join the SNP (including such prominent individuals as Sir D. M. Stevenson, the ex-Lord Provost of Glasgow and a Liberal leader). Others, like Kevan McDowall, left very soon because of the importance they placed on the Empire. Probably many were put off by the requirement that they could be members only of the SNP and not hold joint membership as in the Scottish Party. There seems to have been no gain in membership and there are even indications that it started to go down after 1934. A letter from Dewar Gibb (an ex-Scottish Party man) to Muirhead suggests that nationalist propaganda seems to have lost a great deal of its *élan*.[54] The conclusion seems to be that the SNP may have gained some establishment members but its overall appeal and membership totals did not improve.

The fact that MacCormick was determined to attract these apparently substantial individuals enabled them, because they were more experienced, to force the NPS negotiators to go further than they intended. Unfortunately, however, the Scottish Party people were themselves minor figures. The Duke of Montrose was a nonentity in the Conservative Party although it is always handy to be a Duke. McDowall was very much of an outsider in Scottish Unionist politics and there is no evidence that his revolt on the Home Rule issue spread much beyond the Cathcart Unionists themselves.[55] Dewar Gibb was a competent lawyer but also was not well known. On the Liberal side, MacEwen was a respected figure but the Liberals were by this time in decline and it is, in any case, difficult to find evidence that a large number of Liberals came with him. In retrospect the whole affair seems to have been a bad bargain for nationalism.

Conclusion

These factors must be borne in mind when we consider the effect of these arrangements on political mobilisation. The NPS was small but it was oriented towards a mass appeal. The alliance with the Scottish Party was a return to an older style of politics. The Scottish Party, like MacCormick himself, seemed to believe that elections were won or lost by the appeals of the notables. MacCormick and his new allies paid no attention to the steady work of building up a party organisation and this was of critical importance. In parts of the country where there were traditional social networks with recognised leaders, reorganisation might not have been necessary. With a largely industrialised population and a declining total of leaders, grass roots efforts were crucial. MacCormick's starting point was his success in the small world of Glasgow University Union politics. Where all his electors could be drawn into a hall he was their master. But Scotland was altogether a different proposition.

13 The Scottish National Party

We can view the foundation of the SNP as the achievement of MacCormick's aim. From about 1931 he had considered how the base of the nationalist organisation could be broadened. His first plans to develop a *modus vivendi* with other parties changed to courtship of the Scottish Party but the *quid pro quo* was the same. It was that people who were not determined exclusively on the re-establishment of Scottish sovereignty would be brought into the alliance.

It was consistent with MacCormick's own views that the newcomers should not only be more inclined to Home Rule but that they were prepared to compromise and negotiate. The second point is the more important. Many including Dewar Gibb, Robert Hurd and perhaps even MacEwen, looked for an independent Scotland as the result of a gradual process of devolution. For the majority of the original NPS members this was heresy. Scotland should not beg for its sovereignty. This lay in its own hands. Home Rule was a policy for the Liberal Party or the ILP but not for nationalists. It was, however, more and more in terms of Home Rule that the policy of the party was couched. Thus, for example, we find in the November 1937 edition of the *Scots Independent* an advertisement for workers ending with the message: 'Every new Nationalist means a step nearer Home Rule'[1] and another article in the December issue is entitled 'Home Rule and the Trade Unions'. It was the constant effort of the SNP to make alliances with the other parties to get some measure of Home Rule. Thus, at an SNP conference in October 1936,

MacCormick reported that he tried to come to an agreement with the Labour Party over the Greenock by-election.[2] Most of the effort, however, was directed towards the Liberal Party since there was some sign of sympathy in its ranks. In 1935 the Duke of Montrose resigned the Unionist whip in the House of Lords and became a Liberal. This itself precipitated a storm which will be discussed later. In *Flag in the Wind* MacCormick describes his conversations with Lady Glen-coats and Sir Archibald Sinclair, the leader of the Liberals, who was himself a Scot and much given to wearing the kilt.[3] Finally, contacts were even made with the Communist Party. Under the influence of Aitkin Ferguson of the Boilermakers Union, the Communists became more sympathetic to the idea of Home Rule as compared with the situation when John Maclean was alive. Their 1938 manifesto stated:

> The feeling of nationhood is very strong among all classes of the Scottish people including the workers, another crisis will see it burst out. Another capitalist crisis will certainly see a tremendous upsurge of Scottish nationalism even among the workers—today Scottish national sentiment and the demand for a self-governing Scotland is growing swiftly in the Labour movement.

On the May Day march of that year the Communists wore tartan sashes and carried banners showing Calgacus, Wallace and Bruce.[4] Thus in the period from 1934 until the beginning of the war the SNP was bent on a course of co-operation with any other group in Scotland who had an interest in self-government.

Many developments followed. One of them was that the attitudes of the party to issues other than self-government changed. There were two aspects of this. First, I have already discussed how the emphasis of the argument for self-government changed in the early 1920s. From about 1927 onwards the pamphlets and especially the *Scots Independent* emphasised the industrial collapse, the flight of industry to the south and prescribed a national state as the remedy. The leaders of nationalism, Muirhead, MacCormick and, in the earlier period, Gibson lived in and around Glasgow and it was not surprising that this should be the emphasis. After 1934 the geographical distribution of the leadership changed. The Duke of Montrose was unlikely to be immediately aware of conditions in a Clyde shipyard. MacEwen lived in and was concerned with the

Highlands. One result was what appeared to be a reversion to earlier concerns. In the latter part of the nineteenth century nationalists had spent a great deal of effort discussing legal questions such as the use of the Scottish royal arms and titles. In the first decade of the SNP's existence this concern was revived[5] and Dewar Gibb's main concern was the status of Scots law. He writes a great deal about the violation of the Treaty of Union and the slipshod treatment of Scottish Bills or Scottish sections of Bills due to lack of parliamentary time. In a sense then the new leaders of the party were more concerned with the romantic issues of nationalism than were their immediate predecessors who argued on bread and butter issues in the light of the decline in Clydeside where most of them lived.[6]

This was not the only effect on policy. In the period after 1934 there was a much greater emphasis on building-up policy dealing with matters apart from securing Scottish independence. This was a debate of long standing among nationalists. I have already described how the Douglasites argued that economic freedom had to complete political freedom and therefore the NPS should adopt economic policies over and above the simple policy of independence. Many of those who had come over from the SHRA in 1928 took their socialist programmes with them. Thus, there were certain policies which were supported by the NPS. A great deal was made of the destruction of the Highland communities by the large estates and nationalist speakers supported the idea of land settlement and the development of forestry and fisheries which would provide employment in these areas. The aims of the party as they were accepted at the November 1928 conference were summed up in the *Scots Independent* in December:

The functioning of Scotland as an industrial and commercial unit, the furtherance of the reorganisation of her industries on a distinct national basis, the encouragement of new industries and the stimulation of markets for Scottish goods throughout the world.

Scottish control of national finances and retention of money now spent outside Scotland, thus leading to economy in public expenditure without interference with or at the expense of social services.

National control of credit, motive power and transport.

Development and unification under Scottish National direction of an efficient system of all transport in order to

ensure adequate service at reasonable cost to all parts of
Scotland.

Comprehensive schemes of land settlement, afforestation,
development of water power and rural industries and assistance
of Scottish fisheries.

Provision of decent housing at reasonable rents to meet fully
the requirements of the Scottish people in conjunction with
far-seeing town planning and necessary slum clearance.

Scottish regulation of immigration from whatever source.

Equal educational opportunities for all children.

It might be argued that these policies were vague but in practice
they are not vaguer than those of other parties. In the early
publications of the party, in the *Scots Independent* for example,
there is constant reference to them and even to more detailed
policies such as a Mid-Scotland Ship Canal.[7] There had always been a
group in the NPS, many of them coming from the SNL who believed
that these economic and social policies were a diversion from the
main aim. What seems to have happened after the 1934 amalgamation was that there was a confrontation between the 'single plank'
supporters and those who wanted to develop a reconstruction policy
for use after independence. One of the strongest supporters of the
reconstruction policy was MacEwen. In an article in the *Scottish
Standard* he argued this case.[8] He also declared that the SNP would
welcome co-operation with other parties in furthering these aims.
Another call for a reconstruction policy appeared in the *Scots
Independent* in February 1936. At the party conference in October
John Kinloch proposed a resolution that the party should 'promote
and advocate a policy for Scotland which would form the policy of
the party entrusted with the government of Scotland on the resumption of autonomy'.[9] Kinloch was an associate of MacCormick's and
the idea of developing such policies was associated with MacCormick
and his group. The resolution was rejected but the National Council
was empowered to promote a policy which should be a guide for
candidates and speakers.

The formation of an official economic policy was again pressed in
1938 by Dr John MacDonald,[10] another associate of MacCormick's,
and the conference of that year agreed to do so on the resolution of
F. Cameron Yeaman.[11] The September *Scots Independent* reported
the substance of these policies. They included the development of
lighter industries on the Scandinavian model, rural recolonisation,

231

afforestation and allied works, reconstruction of fishing, decentralisation of industry and rural and urban rehousing.

Finally, the most comprehensive statement of a social and
economic policy appeared on the announcement of a Scottish
National Convention in mid-1939. Howarth comments that this
statement is very similar to that of the Liberal Federation.[12]

To sum up, the SNP came much closer to other parties than its
predecessor by acquiring these official policies. It is reasonable to
suggest that the addition of public figures from outside the old
nationalist tradition strengthened this trend.

With the leaders of the SNP moulding it to be more like an
ordinary British party, it was not surprising that other groups
should grow up. Even before 1934 this started to happen just as
MacCormick directed the SNP more and more towards Home Rule.
The person most associated with these developments is Miss Wendy
Wood. Most of the members of these movements, even those not
associated with Miss Wood, believed in a more 'direct action'
approach to the fight for Scottish independence.

One of the seminal incidents seems to have taken place after the
Bannockburn Demonstration in June 1932. Miss Wood led a group
of demonstrators who took down the Union Jack flying over Stirling
Castle and replaced it (till the guard got there at any rate) with a
Scottish Lion standard.[13] Miss Wood was a member of the NPS at
this time but the party leadership did not support her, as she
admits.[14] The incident gained her a lot of publicity, however, as did
her setting up of the Democratic Scottish Self-Government Organisation (DSSO) immediately after. In her autobiography she writes
that, at that same Bannockburn Rally, MacCormick had sent a
telegram of loyalty to the King. Disgusted by this, some Fife party
members asked her to form the new organisation which she agreed
to do. Whether or not this is an accurate recollection of its origins,
the DSSO was centred mainly in Fife although there also appear to
have been branches in Edinburgh and the Lothians.[15] Its aims were
immediate and complete separation, the overthrow of capitalism
and a Parliament organised on the basis of occupational interests.[16]
Miss Wood wrote 'of such a nature is the Democratic Scottish
Self-Government Organisation. It does not accept Liberals or Tories
as members but only those of Labour interests'.[17] Miss Wood not
only came into conflict with the establishment but also spent a short
time in prison after an altercation with some members of the British
Union of Fascists at a meeting on the Mound in Edinburgh.[18]

Although Miss Wood was an excellent propagandist and therefore obtained a great deal of publicity for the DSSO there is no evidence that it had many members and none that it had much impact on the development of nationalism. She also set up the Scottish Self-Government Federation about 1937 to bring together all the nationalist bodies and the Anti-Conscription League.[19] This latter body seems to have been founded in 1933 and defended the 'right of Scottish citizens to refuse service to Westminster'.[20] It was a revival of a pre-1914 organisation. Her youth organisation, the Scottish Watch, has already been mentioned in connection with the interests of the *Daily Record* and she also seems to have been a leader of the Scottish Defence Force. In a volume of her autobiography this is described as a small organisation 'with a few picked officers, a hidden rifle range and intelligence communication'.[21] Another organisation associated with Miss Wood was the Comunn airson Saorsa na h-Alba (the League for the Independence of Scotland). Starting in April 1939 she edited a four-page spread in several issues of the *Scots Independent* giving the news and views of this organisation. It was explicitly against war and recommended abstinence at parliamentary elections but otherwise it is difficult to understand it other than as a vehicle for Miss Wood's vigorous and publicity conscious personality. It is very easy to dismiss Miss Wood as a buffoon or a trouble-maker, but that would be too facile a judgment. The fact is that she kept up an unremitting campaign for an independent Scotland both at this period and after the war and for many people at many times she *was* Scottish nationalism. The leaders of the SNP may have believed that she brought the cause into disrepute but she certainly made people aware of it and she represented a certain group of nationalists who believed in a militant approach. There were other similar groups centred on the west of Scotland but they were even more shadowy, not having a leader like Miss Wood. Clann Alban appears to have been formed in 1930 as a secret society[22] and the Scots Guard in 1932. This latter, according to the *Daily Record* was a para-military organisation with a careful recruitment policy.[23] In 1934 a group called the League of True Scots was set up with the following policies:[24]

1) The unfettered right of the people of Scotland to determine their own destinies without any reference to any external factor whatsoever;
2) Economic freedom for Scotland and the individual Scot by

the adaptation of a sane economic system based on the reality
of modern scientific production.

In 1938 the Scottish Front and a journal, *Reveille*, were founded by
Major Hume Sleigh.[25]

It must be said that before and after 1934 the NPS and the SNP
represented only the main stream of nationalism and that there were
undercurrents in the form of these other organisations. None of
them amounted to much, which was probably just as well since some
teetered on the brink of violence. The fact is that apart from a few
attempts at sabotage there never was any violence. Instead these
other bodies provided a base from which the official party could be
criticised. There were certainly people within the party who
sympathised with them, especially after 1934. This is shown in a
rather vivid way by the fact that Muirhead, then controlling the
Scots Independent through the Scottish Secretariat, was prepared to
have Miss Wood incorporate *Smeddum* of the DSSO in the *Scots
Independent* during 1939. Many party members felt that the party
was too compromising and, as war approached, many supported a
more vigorous anti-war policy, as we shall see. The best-known of
these organisations specifically against the war was the Scots
Neutrality League which consisted mostly but not exclusively of
nationalists. It will be dealt with later.

It is also worth mentioning that the SNP felt it necessary to set up
one such 'activist' body within its own ranks. In November 1936 the
Scots Independent announced the setting up of the Covenant of
Scottish Action which was to be mostly for younger nationalists. It
had the use of a van in which it undertook propaganda tours of
Scotland but there were hints of other activities which were not ruled
out. In a letter to Miss Wood in April 1937 Muirhead admits that he
had himself looked around Westminster Abbey to assess the
possibility of taking the Stone of Scone and remarks that someone in
the Covenant of Action might also think about this.[26]

At the other end of the spectrum of nationalist organisations there
were several which were more specifically for Home Rule and
supported co-operation in the war effort. Ex-Baillie William
Thomson of Govan set up the League of the Thistle and White
Heather in 1936 and in August 1937 he re-established the Scottish
Home Rule Association.[27] In April 1938 this organisation changed
its name to the Scottish Self-Government Union.[28] This is not to be
confused with the Labour Council for Scottish Self-Government
which was a Scottish version of the London Scots Self-Government

Committee based in Glasgow on Labour Party membership. None of these Home Rule organisations seems to have attracted more than a handful of members.

The smaller organisations were not the only ones to suffer from membership problems. From 1934 onwards these problems also beset the SNP. In November 1934, just after the amalgamation we have a listing of 90 branch conveners.[29] By June 1936 only 59 are listed.[30] There are other indications: an article in the *Scots Independent* of October 1936 indicates the falling attendance at Wallace Day demonstrations at Elderslie and another in August 1937 again commenting on the Scotland's Day demonstration of that year. The November issue carried an article by MacEwen commenting on the situation and urging a membership drive.

It is not possible to conclude that SNP membership was bleeding away to the more militant organisations since they were all tiny. What can be said again is that the 1934 union had no magic effect. Perhaps this had something to do with a lack of dynamism among the leaders or perhaps world conditions drew Scotsmen's attentions away from their homeland to what was happening in Europe, in Abyssinia and elsewhere. It was, of course, precisely these developments which led to a new ferment in the nationalist movement when war seemed imminent. It may be significant that the *Scots Independent* reports a rise in attendance for the first time in several years at the 1938 Scotland's Day celebrations.[31] There is no evidence of increased party membership but clearly nationalism was not confined to the formal organisation.

There were two further issues which came up in the immediately pre-war period. They also illustrate the departure of the party from strict nationalism and what was perceived as democratic values. The first of these concerned the issue of whether SNP members could be members of other parties. It will be recalled that the fourth point accepted by the NPS conference of May 1933 emphasised this point but the wording was, perhaps intentionally, vague. In these terms the NPS and, by implication, the SNP would not be associated with an English party but the possibility of joint membership for individuals might equally be possible. It seems to have been generally interpreted in the NPS that such dual membership was impossible.

The question whether a National Party member could be a member of another party had been discussed in 1932 when talks with the Scottish Party had begun. MacCormick appears to have answered doubters like Gibson that, on this, the line would be held.[32] The issue really arose on the position of the Duke of Montrose. On 4 May 1935 he published a letter in the *Glasgow Herald* proposing that a new party should be formed by amalgamating the SNP and the Scottish Liberal Party. By this time he had changed to the Liberal whip in the House of Lords so the sentiment was understandable but there were two snags. First, he was the President of the SNP and had apparently not consulted that party and secondly it was not generally known in the SNP that he was a Liberal. Many assumed that he followed what they believed to be party policy of being only an SNP member. At the conference which took place a few days later a resolution was proposed: 'No person who is a member of an English-controlled political party is eligible for membership of the Party.'[33] It was defeated. As a compromise MacCormick put up another resolution which was accepted: 'No officer-bearer in the Scottish National Party will take part in the work of an English-controlled party.' This seemed to exclude Montrose from taking an active part in the Liberal Party and it also dealt with the position of Mrs Burnett-Smith (Annie S. Swan, the popular novelist), who became Vice-President of the SNP while being at the same time a well-known member of the Liberal Party. At the conference in 1936 the resolution to exclude members of other parties was again defeated and again a compromise resolution was accepted which was even weaker: 'Only those persons who believe that self-government is the most urgently required political form for Scotland should become members of the Party.'[34] It was by now quite clear that the Scottish Party approach had prevailed over that of the NPS. This development was a precursor of MacCormick's courting of the other parties and especially the Liberals.[35] Several prominent members left the party over this issue, including Gibson.[36]

The other issue concerned the position of the National Council and eventually of the MacCormick group, *vis-à-vis* the annual conference. There was a feeling among some members that MacCormick used the National Council which he could dominate as a tool for controlling the conference. The actual debate concerned the practice of National Council of re-nominating itself as a block. At the 1932 NPS conference it was proposed that federations of branches should elect delegates to the National Council. MacCormick and several supporters spoke against this and the resolution was defeated.[37] It was raised several times again during the 1930s but, by this time, MacCormick was firmly in control.

With the deepening world crisis the SNP could not avoid being involved in the debate. From the first there was no question but that it felt sympathy for the smaller nations attacked by the Dictators. Thus, in 1936, it condemned the Hoare-Laval plan which abandoned Abyssinia to Mussolini.[38] At the same time a considerable section of the members did not want to be dragged into a war. At the 1937 conference a resolution was passed. This conference 'views with alarm the foreign policy of the present government and the apparently purposeless amassing of arms which accompanies it'[39] but it rejected a resolution by the Glasgow University Scottish Nationalist Association which refused to consider conscription,[40] and it condemned the fascist governments. By the autumn of 1938 this situation was considerably worse. In October a manifesto was issued, *Scotland and the World Crisis*. It agreed that:[41]

Scotland would fight with England and the rest of the Commonwealth in a war for ideals appealing to our people— ideals such as liberty and democracy . . . but Scotland cannot voluntarily take part in a game of power politics. . . . We call upon the Scottish nation to unite in defence of their faith. To demand the power to make her voice heard in international affairs. To resist all propagandist efforts to march our people to an imperialist war in the name of these ideals which have been betrayed.

Thus on the issue of joining the war the SNP seemed to agree to it provided that Scotland's voice could be heard among the councils of the nations. This was also the sense of a resolution passed by Conference in May 1939 that the party stood 'in uncompromising opposition to conscription unless and until a clear pledge was given that conscripts and all other forces would be used only for the defence of Britain or to fulfil the moral obligation involved in a real system of collective security'.[42] A glance at the wording shows that it would be easy to justify entering the war effort and, when war broke out, MacCormick gave a pledge of full support on behalf of the party.[43]

The party and the nationalist movement in general was not agreed on this. In particular Arthur Donaldson, who was an extremely able and energetic ex-journalist, established the Scots Neutrality League. The aims of this organisation were:[44]

(1) to secure Scottish neutrality in any war declared or otherwise;

237

(2) to protect against victimisation those who refuse to volunteer for war service.

The League's position was that this was an imperialist war in which no Scotsmen should be killed and, in any case, no other country had a right to declare war on Scotland's behalf. It was an extremely active organisation but, in order to protect members from police attention, there were no membership lists or even a committee. Donaldson was the sole publicly acknowledged office-bearer. He wrote regularly in the *Scots Independent* during 1938 and 1939, largely because Muirhead was sympathetic to his stand, being himself a pacifist. At a National Service Rally in Glasgow and on other occasions the League organised protests.[45]

One outcome of this was that the party executive decided that the *Scots Independent* was showing too much sympathy for the radicals. Pressure was put on Muirhead to hand the journal over to the party as an official organ. It had formally been run as an independent monthly by the Scottish Secretariat since September 1935 when it was discontinued and replaced by the *Scottish Standard*. This ran into financial difficulties and the *Scots Independent* was restarted with money provided by Muirhead on the understanding that it would give news of the whole national movement and would be free to criticise the SNP. This independence began to irk the leadership. By a conference resolution on 27 May 1939 it was decided that it should again become an official party paper and therefore was taken out of Muirhead's control.

The Neutrality League interpreted the 1937 conference resolution to mean that the party had rejected conscription but there is no doubt that subsequent conferences and councils modified this decision. Nevertheless an influential group of nationalists agreed that they should not accept conscription. At a special conference held on 16 September 1939 this resolution was passed:[46]

This party while recognising that the majority of Scottish people have acquiesced in conscription as a necessity in the present emergency, nevertheless considers and will strongly urge that the definition of conscientious objection should be enlarged to include objection based on profound political conviction.

This pointed to a situation which was to have very serious implications. Some nationalists like Muirhead and David Murison, a prominent Aberdeen nationalist, were pacifists on moral grounds which would be accepted by a conscientious objectors' tribunal. Others argued that an English government had no right to call up Scotsmen. The details of the arguments varied, some claiming that the Treaty of Union had been broken but the upshot was the same. The tribunals would not accept the arguments. Quite a few nationalists went to prison when they refused to accept a direction into the forces or into war work but, in particular, the argument was used, in a way which was to contribute to the splintering of the party, by Douglas Young, who was later to become Chairman.

By the beginning of the war there were various tensions within the SNP. These built up to the split of 1942. First of all there was the tension which existed over the war. The majority of members drifted into the forces and to this extent were in agreement with MacCormick's policy. A vigorous minority was against it and got a great deal of publicity through the Scots Neutrality League and through United Scotland, an organisation which seems to have operated mainly in and around Edinburgh under Dr Mary Ramsey but had roughly the same aims.[47] Those who agreed with MacCormick believed that these activities brought nationalism into disrepute. The disquiet over the war did not end with conscription. Especially in Glasgow there was considerable feeling about the forced drafting of female workers into industry in England. The young women were extremely reluctant to go, and nationalists argued that they were being put into dangerous situations, that families were being broken up and that active young people were drained from Scotland. From May 1941 the *Scots Independent* carried a series of articles on this subject and in April 1942, just before the party conference, a particularly strong attack was made.[48]

The stance of the party on the war was, however, only one irritant. More important was the fact that MacCormick and the small group around him had become even more unpopular. About MacCormick himself it was felt that he ran the party in consultation with his 'kitchen cabinet' and with no one else; that he entered into negotiations with other parties unknown to and unapproved by the rest of the party. No doubt these criticisms were made particularly by members who wanted complete independence for Scotland but among the Home Rulers and gradualists too there was a feeling that MacCormick was continually doing things behind their backs; that he was not frank in discussing his contacts with other parties; that he held the whole organisation almost as a fiefdom in which no one

239

else was able to interfere. One of the dissidents explained that they resented 'control of the movement . . . falling more and more into the hands of a small Glasgow group . . . resulting in a gradual freezing of enterprise, bewildering opportunism and a lack of courage in facing national issues fair and square'.[49] This was also witnessed by the attempts to loosen the hold of the Secretary over National Council and by giving branches direct representation, an attempt which failed. Thus, after the 1942 conference a letter from Robert Hurd to Dewar Gibb, both ex-members of the Scottish Party, and certainly not radicals, makes it clear that both men distrusted MacCormick as an intriguer.[50] Hurd at least voted with the anti-MacCormick faction.

There was finally the issue of where the party stood on Home Rule versus independence. As early as 1937 MacCormick had suggested that the SNP should operate more like the old SHRA working through and in alliance with other parties.[51] This was wholly consistent with his approaches to the Liberals and his attempt to organise a Scottish National Convention in 1938-9. In his report to the 1942 conference he noted that the Labour and Liberal Parties seemed to be coming back to the idea of Home Rule and, in the course of the debate at the conference, it became clear that the Secretary and his associates were proposing that the SNP should become a pressure group to work in and with the other parties to achieve Home Rule.[52] In short they were planning that the SNP should become the sort of organisation that the Scottish Convention later became.

One has to say that, while the war issue may have brought the internal argument to a head, there were other longer standing issues involved. It was the issue of the party leadership that really split the party in 1942 as is evidenced by the anti-MacCormick stance of people like Hurd and Dewar Gibb who were helping the war effort and were sympathetic to a gradualist approach to independence.

The conference took place at the end of May. MacCormick stood down as Secretary as he recognised that the situation was difficult. His nominee as Chairman was William Power, a well-known journalist. There was, unusually, another nominee, Douglas Young. Young was an Assistant to the Professor of Greek at Aberdeen. He had a reputation as a poet as well as a classicist but his best known characteristic at this time was that he had refused conscription on the grounds that the British government had no right to call up Scotsmen. For this he had spent a few months in jail and a certain amount of publicity had been given by the newspapers.[53] Young was certainly an active member of the SNP in Aberdeen and, although he was a young man in his twenties, he was a very attractive and forceful personality. It could not be said that he was in the front line of the leadership of the SNP. Neither could it be said that he was a hard line nationalist. On the contrary, an article which he published in the *Scots Independent* in January 1940 argued for a Federal Union of Britain on the model of the Lowther Commission of twenty years earlier. His voluminous personal correspondence in the National Library of Scotland shows that he never moved from this position and his later support for MacCormick's Scottish Convention also demonstrates this.[54] Furthermore, the occasion of his resignation from the SNP in 1948 was that he wanted to be a member of the Labour Party as well as of the SNP. In other words, he took a 'MacCormick' line in most of the classic controversies of the SNP. What seems to have happened was that he was used as a figurehead for a group, mostly of hardline nationalists, in order to beat MacCormick's nominee, William L. Power. There is little evidence of an anti-establishment caucus to defeat Power although another young nationalist, Robert MacIntyre, may have been active. Power was defeated by the close margin of 33 to 29 because of the Secretary's unpopularity.

There was a bitter argument after Young's election and MacCormick called upon his followers to leave with him to consider further action. About half the delegates did so and, in the Roxburgh Hotel close by, where a room had been booked, they established a body which became the Scottish Convention.

The 1942 conference was a major event in the history of nationalism. On the one hand it split the movement almost in two. Because MacCormick had the contacts and political skill he was able to build from his followers a large movement which eventually ran the Scottish Covenant of the early 1950s. As one would expect from his activities from 1937 onwards, this was dedicated to Home Rule. What was left in the SNP was largely, but not exclusively, the element that worked for complete independence and these members were strengthened by other 'hard line' nationalists who had drifted out of the party from 1933 onwards, for example, Tom Gibson, Elma Campbell, Hugh MacDiarmid and Wendy Wood. The SNP thus became a much smaller organisation than the Scottish Convention because it was putting forward a much more radical policy which was not as palatable as Home Rule. In practice it meant that the SNP suffered from the sickness of all small movements with a gospel no one heeds. It became inward looking and this tended to make it even less successful. When the Scottish Covenant was gathering well over a million signatures, the Nationalists were not represented at many elections and were doing disastrously badly.

There was a positive side for the Nationalists. Under the leadership of MacIntyre, who became the Secretary and later President, and Arthur Donaldson, the party line on the core issue was strictly defined. The aim was to be the re-establishment of full Scottish sovereignty. There were to be no alliances or compromises with other parties which took away from this. The years of intrigue made the new young leadership determined that they would have nothing short of a programme of national independence. Several remained in the party who would have been content with gradualism but it was not their stamp which now moulded it. Although this may have been a limit on their appeal, in the short run it meant that in the 1960s, when the attraction of the traditional parties was waning, the Nationalists presented a real alternative.

The unpopularity of the SNP did not become immediately apparent during the war. In 1939 the major parties agreed that there would be no contests at by-elections during the war. The party which held a seat would put forward a candidate who would not be opposed by a candidate of another party. The SNP had not been invited to become a party to this truce. Thus in October 1939 the *Scots Independent*, now an official paper, carried an article to the effect that by-elections would be contested and appealed to all branches to keep together. Thereafter, in several contests, the Nationalists did quite well as the sole opponent, or almost the sole opponent, of the government. In Argyll in April 1940 William Power gained 37 per cent of the vote; in Kirkcaldy Burghs in February 1944 Douglas Young gained 6,621 votes as against the Labour victor's 8,268. In Motherwell in April 1945 Robert MacIntyre won the seat although he lost it at the subsequent general election in June. It was at this point, with only 1·27 per cent of the Scottish vote and the loss of their only seat that the euphoria of the war-time by-elections was dissipated.

Thus at the end of the war the SNP was reduced to a very small group of intransigent nationalists. They were led by people without a great deal of political experience. They shared with MacCormick a lack of willingness to build up a grass roots organisation but they had none of his speaking skills or power to attract supporters.

The Scottish Convention

For the Scottish Convention too, things were not straightforward at first. About half of the members of the 1942 conference left, including the majority of those who led the party. In July 1942 circulars were sent to all SNP branches, to council members and to *Scots Independent* subscribers to explain the position of Convention and their view of the conference. This was not noticeably successful. Langside and Cathcart branches appear to have gone over as did Hardgate and Kirkintilloch but these are virtually all of which it is possible to get a record.[55] In September another letter was sent to branch secretaries offering a visit by Robert Grey, a leading member. By that time they had attracted 312 individual members and the numbers appear to have gone up to 743 by March 1943 when precise numbers cease to be recorded. The minutes comment, however, that a large proportion of these came from outside the party. Lady Glen-coats joined in 1942 as did Naomi L. Mitchison and her husband George, who was a Labour MP. By 1943 MacCormick himself had joined the Liberals and it was the policy of Convention to infiltrate other organisations and parties.[56] In particular, the Liberal Party was a target partly because of personal contacts, partly because of a joint interest in Home Rule, and partly because it was felt that since it was the weakest of the parties it could be influenced.

Given that it was committed to Home Rule rather than independence, what were the activities and programmes of Convention? The idea of a Scottish convention was an old one. We have already seen that the SHRA organised one in the 1920s and MacCormick himself had made two attempts which had been unsuccessful. In August 1932 it was announced that the NPS would call a National Convention in the following February.[57] It was to consist of representatives of Scottish institutions such as burghs, trade unions, business, the kirk and so forth and was to approve a draft Bill for the setting up of a Scottish Constituent Assembly and the repeal of the Act of Union. With the arrival of the Scottish Party this project was dropped in favour of negotiating for amalgamation. In January 1938 the *Scots Independent* again announced that a Scottish National Convention was to be organised from among the same sorts of groups and all others who were in favour of Home Rule. Again a short Bill was published to give authority for the setting up of a Constituent Assembly. In March 1939 the *Scots Independent* announced that

243

the convention was to be in the Glasgow City Halls from 30
September to 1 October 1939, but this too did not take place as the
timing obviously was bad. But the idea did not die. On 21 December
1940 Muirhead, the man who organised the 1926 Convention,
suggested to National Council that it might still be held.[58]

There was, thus, a long history to this project. At the early stages
the new organisation concentrated on individual members and a
great many meetings were held. In Glasgow itself monthly meetings
were held in the Cosmo Cinema during the war. MacCormick, as
Chairman of Convention, presided. At this time Convention worked
closely with other Home Rule groups such as the London Scots
Self-Government Committee and a number of pamphlets were
published on various aspects of Scottish Reconstruction.[59]

MacCormick and his colleagues worked hard to bring all the
parties together to solve Scotland's problems. Members were urged
to join political parties in order to affect policies and contacts were
made at both ends of the political spectrum, at the Young
Communist League Congress in 1946 and on a deputation to
Conservative MPs at Westminster also in 1946. The *quid pro quo*
here was, of course, that Convention would not put up parliamentary
candidates; it no longer regarded itself as a political party.
MacCormick himself stood as a Liberal candidate in the 1945
general election.

In 1947 the first Scottish National Assembly was held. With
around 600 delegates it was extremely successful. The *Scotsman*
described it as 'perhaps the most widely representative meeting ever
held to discuss Scottish affairs'. Invitations had been sent to every
Church of Scotland presbytery, every chamber of commerce and
local authority and to every trade union. Accounts describe it as
largely a middle class affair. There was only one well-known trade
unionist, Michael Byrne. What has to be remembered is that it took
place during a time of Labour government and indeed, towards the
end of the 1940s the Labour Party was very unpopular owing to raw
material shortages and the austerity measures. Labour supporters
recall that there was strong pressure on MPs not to take part in the
meetings.[60]

From middle class Scotland, however, there was support. The
meeting was opened with a prayer by the Minister of Glasgow
Cathedral, a very senior clergyman, and there were also several
members of the aristocracy in attendance, including the Countess of
Errol, Sir George Ogilvie-Forbes and Lord Belhaven. This first

meeting of Convention appointed a committee to draw up a 'Blueprint' for Scotland which was submitted to the next assembly on 20 March 1948.[61] With MacCormick's flair for publicity there was a great deal of press coverage and the whole affair became of interest in Scotland. It was at this assembly that the idea of national plebiscite, or, what later became a covenant was publicly discussed. The first ideas for this were as follows:[62]

1. We have no desire to impair the essential unity of the United Kingdom but we are satisfied that the existing constitution cannot serve the best interests either of Scotland or of the United Kingdom. Without self-government a nation can have no adequate focus for the expression of its spiritual, cultural or economic life. . . .

2. The existing legal machinery is heavily overburdened with the result that it is impossible for Parliament to give due consideration to matters of great importance.

3. Scottish representation suffers from the fact that many bills affecting the whole of the UK are drawn up primarily with English law and conditions as their framework and background. . . .

5. The Scottish Grand Committee is not representative of Scottish opinion. . . .

7. Administration is over-centralised.

On the basis of this argument the *Blueprint* recommended among other things that:

1. The Scottish Parliament has final power over Scottish affairs except for the Crown, peace and war, defence, foreign and dominion affairs.

2. The Scottish Parliament shall have power to alter its own constitution but no amendment shall be made to effect the altering of its relation to the United Kingdom Parliament until such an amendment shall have been considered by a joint commission representative of the UK Parliament and the Scottish Parliament. . . .

6. Disputes shall be solved by the Judicial Committee of the Privy Council.

It is clear that this was at the very least a proposal for a federal system and contained a clause which could take it far beyond this.

The idea of a covenant was not new. It went back to the Solemn League and Covenant of the seventeenth century but it had been discussed much more recently than that. There had been a proposal for such a covenant in 1930. In February 1939 the *Scots Independent* carried an article canvassing the idea and MacCormick himself had referred to the matter in speeches. At the Third National Assembly held in the Church of Scotland Assembly Halls in Edinburgh this covenant was produced. It was couched in more general terms than the *Blueprint.*[63]

We, the people of Scotland who subscribe to this Engagement, declare our belief that reform in the constitution of our country is necessary to secure good government in accordance with our Scottish traditions and to promote the spiritual and economic welfare of our nation.

We affirm that the desire for such reform is both deep and widespread through the whole community, transcending all political differences and sectional interests and we undertake to continue united in purpose for its achievement.

With that end in view we solemnly enter into this Covenant whereby we pledge ourselves in all loyalty to the Crown and within the framework of the United Kingdom, to do everything in our power to secure for Scotland a Parliament with adequate legislative authority in Scottish affairs.

About 1,200 delegates attended this Assembly and signed the Covenant on 29 October 1949. The Duke of Montrose was the first to sign at the meeting and he was followed by many others well known in Scottish life, among them Robert MacIntyre of the SNP. Although there was no official relationship between the party and the Scottish Convention there was a great deal of personal goodwill. The Covenant forms which then went out headed by the 'Undertaking' were circulated by many people including those who were active members of the SNP.

The ironical fate of the Covenant was that it quickly became too popular. In the first weeks after the National Assembly there was a totally unexpected rush to sign it. Very quickly supplies of Covenant forms ran out and there was a frantic rush to print more. People queued in the streets to sign and again there was immense publicity. In short, this was another example of MacCormick's talent for starting off a popular and exciting project married to an inability to organise or follow through on anything like the same scale. The

Covenant ran away with its sponsors and their tragedy was that they did not know how to handle it.

A great deal has been made of the claim that two million Scots signed the Covenant. There is no way of knowing this since it was never completely audited and it would be difficult to know how to do this in any case. Many people below voting age, for example, might have signed it and it would be impossible to check this fact. Whatever the number was, the support for the Covenant was very large. Nor, considering the events which had preceded the signing, was the support so surprising. Nearly all the major institutions with the exception of some business organisations and the leadership of the Labour and Conservative parties, had supported Convention and attended the Assemblies. Second, the trial ballots which had been held in small Scottish towns like Kirriemuir and Galashiels also showed that there was a great support for a Home Rule programme.[64] Over and above all those who reacted positively to the idea of Home Rule there must have been others who felt that the Covenant was about a better deal for Scotland. We know from the election studies that people do not usually vote for a party with clear ideas even of its main planks. There is no reason to think that they should have done otherwise for the Covenant. I have already pointed out that 1949 was a time when the Labour government was unpopular. It may well be that the signing of the Covenant expressed this.

It was commonly said of the Covenant organisers that they did not know what to do with their immensely successful petition. Commissioners were appointed to negotiate with the government. The Prime Minister, Attlee, would not meet them and, instead, they had an interview with Arthur Woodburn, the Secretary of State for Scotland. He pointed out that if Scotland truly did want Home Rule then to sign a petition was not enough. They would have to vote for it. The reaction of James Stuart, the Chairman of the Scottish Unionist MPs, is recorded and it is worth quoting:[65]

> We cannot hold the view that such extremely complex matters can properly be determined either by plebiscite or by reference to the number of signatures affixed to a document. The constitutional methods by which the people in our democracy can make their wishes known and effective are well understood, generally respected, in constant use and available to all shades of opinion.

It did not help the cause that the elections of 1950 and 1951 were

247

immediate and negative tests of whether the people of Scotland intended to do anything more about Home Rule.

There followed a discussion about putting up Home Rule candidates. The Scottish Covenant Committee, which circulated the Covenant forms, was organised into the Scottish Covenant Association in May 1951. This was set up on a constituency basis and incorporated the existing organisation of the Scottish Convention and the local Covenant Committees. Several of these associations urged that they should run candidates and some national leaders were sympathetic. In March 1951 the National Covenant Committee considered a resolution that all MPs who would not sign a pledge to support Home Rule should be opposed by Covenant candidates. Nothing came of this.[66] It was considered again at the first general meeting of the Covenant Association on 27 October 1951 but was rejected. Later both Dewar Gibb and Dr John Macdonald urged this method in the *Scottish Covenant Newsletter* (May 1954 and January 1955 respectively) but by this time the whole thing was dead. The 1951 Assembly meeting on 23 June slipped to 200 delegates from the 1,000 or so who had attended in 1950. The drive had gone and from then on the Covenant continued to decline. MacCormick was deeply hurt and never again tried to get the Home Rule movement off the ground. He died in 1961 and with him the Covenant Association finally died too.

It is very difficult to assess the long-term importance of the Covenant Movement. On the one hand it can be said to have split the SNP but on the other hand it did make some form of Scottish self-government a well-discussed and popular programme for a great many Scots. It appears that many SNP people drifted into the Convention, and later after the war, the Covenant Association, but equally many came from the Covenant Association to the SNP in the early 1960s. James Porteous, the economic expert of Convention, is but one example and William Wolfe, the Chairman of the SNP, is another. It can thus be argued that the Covenant Association acted as a stepping stone towards the SNP. It was the Covenant Association that made the running in commenting on Scottish affairs in the late 1940s and early 1950s, on the question of the building of a Forth Road Bridge, the rocket-testing range in South Uist, the closing of the Clyde piers, the question of the numeral in the Royal title Elizabeth II or Elizabeth I.

It was Convention through MacCormick which was involved in the 'lifting' of the Stone of Scone from Westminster Abbey. What must finally be said about Convention and the Covenant movement is that in spirit it was nationalist and not simply concerned with devolution for administrative convenience or even for democratic representation in the strict sense. A cursory glance through the publications or the *Scottish Covenant Newsletter* shows a great deal of attention paid to Scottish culture and national feeling. MacCormick and his colleagues may have had a picture of Scotland within the United Kingdom but it was a Scotland conscious of itself as a national unit, and, as such, with a right to govern itself. In terms of the modelling of Scottish voters for nationalism, the construction of the Covenant was, at best, long term. It kept alive the idea of self-government but it leads us further to understand that there had to be a long term effort to secure Home Rule. The branches of the Covenant Association were set up as an afterthought when the petition had been rejected by the government and there was never any leadership to tell the organisers what they ought to be doing.

The SNP in the doldrums

We turn now to what was happening in the SNP. Some of the effects of the 1942 split have already been mentioned. Most of those who were left were dedicated to the struggle for complete independence. There was a very considerable shift in the balance of the party. Whether related to the new orientation or not there was also a rise in the number of branches. Some branches, but only a few, went over to the Covenant and others collapsed with the pressure of war conditions but by December 1942 the *Scots Independent* was carrying names of thirty-two branch secretaries as opposed to about twenty at the beginning of the year. This issue of the journal also reports the paying of the debt of about £100 on the *Scots Independent* and a rise in the circulation figures. At the next annual conference it was announced that membership had increased by about 60 per cent since the last conference and there had been an increase in the sales of the *Scots Independent* by 13 per cent.[67] This trend is confirmed by the papers in the Muirhead collection.[68]

Part of this success may have been due to the general rise of interest in a protest against the large parties in the coalition government. It is worth saying, however, that this does not mean that the SNP was moving forward inexorably. I have already pointed out that it did well in by-elections but there were divisions among those who had moved back to the party. After MacCormick left

249

some gifted but often very troublesome individuals joined. Although Douglas Young became Chairman he was something of a titular head. The real leadership was given by men like Robert MacIntyre and Arthur Donaldson. Neither of these had the sort of charisma of MacCormick or Douglas Young but they were deeply dedicated to the cause of an independent Scotland and they were determined to achieve it by establishing a serious party which would fight parliamentary elections. There were several in the SNP who believed that other methods were legitimate and they were often vociferous in putting their case. The new leaders were convinced that there had to be party unity and no deviation from agreed tactics. With these beliefs they ruled with a firm hand.

Such an approach was expressed especially in the years following the war when many of the dissidents were expelled or edged out of the party. What was left by 1948 or thereabouts was a very small group who agreed that the aim of the party should be complete independence for Scotland and that this should be done by parliamentary means by fighting at elections as SNP candidates. Apart from the 'unclubbables' this also discouraged, for example, those who thought that extra-parliamentary methods might be necessary. In the *Scots Independent* for January 1946 Roland Muirhead, now the President of the party, argued that the lesson of 1945 was that some 'direct action' methods might be useful. He suggested some type of non co-operation with the English bureaucracy. Later he went on to form Scottish Congress. It goes without saying that all who favoured a form of self-government short of complete independence would now be likely to work with Scottish Convention. Finally, at the 1948 conference, the issue of dual membership of political parties came up. Douglas Young had flirted with many moderately left wing organisations including the Labour Party. He opposed a National Council resolution which said, among other things: 'Members may not at the same time be members of any other political party. In all cases the National Council shall decide which bodies are to be considered as political parties.'⁶⁹ The resolution was passed and Young left the SNP although he always remained sympathetic.

This process of clarifying the lines of development of the party also took the form of a demand for policy. The *Scots Independent* of July 1946 contained a complaint that it was impossible to find out party policy other than by scratching through resolutions at various conferences. A committee under Frank Yeaman was, therefore, appointed to draw up just such a document which would be submitted to a special conference of December 1946. This is the first of the major statements and forms a basis for today's SNP. With the pressures of Covenant it was inevitable that some members' attention should turn to this. It was also important that the Labour Party was busily engaged in running policy statements and this also seems to have been an influence. One point to which we shall return is that, despite the shake-out of the Home Rulers, the 1947 programme was still one that recognised the importance of the relationship with England and especially the necessity of economic links. It could not be said at this time, or at any other, that the SNP was a totally separatist party. Many of the old ideas for small rural industries and for the control of credit were revised and put in a more systematic form. It was this revision of the policy which also led to the revision of the constitution and part of this was the tightening up on the membership question. Just as important was the fact that the Nationalists now started to become involved in local government elections. In the 1920s and 1930s they had taken part in parliamentary elections. Perhaps as a result of the 1945 disaster, however, an effort was now put into these other contests. The best-known success was that of Robert MacIntyre, who became Provost of Stirling, and Donaldson, who became Dean of Guild of Forfar and a member of the Angus County Council. Scotland's youngest Provost, in Alva, was the Nationalist Robert Curran. This was small beer compared with contests for Westminster and in those the SNP did not do very well. Very few candidates were put up: only eight in 1945 and four in 1950. In 1951 and 1955 there were only two. It was in these years from 1945 until about 1960 that the SNP went through its darkest years. They were the years of austerity, the Cold War and Korea. Later they were the years of 'never having it so good' and Butskellism. Whether the situation was austere or prosperous there was an effect of drawing people's attention away from Scotland. The political struggle was portrayed in terms of a Conservative-Labour contest and what attention there was for Home Rule was devoted to the Covenant. Party meetings were small and, with the remoteness of success, the party became introverted. There were several attempts, especially in the 1950s, to overturn the existing leaders and this gave many the feeling that MacIntyre, Donaldson and their colleagues were dedicated to control for themselves and for no other reason. Two very important lines were, however, maintained in these years. The first was that the SNP leaders did not ignore the importance of keeping an organisation going. It might be small and weak but the SNP was not run by a clique meeting daily in a Glasgow coffee room as had been the case before 1939. Secondly, they were absolutely clear that the aim of the party was independence. There could be no compromise over that and any suggested deals with other organisations were regarded with enormous suspicion.

The strictness with which MacIntyre and his colleagues led the SNP meant that several splinter groups were organised in the 1940s and 1950s. During the war two youth movements came into being. At first Young Scotland was linked to the SNP but in 1944 it appears to have disaffiliated. Much more long lived and interesting was Fianna na h-Alba.[70] It appears to have been two sections for boys, from twelve to fifteen, and then for those from sixteen onwards and was exclusively based in Glasgow chiefly among working-class children. Its programme included nightly meetings during the week and a weekend devoted to hill walking. Every evening's meeting started with fifteen minutes compulsory Gaelic. At any one time a maximum of about seventy would have been involved. As the name suggests there was some conscious modelling of this organisation on Irish examples and there was even a suggestion that violence might be used to secure Scotland's rights, although this was never condoned by the leaders. This quasi-violent tradition has gone on since the war. There has been talk of the Scottish Republican Army, a Tartan Army, a Border Clan and so forth. It is never clear that such organisations really exist or whether they are a fiction created by some policemen, isolated individuals or the imaginings of popular newspapers. The most important point in this respect is that, apart from these rather questionable and very unimportant groups, violence has never been an aspect of Scottish nationalism. The Fianna seems to have died out in the 1950s.

The Scottish Congress

The most important of the fringe organisations was Scottish Congress, largely the creation of R. E. Muirhead. After MacIntyre's loss of Motherwell, Muirhead argued strongly, as we have already seen, that extra-parliamentary tactics were required. After the end of his term of office as SNP President he founded Congress in 1950. He himself never left the SNP although most of the members of the organisation which he then set up were non-members. A fair proportion had been expelled.

Muirhead founded Congress along the lines which, he believed, guided the Indian National Congress of Gandhi. It concentrated on a programme of propaganda and political education and, because he believed that there could be no success through the ballot box, a programme of non-violent disruption and non-co-operation was planned; indeed, one of the journals which it produced was called the *Non-Violent Scot*.[71] The second point which Scottish Congress shared with its Indian forerunner was that it was to be an alliance of organisations. Several of these already existed and have been mentioned. United Scotland had been set up in the 1940s led by Dr Mary Ramsay with the object of opposing conscription among other things. It continued into the 1950s holding rallies against the Korean War and British colonialism in Cyprus and, in this, was supported by Congress. They also co-operated in the support of some individuals such as Michael Grieve, Hugh MacDiarmid's son, who refused to be conscripted into the British army. Another constituent organisation was the Scottish Socialist Party which was set up in the early 1940s. For the most part it seems to have been a vehicle for the energies of Oliver Brown, an able and indefatigable open-air speaker and pamphleteer. It is difficult to find any statement of policy and it probably had very few members. A final constituent organisation which should be mentioned was Wendy Wood's Scottish Patriots, which still exists. Miss Wood appears to have left the SNP about 1949 and founded the Scottish Patriots. This was a movement similar to her Democratic Self-Government Organisation of pre-war years in that it, or she, tended to make left wing pronouncements and again it seems to have been largely a vehicle for her extremely forceful and attractive personality and her ability as an open-air speaker. She operated mostly in Edinburgh, while Oliver Brown operated in Glasgow.

This was the mixture in Scottish Congress. It was 'hard line' on nationalism and it was radical both in its tactics and in its pronouncements on social and economic affairs and the issues of conscription and colonialism. The radicalism came out in the title of its longest running paper *Scottish Forward*. (Muirhead had been a director of the old ILP paper *Forward*.) It was agreed that Congress would not put up parliamentary candidates of its own since this would cut across the role of the SNP and many of its members wanted also to be members of the party.

Perhaps the most important thing about Congress is that it was held together by Muirhead both by money and by the attention he was prepared to give it. The organisations in it showed that Congress was made up of a group of highly articulate individuals even though they might prefer to masquerade as organisations. Bodies like the Scottish Patriots were, and are, small groups of acquaintances gathered round particular leaders and this was true of Congress itself.

The Scottish Secretariat was, as in 1926 when it had been founded, a publishing concern owned by Muirhead which he used to circulate the pamphlets and journals associated with Congress and its related bodies. When Muirhead died the Scottish Secretariat and Congress disappeared (although the name 'Scottish Secretariat' is still carried on through the work of Dr Archie Lamont).

Congress itself had various branches with an existence separate from the constituent organisations but the activities were mostly centred on Glasgow as Muirhead himself admitted on several occasions.[72] It held a great many open-air meetings: again mostly in Glasgow and conducted several campaigns such as the 'Buy Scottish Goods' exercise of the early 1950s. One of its final activities was to run a Scottish Constituent Assembly.[73] A draft constitution was produced and it was discussed at the Assembly on 21 April 1962.[74] This was attended by 110 delegates only and did not form a very convincing body to decide the future of the nation. The experiment faded away.

At first relations between Scottish Congress and the SNP were friendly. Muirhead was, after all, an important connecting link. As time went on, however, relations deteriorated. MacIntyre was determined that the SNP should be a fully respectable Scottish party and certain members of Congress were rather shrill. As a result Congress was declared a prohibited organisation in March 1958. The occasion was a Congress request to the Soviet Union to present Scotland's case at the UN. According to the SNP resolution this indicated that Congress had become a political party. After a few years quite a few of the old Congress members joined or rejoined the SNP and after 1964 Congress disappeared altogether.

Although it occasionally gathered some publicity Congress played a very small role in the Scottish national movement. It provided a home for radical dissidents and it produced a number of competent pamphlets and journals. In this way there was a possibility for a nationalist but independent critique of the SNP and this was itself an important function to perform. The *National Weekly* especially, had some very high quality material. The problem of Congress was that, although it was dedicated to non-violent tactics and direct action, it consisted mostly of older people for whom the strains of this approach were really too great. Experience from other such movements suggests that this takes youth and the stamina of youth to achieve success. Most of the leading members of Congress were ageing prima donnas. Few had real political or organisational skills. For some reason, the young people attracted to nationalism in the 1940s and 1950s went to the SNP rather than to Congress and it was mostly in the SNP that the struggle was carried on.

One final 'extraneous' organisation should be mentioned: the Nationalist Party of Scotland. By 1954 a new generation of young people had joined the SNP. It may have been that the incident of 'lifting' the Stone of Destiny was associated with this cause and they had the irreverent attitudes of youth. The main concentrations were in Glasgow and Edinburgh where the membership of the party was concentrated in any case. There were not many of them but in any case the SNP was a small party and it did not take many to have some impact. Some of them joined from youth organisations such as the Fianna. Other young people came from the student organisation in Edinburgh but they were similar in two respects. One was that they were extremely hardworking. The other was that they felt the leadership was not active enough. As happens in all organisations, the people who led the SNP had turned inward somewhat and had something of a possessive attitude towards the organisation. For some of the young recruits a new policy of activism meant that the old guard would have to go. Thus it was that around 1954 the most active elements in Glasgow and Edinburgh were committed to bringing down the leadership of MacIntyre and Donaldson or at least to making them share the power. Inevitably these new party workers became prominent in the central organisation and one person who was associated with the Edinburgh group, James Glendinning, became editor of the *Scots Independent*. At the same time they tried to infiltrate existing branches and set up new branches so that their attitudes would be successful.

In making all these points, however, it is important to say that the Glasgow and Edinburgh groups never amalgamated. They were both rather informal bodies and they decided on an informal alliance called 'The 1955 Group' dedicated in practice to winning party offices at the conference. In a statement they said:[75]

The 1955 group is those members of the SNP who are dissatisfied with the conduct of the 1955 Conference, the administration and incompetence of Party HQ, the failure of the Party to show results after thirty-seven years . . . and the dictatorial methods used by office-bearers to stifle free disagreement and criticism of any kind.

The main source of dissatisfaction for the 1955 Group was that their candidates had not been elected at the 1955 conference. They believed that this had been done by the manipulation on the part of the leadership and, indeed, this was a belief shared by other nationalists. As a result of the really major clash which took place at that conference, a number of other break-aways occurred. The Scottish Nationalists (Aberdeen) was formed by a break-away from the Aberdeen branch. Later it was associated with an Aberdeen Congress Branch.[76] Similarly, in Greenock there was a break-away organisation.

Thus the frustration of certain, mainly young, members came to a head at the 1955 conference. Certain splits took place and the Nationalist Party of Scotland was set up. This Edinburgh-centred organisation was only one part of the discontent. It was the most articulate and the best known but its views on issues other than the ousting of the leadership do not seem to have been shared by the other dissidents. In particular, the Nationalist Party of Scotland indulged in some rather vigorous anti-English propaganda which is virtually unique in the whole story of Scottish nationalism. Thus, in the pamphlet *The English: are they human?* there is a long list of atrocities committed by the English in the colonies and they are described as 'the end of a society rotten and putrid to the core. Rotten with class privilege and class war. Putrid with sexual perverts and shameless adulterers in high places'.[77]

In open-air meetings in Edinburgh similar sentiments were expressed but there is no evidence that they were racialist in any other sense. A statement published by the Nationalist Party of Scotland read: 'We, the undersigned citizens of Scotland, mindful of our national tradition of freedom, congratulate Col. Nasser, President of Egypt, on the courageous stand his people have taken against English Imperialism.'[78] Nevertheless, it was this aspect of their statements which was heeded. In October 1953 the National Council of the SNP passed the following resolution: 'Racial and hate propaganda is contrary to the policy of the SNP being alien to the best Scottish tradition which it is our duty to defend. . . . Acts of violence or encouragement to acts of violence . . . is (sic) contrary to the policy of the SNP.'[79] On 5 November the *Scots Independent* announced that the 'hate dissidents' had left the party and some had been expelled. Thus a major threat to the existing leadership of the SNP was averted. It did not end the internal squabbling but for some time there was no other focused opposition to the leadership. The importance of the events of 1955 is mostly negative rather than positive. They illustrate the control held by the existing leaders. It may be that the leadership was stodgy and not prepared to take up some of the new ideas but the 'young Turks' did not show that they were capable of any co-ordinated action and there can be no doubt that the anti-English propaganda of one group, the Nationalist Party of Scotland, was ill-judged. The other lesson is that the party reacted with such speed and definition to the element of anti-Englishness. It is not part of the tradition of nationalism in Scotland and it was anathema to the sort of party which MacIntyre and Donaldson were trying to run—a moderate, reasonable nationalist party dedicated to complete independence for Scotland.

The attitudes of new, young and frustrated members had been contained in 1956. The paradox was that, if the party was to go anywhere, these energies had to be encouraged and the number of members having them had to be increased. It was not long before the problem was to arise again.

The New Departure

Around 1961 a new group of members were beginning to make themselves felt. It is difficult to explain why they started to come in about this time. It may be significant that the Scottish Covenant Association finally collapsed about this time with MacCormick's death. In an extremely interesting article Dr John MacDonald, one of the best known and most able leaders of the association wrote:[80]

As you know, in the past I have supported the idea of moderate legislative development believing that any kind of separate parliament in Edinburgh could be a stepping stone to greater independence.

In my view the position is now radically altered. Because of the extreme gravity of the international situation and also because of the threatening outlook on the economic front, I feel that if Scotland is to survive she must have full freedom and that soon.

This was a time when, as we have seen earlier, the economic situation in Scotland was becoming particularly bad. It was only a year before the winter of 1962 when the unemployment figures led to the issuing of a white paper on the situation in central Scotland.[81] A number of people who had been prominent in the covenant joined Macdonald in the move over to the SNP. Thus, a section of Scottish opinion, already aware of the issue of self-government, moved over to the SNP.

This is not the only explanation for the influx of new members. Another quite straightforward one is that in 1958 the National Council decided on a membership drive.[82] A system of business reply cards was introduced. Large numbers were to be distributed by branches and some results were obtained.[83] This campaign was very much intensified from 1960 onwards after Arthur Donaldson became the Chairman and has been used quite continuously ever since. From 1960 onwards a positive and constant effort was made to bring in members.

It may be objected that the impetus to join came not only from an effort from the party but also because the political moment was right. It is certainly true that Labour had gone down unexpectedly at the 1959 election and many, even among the Shadow Cabinet, feared that this might be taken as fundamental failure of the movement.[84] It may be significant that the two by-election 'successes' of this period were Glasgow, Bridgeton and West Lothian, both Labour seats. There is an argument to suggest that some Labour supporters at this time felt that a new political force was needed in Scotland.

These are speculations. What is not in question is that on 16 November 1961 an SNP candidate won 18·7 per cent of the vote at a by-election in Bridgeton. This was the best result the Nationalists had had for a long time. What was different about this by-election was that the active group of young workers who had been dis-illusioned by the events of 1955 and 1956 had begun to drift back into activity and, in Ian Macdonald, they had a candidate of enormous energy and considerable organisational skills. On the one hand the activists provided a dedicated work force which had not been tried at a by-election for some time. Ian Macdonald got this group to approach the campaign in a vigorous fashion. Almost for the first time a constituency was worked systematically street by street. It was leafletted and canvassed and successful efforts were made to persuade the Press that the SNP was seriously contesting the election.

What happened after Bridgeton was at least as important as what happened at the poll. Where before Nationalist candidates might have fought hard at the time of the election, they pulled out afterwards. Macdonald and his colleagues decided that advance depended on the regular building-up of branches. People who had voted Nationalist must be considered potential members and thus the policy was established of setting up branches in every constituency or local government ward where a contest took place.

This was only part of the major organisational effort which now followed. There were many dedicated people in the party: people who had sacrificed their careers and family lives and who had spent night after night in the service of the party. Essentially, however, the organisation was run by amateurs. At the time of the Bridgeton by-election Ian Macdonald was farming in Ayrshire. He decided to sell his farm and live on the income from this sale and a very small fee paid by the party so that he could work as the National Organiser. For the first time in many years the SNP had a senior full-time official and, moreover, one with enormous enthusiasm for the movement and considerable skill at building up the branch organisation. The importance of this cannot be overstated. It may well have been that the time was right for a swing over to the Nationalists. It may also be true that a group of dedicated amateurs could have done it. What is historically true is that Macdonald himself now toured Scotland setting up branches everywhere he could. In this way the wave of enthusiasm for nationalism was converted into an organisation where before it might simply have fallen back again. The fact that branches began to be built up in some areas meant that it became that much easier to get others going.

Macdonald's techniques were simple. In the years up to 1960 very few branches existed, probably not more than half a dozen working properly. Party membership was between one and two thousand and most of those joined as 'headquarters' members. Macdonald wrote to each of these headquarters members asking if they would consider setting up a branch and offering to help them with the organisation of the first meeting and future support. Quite a number replied and the pattern of each meeting was similar. The National Organiser visited the local people and delivered a standardised speech of encouragement. Branches were set up if there were a minimum of twenty members. If less than that number turned up an 'Interim Committee' was established. In either case they were issued with stocks of business reply cards to be sent around the area and some new members were gained in this way. In his first year of office Macdonald set up twenty fully operational new branches. There was a clear effect on party morale at the next conference.[85]

When a branch was fairly well established it was encouraged to set up other branches in neighbouring areas or to split itself. Thus a town branch in a burgh might set up another in a neighbouring village or split into two: one each for the north and south of the town. There was another important characteristic of the organiser's technique. At the initial meeting when a branch or interim committee was set up, Macdonald insisted that as many people as possible should be given a task. In this way the maximum number were involved. This has remained a characteristic of the party ever since and has been a major factor in building enthusiasm and in the subsequent electoral success.

This was the start of the climb to become a major party. The two components were a change in the tenor of Scottish politics and a vigorous system of organisation. Neither could have worked alone. It was at the West Lothian by-election that this process began to pay off in an obvious way.

West Lothian is a mixed agricultural and mining constituency in the eastern part of the Scottish central belt. It had been held by the Labour Party since 1945 but at the by-election in 1962 there were important changes in the situation. For the first time a representative of the SNP stood (Billy Wolfe) and he made a considerable impact. As Table 13.1 shows, the Conservative vote suffered and has never again reached its old level.

Table 13.1   The vote in West Lothian

	Labour	Conservative	SNP	Liberal
1959	27,454	18,083		
1962	21,266	4,784	9,450	4,537
1964	24,933	8,919	15,087	
1966	26,662	5,726	17,955	
1970	29,360	10,048	15,620	
1974 Feb.	28,112	11,804	21,690	
1974 Oct.	27,687	6,086	24,977	2,083

Although West Lothian was not particularly noticed by the Press it was well chewed over in the party and it gave a great deal of encouragement to activists. While the result in 1962 undoubtedly owed a great deal to the general discontent with the Conservative government and, in particular, to the closing of the shale oil workings which had employed many men in the constituency, one cannot ignore the fact that the Organiser, Ian Macdonald, and the candidate, Billy Wolfe, were members of the new wave in the party. There were no sacred cows for them in the form of beliefs which the old parties held about the manner in which an election should be run. They ran it energetically and thoroughly, bringing forward a great many new ideas. There was another factor. For West Lothian, if for nowhere else, it was now clear that the SNP was not simply a rather odd group on the periphery of British politics but was actually able to put up a good showing at national elections. Like other elections after it, the West Lothian by-election was an event which crystallised the situation and made the way ahead a little clearer. In Smelser's terms it was a precipitating event for many voters in Scotland and especially for several who later became SNP activists.

At the next general election in 1964 there were clear signs that the Nationalists had taken heart from their earlier performances. Whereas at the 1959 election they had put up only five candidates, of whom only one kept his deposit, in 1964 there were fifteen Nationalist candidates, of whom eight saved their deposits. In 1966 there were twenty-three candidates, of whom sixteen kept their deposits. For those who had eyes to see it was clear that things were moving but, in fact, very few seemed to have this faculty. This may have been the reason why the Hamilton by-election of the next year came as such a shock. There had, in fact, been a harbinger in that the SNP did extremely well at a by-election in Glasgow, Pollok, in March. Table 13.2 shows the extent of the move to Nationalists.

Table 13.2   The vote in Glasgow, Pollok

	Labour	Conservative	SNP	Liberal
1966	21,257	19,282		
1967 (by-election)	12,069	14,270	10,084	735

At Hamilton, not far from Glasgow, the voting was even more striking, as shown in Table 13.3.

Table 13.3   The vote in Hamilton

	Labour	Conservative	SNP	Liberal
1966	27,865	11,289		
1967	16,598	4,986	18,397	

Hamilton had always been considered a safe Labour seat, and the size of Mrs Ewing's SNP vote was, therefore, even more remarkable. It had a tremendous impact on Scottish public opinion. Overnight popularity was helped by the fact that both the mass circulation dailies in Scotland: the *Daily Record* and the *Scottish Daily Express* ran columns by Mrs Ewing and she made frequent appearances on television. This election really marks the arrival of the SNP for the majority of the Scottish electorate as a party with a serious political future.

The next development was the performance at the 1968 municipal elections. *New Scotland*, a Conservative journal, had the best summary of the position, as shown in Table 13.4.

Table 13.4   Gains and losses at the Scottish municipal elections, 1968

	Gains	Losses
Conservatives	15	
Progressives etc.	18	13
Independents	9	33
Socialists	4	88
SNP	103	2 (June 1968)

The SNP performance in Glasgow was particularly striking with a win of thirteen seats.

From the beginning of the decade until 1968 the SNP made regular advances among the electors of Scotland. If we refer to Tables 13: 1-3, in which the votes cast in West Lothian, Pollok and Hamilton were laid out, various points are exemplified. The first is that the Conservative vote is badly eroded. It is worth remembering that the Conservatives are the only party to have gained a majority of Scottish votes in this century. In the 1955 election they received 50·09 per cent of the Scottish vote. A glance at the vote in West Lothian shows that, at the beginning at any rate, it was the Conservative vote which fell while the SNP vote rose. After the Labour Party had come into power in 1964, however, there was a similar erosion in the Labour vote. In 1966 Labour was able to claim the support of 49·9 per cent of the Scottish electors but by October 1974 only 36·3 per cent of the electors voted Labour.

Up to this point it seemed that everything was consistently a success for the Nationalists. In 1969 the situation changed. The reasons for the downturn in the popularity of the SNP are complicated and only an impression can be given here. There are, however, several factors which are worth mentioning. The first is that the rapid expansion of the party both in votes and in membership and branches was probably too much to be controlled. Although there was a grass roots organisation it took considerable skill to control what was happening. In another sense, too, the expansion over-extended the party. The heady days of Hamilton and the 1968 municipal elections led many people to believe that independence was just around the corner. Many others probably believed that the SNP victories were a certain recipe for an improvement in Scottish economic conditions. When neither of these events occurred there was a certain amount of disillusion. Since many came into the party very recently they were not fully socialised into the necessity for a fight in order to gain political ends. Perhaps most important of all was the performance of the SNP councillors on Glasgow Corporation. Most of them had very little previous experience of politics. Probably quite a few did not expect to win. For whatever reason they were not prepared for the demands of being a member of a major local authority and the Press soon began to write about their difficulties. A clear indicator of their inexperience was that they seemed to have no idea of the demands that would be made on their time. Several became very bad attenders. Of the thirteen no less than eight lost their jobs when their employers realised what their civic duties would mean in terms of working time lost. In 1969 the Nationalists passed into a very bad period indeed. Partly this was indicated by their showing in the 1970 election. Although they still made an advance in the number of votes cast for them, the increase was not nearly what one would have expected from the by-election results. Exactly how many members left the party is not clear but it was a considerable exodus. On the credit side, however, was the fact that not many branches disappeared completely. Many of them were kept in being artificially by appeals from headquarters to maintain a presence. This often meant that the real number of activists was reduced to one or two but this left a nucleus around which a branch could be organised when things got better.

Perhaps the most important process which took place in the period from 1969 to 1972 when the party was not doing well at the polls was that a certain element of its internal strength was built up. Although it was and is often said that the Nationalists have no policy but independence for Scotland, in fact there have been several policy statements covering wider ground, as we have seen. At the same time it is fair to say that the salience of these other policies for the majority of SNP activists was about as great as the salience of policy for activists of most parties, which is not much. In 1968 groups in Edinburgh and Glasgow had published 'Blueprints' for these cities which were detailed considerations of the conditions there and proposals as to the ways in which the local authority should take action. Partially building upon this, 1969 saw a great expansion in the degree to which the party was prepared to consider policy. Leaders like Billy Wolfe and Margo Macdonald were convinced that, if the party was to have stability, it was necessary that it should start to think politically rather than concentrating all its attention on one final aim. It was in this period that a large number of policy committees were set up. This process had two effects. One was that in these difficult years the party was kept together in a way which might not have been possible if its sole aim had been independence. In 1969 independence seemed a long way off. The people who worked on these policies became committed to them and to the party which was, they hoped, to implement them in a way which had not been true before. Apart from this integrative function the concentration on policy also had the effect of making the SNP a much more political party. Whereas up to 1968 the typical SNP activist seems to have been an individual without much of a grasp of political requirements and the political situation, the long and sometimes tedious arguments about policy and its implementation were a critical educational process.

At the 1974 elections the SNP at last was able to create a parliamentary party. From now on there could be no doubt that they were a serious part of British politics. The argument of this chapter has been that a major contribution towards this situation was made by organisation and that the difference between the SNP's lack of success at earlier periods and its success at this time can only be explained by taking the organisational effort into consideration. In order to explore this further the next chapter will be devoted to the organisation of the present day SNP.

14 The Present Organisation of the SNP

Introduction

Organisation was one essential element which changed the performance of the SNP in the 1950s to its performance in the 1960s and 1970s. Organisation worked along with the changes in the British political atmosphere to remould Scottish politics. It might have been ineffective without these changes but without an improvement in organisation, the party would have been unable to grasp the advantages which were being offered. Richard Rose points out that organisation creates political resources. Without organisation, a politically active citizen has no means of collective influence.[1] This is borne out by the experience of the Scottish Covenant in the early 1950s. MacCormick had the support of a majority of the Scottish electors but he was too late in creating a machine (the Covenant Association) which could exert pressure on the government. As we have seen in Chapter 13, the support of the one or two million signatories was simply allowed to leak away. Organisation creates the stability on which further campaigning can build. This was the lesson which the SNP began to learn in the early 1960s.

We may also ask what is the importance of organisation for a party in terms of votes lost or won. Conventional wisdom has it that good organisation is not worth many votes. Elections are won or lost by trends of opinion which are uniform across the country. The very success of the SNP seems to put a question mark against this point of view. In fact, there is little hard evidence either way but even among political scientists who have been doubtful about the

265

importance of organisation, there are now some who are less sure. Butler and Pinto-Duschinsky, in their study of the 1970 general election, express these sentiments,[2] as do Bochel and Denver,[3] and Richard Rose concludes that there may be some long term effects of good organisation.

It is the purpose of this chapter to describe the organisation of the SNP in terms of previous discussions of party organisation and also in terms of its contributions to the building up of the Nationalist vote. Thus this chapter contributes to the second aim of this study: the description of the party, but it also plays its part in explaining the electoral strength of the party; its power in mobilisation. These two aims are related but are not identical since there are several new features of party organisation illustrated by the Scottish Nationalists.

The most discussed question in this field concerns the place of leadership. Michels based his study mainly on the development of the German Social Democratic Party and showed how power inevitably seemed to fall to those who had control of the organisation: the party bureaucrats, to the detriment of the electors and of their representatives in Parliament.[4] It might be argued that the Scottish Nationalists were in a situation very similar to that of the continental socialists. From a small movement they had become a mass party. For the Germans this strengthened the power of the central organisation. Has a similar move meant a similar change in power location for the SNP? Has it also meant, as Michels observed on the continent, that concern for the principles of the old movement is replaced by a desire for electoral success, for the maximum increase in membership and for both of these at the price of any compromise in principle.

Any of the standard texts on British parties gives us an account which shows that something different has happened in the United Kingdom.[5] Parliament has had such a dominant position in the country that party power has been in the hands of its parliamentary leaders. Since 1974 the SNP has had a parliamentary group. Does this mean that the major decisions will now be taken by the MPs rather than by those elected to be officials in the party? In either event, what is the position of the ordinary party members? What role do they play in decision-making? Whether this concerns parliamentary or non-parliamentary leadership, is there any sign that people placed in this position are put on the sort of pedestal which, Michels argued, is usually the fate of mass party leaders?

Bryce had a different perspective on party organisation: 'The chief thing is the selection of candidates.'[6] We must, therefore, ask: who selects the candidates, what sort of candidates are acceptable, what sanctions exist to ensure that candidates who are chosen do not present a disharmonious front to the electorate? What effect does this have on the distribution of power between the central leadership and the rank and file of militants?

This last question of the selection of candidates is then related to that of leadership as is the consideration of the place of policy. There are many examples of small left wing groups who are passionately concerned with the definition of a programme; even with the minutiae of a programme. In the same way, the early years of the SNP were full of bitter controversies. Where a party has grown from a tiny band of true believers to a mass organisation, concern for policy has often given way to the desire to build membership. Is this true of the SNP? Has the locus of policy making moved upwards or downwards? What organisational arrangements exist in the SNP for dealing with policy and what does this tell us about the party?

The theme which will be developed in this chapter is that the organisation of the SNP is one which is particularly open and ready to take a great deal of guidance from the grass roots. As in every other organisation, there are strong individuals who have tried to set the organisation on a particular way and who have met with opposition. What is noteworthy, is the extent to which the participation of the membership has been built into the structure. In this it is different, if only in degree, from other major British parties.

At the outset it is worth saying that the SNP has always had the organisation of a mass party as compared with, for example, that of a caucus party. Although it was to be forty years before it had a mass membership, the type of organisation which was set up assumed that its base would be upon a large proportion of the electors of Scotland. There is an interesting comparison in structure between, on the one hand, the SNP and its predecessor the National Party of Scotland, and the Scottish Party on the other. The last named was an excellent example of a caucus party.[7] It had no mass membership and made no attempt to recruit one. Instead it depended on the leadership of a small group of well-known people; they *were* the Scottish Party with the addition of a few supporters, mostly from the same class and background of public life. Where the NPS and the SHRA and even the SNL worked in terms of setting up a network of branches, the Scottish Party assumed that an appeal from public figures would attract votes at elections with the help of some *ad hoc* local support.

Why has the dominant model been of a mass party rather than a caucus party? In the first place there simply were not sufficient sympathetic 'public persons' of sufficient prestige to make a caucus party work. I have already referred to the fact that, although they had more political experience than the leaders of the NPS, the men of the Scottish Party were a 'third eleven' in their spheres of public life. Perhaps more important than this was the fact that the idea of a democratic or quasi-democratic mass party was the dominant model of the time. Even parties which had not started out as democratic mass parties were forced to assume some of the trappings of democracy. Conservative parties both in Britain and on the continent were, at this time, setting up divisional associations or their equivalent. The most direct reason of all, is the fact, again mentioned before, that most of the leaders of the NPS came from a Labour or ILP background. It seems quite clear that there was a diffusion of basic organisational ideas from the Labour or radical movement to the nationalist one. It is worth noticing that the SHRA even had an 'indirect' type of membership in trade union branches and co-operative societies which was, of course, taken directly from the example of the Labour Party. Duverger draws our attention to the fact that the idea of enrolling a mass membership and getting them to sign an undertaking to follow the aims of the party is a socialist invention as is the whole idea of a branch in which serious political topics are discussed.[8] This has been a feature of the Scottish nationalist organisations since the beginning. The aims have changed slightly but there has always been a requirement that members formally accepted them. Finally and most obviously, a nationalist party appeals to the nation. It must have the mass behind it in order to achieve its aims. Unless it assumes an extremely aristocratic view of leadership it will want to recruit all the nation into the nation's party.

The structure of the organisation

In order to understand the present organisation it is as well to refer to the early arrangements. Many existing features are explained by their origins rather than by contemporary demands. Perhaps the most striking of these is the nature of the basic unit of the SNP: the branch. In the other major parties, organisation is based on electoral divisions. The ward Labour party or branch is the unit which a new member joins. In the Conservative Party there are branches which cover areas smaller even than local government wards but these are not organisations with a major political job and meetings are infrequent and dedicated to social arrangements, money-raising and electoral activities. The SNP and its predecessors were organised before there was any hope of electoral success. The area covered by the grass roots organisation was determined, not by the boundaries of the seats to be won, but by the presence of activists and their feeling for the community to which they belonged. A branch might cover the whole city of Glasgow with thirteen constituencies or a small Fifeshire mining village which was only a fraction of a local government area. At election times *ad hoc* organisations were set up to fight constituencies but these seldom survived. When Ian Macdonald became National Organiser in 1961 it was on this model that he expanded the grass roots organisation of his party. We have already seen that he contacted activists wherever they were and persuaded many of them to set up local branches. An organisation of twenty members was entitled to be recognised as a branch if it was fully paid up. If there were less than twenty members, the organisation was regarded as a 'group' which had fewer rights in terms of elections to higher bodies. Macdonald encouraged large branches to split so that as many basic units existed as possible. He argued, as do many in the party today, that the branch structure leads to an intimacy and the encouragement of new members. In a small branch organisation it is much easier to pull people together to discuss policy, raise money and organise canvasses and leafletting.

It is very important to realise that the branch does perform these important functions. It is also the body which elects delegates to national conferences whereas in the Conservative and Labour Parties this is exclusively the job of the constituency associations. Furthermore, when the SNP has tried to evaluate its own performance it has done this not only in terms of votes and members but also in terms of branches. Thus, in a private memorandum to the National Executive Committee (NEC), John MacCormick outlined the situation after the Scottish Party and the NPS had amalgamated.[9] He listed 45 branches which were fully paid up and had the required number of members. This seems to have been a pre-war high. The number of branches seems to have tumbled until at the end of the 1950s some reliable sources have estimated that there were only 2 branches fully operational in the whole country. With the 1960s, once again branch numbers rose. In May 1962 there were 18 branches with 867 members recruited in that year. At the next conference in May 1963 there were 41 branches.[10] By 1965 there were 140 recognised branches; by December 1966, 205 with 42,000 members, and by December 1967, 484 branches with 125,000 members. At about this time the numbers of branches and members stabilised since the whole of Scotland was covered. In April 1969 the target of 500 branches was reached but it was also around this time that the party suffered a downturn in popularity probably as a result of the bad publicity given to the performances of SNP councillors after their spectacular victories in 1968. Many branches collapsed or were amalgamated. At the end of 1970 efforts were made to re-establish branches, and by March 1971, 518 branches were recognised with most of the lost ground made up.[11]

As the party grew stronger and it was easier to believe that it might win elections, some members recommended the reorganisation of the party so that the basic organisation would be the constituency party. The idea has been discussed at several conferences and sessions of National Council but the campaign to build up branches in the 1960s was too successful for this other structure to be attractive. The large mass membership has a loyalty to its branches which would be very difficult to disturb.

This does not mean that there is no constituency party organisation in the SNP. On the contrary, its importance is growing. As Rose points out we should expect this to happen in a growing party.[12] The first real pressures to replace the branch structure with one based on constituencies came in 1965 in a report of the Organisation Committee of the NEC.[13] In 1966 this was brought forward again but this time the proposal was more in the form of a recommendation that constituency parties should be built up to stand alongside the branches. This point of view was strongly endorsed by Billy Wolfe, who had come to prominence at a parliamentary by-election in 1962 in West Lothian and who was again a Parliamentary candidate. The older members of the NEC seem to have been keener on building up branch membership. Nevertheless, from 1966 onwards, there has been a successful campaign to establish SNP constituency organisations in every constituency. By the end of that year seventeen constituency organisations existed; by the end of 1967 there were organisations in every Scottish constituency but two. At the present, of course, every constituency is covered.

It is fair to say that the relation between the branches and the constituency might still change. It is the branches which raise party funds, distribute the *Scots Independent* and the *Newsletters* and do the canvassing. It may be that they are a hangover from the 'movement' phase of the SNP but they are extremely popular with the activists and, in a movement which is still crusading and looking for new converts, branches offer an intimacy which makes it possible to bring in neighbours and to know what is going on in the immediate area. The party relies on the branches for information about local events which might have a party significance such as factory closures or planning controversies. The branches contribute the greatest proportion of delegates to the annual conferences with two delegates for the first fifty members and one for each fifty members thereafter up to a maximum of ten. Constituency organisations have only one delegate each. National Council is also made up mainly of branch representatives. On the other hand, one has to say that the small scale of most branches leads to a kind of introspection which can be unhealthy. More and more the political role has been taken over by the constituency. One sign of this is that the National Assembly which, as we shall see, is the Scotland-wide organisation where policy is first discussed, is made up of constituency representatives; two from each constituency with the addition of the prospective parliamentary candidate. The constituency is obviously the body which discusses election tactics even for local government elections. The constituency itself is made up of equal numbers of delegates from each branch. The actual number depends on the number of branches and it is up to the constituency to decide but usually there are three or four delegates from each branch.

It is a measure of the increased importance of the constituency that this relatively new body exercises a degree of supervision over branches within its area. It has the responsibility for covering the whole of the division with branches and of showing that branches are working well. There is always an industrial organiser at constituency level and, if there are industrial organisers in the branches, they report to the constituency industrial organiser as well as to their own branches. Similarly, at an election, the constituency organiser often becomes the agent with branch organisers acting as sub-agents. Even outside election times it would be usual for the constituency organiser to pinpoint any weak spots in branch organisation or coverage and to try to remedy the situation. Constituencies also co-ordinate general policy within their areas. They are responsible for an annual report to headquarters listing branches and members

271

and making an assessment of the political situation. When all this is said, however, it is still true that the primary loyalty of the SNP member is to his branch and most of his activities are likely to be carried out in his branch. The constituency is more important than it was in the 1960s but the relationship between the two levels has now probably stabilised. Basic fund raising still remains the job of the branch and for the SNP this is particularly important.

There have always been intermediate arrangements between the branch and the central leadership. In the historical chapters we saw that there had been a South Eastern Federation of Branches which was expelled from the National Party of Scotland just before the merger with the Scottish Party. In the later 1930s and up to the end of the 1950s there were not sufficient members of branches to make an intermediate structure meaningful but it always seems to have been true that branches were in contact other than through the leadership. Although, as we shall see, leadership was fairly centralised in those years, branches still had enough independence to develop their own individuality and even to make alliances among themselves. In 1962 a system of area councils was set up and in 1967 this was changed to regional councils. When local government was reformed in 1972 a regional and district structure was inaugurated to parallel the local government divisions but these are not particularly important units. They are based on delegations from the branches and they meet monthly but are most important at election times.

Most political parties have an annual conference to determine policy or to rally the faithful. One characteristic of the national party ever since the NPS was set up in 1928 is that a National Council exists alongside Conference. In the early days there were at least two meetings of Council every year but now there are four every year. Broadly Council has the same function as Conference in making the final decisions about policy but it looks after such matters between the annual meetings of Conference. The very fact that there is such a regular means of consulting the membership is significant as compared with the infrequent and often ritualised meetings of other parties. Again it is significant in terms of contact with the grass roots that the bulk of the members of Council are from the branches. It consists of all the national office bearers elected at the annual conference, all members of the NEC and one delegate from each branch. In 1967 there was an attempt to add delegates from the constituencies but this was defeated.[14]

In terms of its broader representation and its right to appoint the officers of the party, Conference is the supreme body. There is no formal directive, however, which demands that the more important policies go to Conference and the less important areas to Council. In practice Council is the place where the more important policy decisions take place. Conference is very large and its meetings are complicated by the fact that they are social occasions where a great many people attend to see old friends. The type of people who turn up at Conference is also affected by the fact that expenses for attendance are not paid. They tend to be older and better-off. The branch or constituency meets expenses for attendance at Council or Assembly. Conference is now surrounded by a blaze of Press publicity and this also affects discussion. Up to the Oban conference in 1969 there was no attempt to impose strong platform guidance on SNP conferences. The motions for discussion were not selected with a view to creating the best press. This conference was a turning point. It took place just at the point when the party was experiencing a reverse. Whereas SNP gains and personalities had been front page news in 1967 and 1968, in 1969 SNP councillors had shown that several of them were not fully capable of fulfilling their functions. This also became front page news and the Press went into a phase of searching out the problems of nationalism. There were several incidents or debates which brought comment in the Press: one of them was the performance of the councillors and another was the party's employment policy. Afterwards it was decided that a tighter rein would have to be kept on debates. Before the Motherwell conference in 1976, however, there appears to have been a decision to open out discussion and the effect was marked. There was a vigorous debate on industrial policies and on devolution. The difference between this and the time of the Oban conference was, of course, that in 1976 the SNP was confident and expanding. Thus the party has gone back to its traditionally open method of dealing with policy.

It should not be thought, however, that Conference has now become the most important body dealing with policies. As I have already pointed out, in a body of this size—the Motherwell meeting had over two thousand attending—meaningful debate is difficult. Most people have come for the socialising or to speak on one or two topics which interest them particularly. One has to say that the vast bulk of the policy decisions are finally taken by National Council. Virtually every decision taken to Conference has first gone through

273

Council and it would proceed to Conference only if it was particularly controversial or it was felt to have particular, often symbolic importance. In the 1976 conference examples of this were the industry policies which were felt to represent a right-left split and the policy over devolution in which there was a general discussion throughout the party upon whether one ought to go gradually through the Scottish Assembly then being offered by the Labour government, or whether one ought to reject this and struggle for complete independence with no half-way houses. Such issues were so widely canvassed in the party that it would have been easy to have the final decision in Council. It is still true that in Council they had their most serious consideration.

The discussion of policy brings us to the National Assembly. In the mid-1960s the pressures of the expanding party were beginning to tell on the existing structure. In particular this was felt in the NEC. This body will be discussed later but, broadly speaking, it is the main small managing body of the party similar to the NEC of the Labour party. At this time it was expected to deal with policy as well as administrative matters and strategy. Given its size and the demands of the situation this was too heavy a burden and policy tended to be left out. The first proposal was to expand the NEC to 100 members. It was later agreed that the functions of the existing executive should be split. On the one hand there would be the NEC which would run the business of the party and make decisions on strategy or tactics subject to National Council or Conference. On the other hand there would be an entirely new body. This was to be called the National Executive Assembly (now called the National Assembly). This would be the body to discuss policy. Assembly receives reports from the policy committees covering a wide range of subjects. It considers them, often at great length, and they are then passed on to Council or Conference. Assembly does not make final decisions about any topic. It merely provides a forum for the preliminary discussion of policy. As such it has become a rather sophisticated political body. It is made up of two representatives from each constituency association. This again points to the important political role of the constituencies.

Finally we come to the National Executive Committee. This is a relatively small body meeting monthly and consisting of the office bearers and of members elected by the National Council at their first meeting after the annual conference. It carries on the work of the party from month to month and it is at the centre of a network of reports and calculations. Inevitably it is at the nerve centre of the party. Although it does not ignore policy it is not primarily concerned with it. As we have seen, National Assembly is the body which examines policy and makes recommendations to the final decision-making bodies: Council and Conference. The NEC is not concerned with the details of administration. On 22 December 1967 the General Business Committee was set up as a sub-committee of the NEC to look after administration: the staffing of headquarters, reviewing salaries, fund raising, membership and overseeing the work of the Finance, Organisation, Conference and Membership Committees. It is chaired by the Vice Chairman for Administration. The NEC does not have a formal remit, but in practice it exercises the functions of Council between meetings of Council. It keeps matters of policy under review even if it is policy in general terms. It supervises administration and it initiates the strategy and tactics of the party. There can be no doubt that this is an extremely important committee. One indication of its importance is that its recommendations to Council or Conference are seldom overturned. There is no record of any major recommendation of the executive being refused by Council or Conference. The full-time officials: National Organiser, Research Officers, Press Relations Officer and so forth are responsible to the NEC.

Finally in this formal review of the structure of the party, we come to the officers. They are elected at annual conferences. There is a President and three Vice Presidents. These are largely honorific positions in the sense that they are usually filled by people who have served the party in prominent positions for many years. In 1976 the President was Robert MacIntyre, the party's first MP (in 1945), and for many years their Chairman. While these people may not have a clearly defined function they undoubtedly act as elder statesmen and are regularly consulted. MacIntyre carries weight in the party, especially at Conference, and is still tireless in attending meetings and social events all over the country. It is important to say that these positions are not *solely* honorific. This was brought out clearly in 1963 when Gordon Wilson wrote a report on party structure. At that time it was by no means clear what was the division of functions between the Chairman and the President. By consulting the incumbents, Arthur Donaldson and Robert MacIntyre, Wilson elicited the opinion that the Chairman was the executive head of the party. This has been the position ever since.

There can be no doubt that the Chairman has a very heavy

burden. At one time (in 1967) there was some discussion about the possibility of a full-time Chairman but this idea was abandoned. One may contrast the position in the other parties where, in opposition or government, the Leader of the party is given facilities to devote himself to this work full-time. In the SNP however, both the Chairman and the National Secretary, again full-time in other parties, are people who have to earn their livings outside the party structure. This is also the case with the Senior Vice Chairman and the four Executive Vice Chairmen. These latter are elected at conferences and they are elected to specific responsibilities. In 1976 there were Executive Vice Chairmen for Organisation, Administration, Policy and Publicity but the specific remits have varied with the needs of the party. The system of Executive Vice Chairmen was started in 1964 on the basis of a recommendation in the Wilson report on party structure. At that time a number of committees existed for particular jobs but they were notoriously inactive. The system of appointing two, and then, in 1966, four Executive Vice Chairmen, was that particular individuals would be given responsibility for particular aspects of the party's work. In this aim the system has been successful. Each one usually works with a committee which he or she appoints. The Executive Vice Chairman for policy appoints a large number of committees to examine and present to the National Assembly policy documents in as many fields as seem appropriate. In 1976 there were twenty-three committees. This is the mechanism whereby policy is first formulated and again is an illustration of the open nature of decision-making in the party. The very number of committees indicates the extent to which large numbers of people in the party are involved. This is underlined by the fact that it is quite easy to become a member of a committee in which a party member is interested. Thus through the structure of policy committees and the National Assembly, the open nature of the SNP, in particular in its policy making role, is demonstrated.

The question of leadership

These are the bones of the organisation. It is now time to ask how it moves as a living political organism. It is most appropriate to say something first about leadership. A cursory reading of the classic texts such as Michels might suggest that the early days of mass parties were marked by openness and democracy but that, as parties grew, the leaders took on more and more of the job of direction. In the early days of the nationalist movement, this openness could be detected. Muirhead, Erskine and Gillies were leaders but there was an open debate about policy and strategy and no single man or woman was dominant: the movement could not even be described as being run by an oligarchy. After 1928, the situation changed. MacCormick became the leader both in terms of real influence, decisions and of his public prominence. There were several reasons for this. One was that he was available for the job. Running a political party is time consuming and there are few jobs which are compatible with it. As a solicitor, MacCormick was the master of his own time. At least as important was the fact that he was a man with his own ideas and an ability to manipulate others to achieve them. His immense ability as a speaker meant that he was able to command sessions of Conference and Council as well as public meetings and he used this ability very effectively. Whether one agrees with MacCormick's approach or not there is no doubt that, while he was the Secretary, the SNP was dominated by its leadership. Dalton points to the importance of friendship cliques in the early development of social movements.[15] As we saw above MacCormick worked very much in the context of a small group of friends who met daily for coffee or drinks to discuss politics and the tactics of the movement. He carried on this approach to leadership after he had left the SNP when he led Scottish Convention and the Scottish Covenant Association. He shared his ideas with people like John M. McNicol, Robert Gray and Dr John Macdonald but there is no doubt that he was the dominant figure among them. MacCormick was not tolerant of opposition. His most vocal opponents in the issue of the merger with the Scottish Party were expelled and other critics were excluded from positions of influence.

Thus in the 1930s and early 1940s one individual was the identifiable leader of the SNP. From 1942 until the end of the 1950s, power was still fairly well concentrated. It is worth re-emphasising that, from 1945 until about 1961, the SNP was a tiny organisation. Most of its best known members had gone with MacCormick into Scottish Convention. After 1945, however, there was one well-known leader: Dr Robert MacIntyre who had won Motherwell at a by-election. It was understandable that he should be recognised as the leader. It was not simply that MacIntyre was elected as Chairman but that he was a Chairman whom party members respected for his achievement. In a tiny organisation his parliamentary experience put MacIntyre beyond the other party figures in public esteem. There was another important contribution to the centralisation of power. With MacCormick most of those who believed in a gradualist approach to independence or Home Rule by political negotiations and strategy had left the party. Most of those remaining were 'true believers' who would fight hard to keep party doctrine pure. It was not surprising that the central leadership of the party should concern themselves with affairs in the branches to ensure that there should be no backsliding. Thus, while power in the party was centralised after 1942 as before, there were some differences. The main aim of the leaders after 1942 was to maintain the doctrine of the party. Secondly, MacIntyre did not seek to occupy the position of sole leader which had effectively been exercised by MacCormick. The SNP in the 1940s and 1950s was led by an oligarchy consisting of MacIntyre, Tom Gibson and Arthur Donaldson principally, with other figures such as Mary Dott and James Halliday. It is probably due to the fact that this small group of people demanded adherence to the idea of complete independence and constitutional means to achieve independence that the party was later able to build its success. They may have appeared restrictive and needlessly cautious but, had they not taken their strong stand, an entire new nationalist movement would have had to be built in the 1960s. The fact that the new movement had a base of organisation on which to build was due to these people and probably more than anyone else to MacIntyre.

With the beginning of the 1960s the situation changed. We have already seen that the party mushroomed in size and with this came a new informal structure. Whereas it had been fairly easy to control a tiny organisation, the established oligarchy of the SNP found the party flooded with new members. While their stand on party doctrine for twenty years made it clear what were the main policies of the party, there came to be wide discussion in the party over a whole range of topics. It would have been impossible for the leaders, even if they had wanted, to dictate the line on these topics. More than this, a whole set of new leaders suddenly came into the party. Billy Wolfe was unknown to the NEC when he was proposed as candidate for West Lothian in 1962 but within a year he was a member of this committee and by 1969 he was the Chairman of the party. Winnie Ewing, Margo Macdonald, Ian MacCormick were all young people who were not associated in the public mind with the SNP at the beginning of the 1960s but by the end of the decade they had become household names. As far as the informal organisation of the party was concerned, this meant that there was no longer an oligarchy able to control every step along the road. Instead, a large group of people came to prominence who often argued amongst themselves and saw no reason to deny that many vigorous debates took place in the party at all levels. As compared with the SNP in the 1950s, today's party is more open. In part this is due to the explosion in size and the related fact that the party now contains a wider spectrum of views on the future of Scotland. In the same way, while it may have been possible to control what was going on in a dozen branches, supervision of more than 500 is an entirely different question. Probably the debate over party policy towards the BBC helped members to realise that it was possible to disagree on a major issue and still remain together. Eldersfeldt describes the party system in Detroit as a 'stratarchy'.[16] While it is not true that the SNP has such a number of distinct power bases as might exist in United States parties with their machines and caucuses, it is still true that one could describe the SNP as a 'mutual deference structure'. There is a great deal of independence among the branches *vis-à-vis* the officers of the party and this is shown in the general attitude to the leaders. In an introductory chapter, I have already noted that the SNP, unlike populist movements, had not placed one leader on a pedestal. It is certainly true that many of the well-known figures are popular and are cheered at Conference or National Council. On the other hand, it cannot be said that any one member of the party is the leader whose guidance the party would unhesitatingly accept. To some extent this situation exists because there are two major alternative sources of power: the NEC including the national office bearers, and the parliamentary party. On the other hand, this situation existed before there was a parliamentary party. Perhaps because of the memory of the MacCormick domination, perhaps because the SNP is a new party in terms of its members and considers no members better than others, perhaps because of the democracy of Scottish society where few have been affluent enough to be very far set apart from their fellows, one cannot describe the SNP as a party built on a charismatic or unquestioned leadership. Duverger gives an example of leadership of this type when he describes the Communist Party in France running a membership campaign in which voters were asked to pledge themselves to 'the party of Maurice Thorez'.[17] It is unthinkable that SNP voters would pledge themselves to 'the party of William Wolfe'. Whatever the reasons one has to say that the development of the SNP into a mass party has made for more openness and participation in the structure rather than less. The contests for the leading positions are genuinely open and are fought at each annual conference. The Chairman is regarded as an equal and no special arrangements are made to give him a special status in the party other than that democratically given him at his election. In the discussion of policy or tactics neither the Chairman nor any other leader's views are automatically accepted. At Conference and National Council the reports of the Chairman, the parliamentary leader and the other officers are often fiercely debated and are not regarded as statements to be accepted automatically with acclamation.

As a footnote to this discussion of the leadership it is appropriate to note the relationship between the NEC and the officers on one hand and the parliamentary party on the other. MPs are entitled to attend the NEC and up to ten can be present at meetings of the National Council. In practice attendance is much slighter. The leader of the parliamentary group rarely attends the NEC. Two members of the NEC travel to London about once a month during the parliamentary session to meet the MPs and there is daily telephone contact especially between the Chairman and members of the parliamentary party. Despite some attempts by the Press to suggest that there have been arguments, there is no real evidence of serious controversy between the two sides. It may be that, if the SNP takes power in a Scottish Assembly, the parliamentary group there will capture power in the party. At the moment the Westminster MPs certainly do not have this status. It is significant that political broadcasts are not handled chiefly by MPs and the real debate in the party takes place outside the ranks of the parliamentarians.

The selection of candidates

Despite the relative importance of the parliamentary party in the SNP, the method of selecting candidates still tells us a great deal about the distribution of power in a party and its attitude towards politics. Once again we see the openness of the Nationalists and the degree to which as many party activists as possible are brought into the process of selection.

Any member who is interested in becoming a parliamentary candidate or who has been persuaded to stand, writes to the Election Committee. The individuals concerned are then interviewed, usually over a weekend, and the Election Committee then recommends acceptance or refusal to the NEC of which it is a sub-committee. If the NEC accepts the member, his or her name is put on a list which is circulated to all branches and constituency associations. Up to this point the leadership acts as a gatekeeper and it is progressively more careful about the people who are admitted to the list. There have been several cases in the past of candidates who have been incompetent and others who have been involved in splinter groups. Like all radical movements the SNP attracts people who are unbalanced or who have clandestine associations. It is one of the successes of the leadership that they have kept the numbers in these categories to a minimum.

The first stage in selecting a candidate takes place when the constituency secretary writes to all branches in the constituency asking for nominations. Branches can nominate as many candidates from the list as they like. From them the constituency forms a short list if this is necessary and members on this often go around the branches addressing them or answering questions. In addition to this there is a constituency meeting which all members in the constituency can attend. The branches then meet to decide on their preferences and their delegates to the constituency are mandated on their branch's choice. In some cases an alternative choice is made in case the first choice is eliminated at an early stage and constituency delegates are mandated for the second choice as well. Candidates are then chosen by a simple majority vote by the constituency party made up, in the usual way, of branch delegates.

It seems clear from the description of this procedure that the SNP, as I suggested earlier, involves more of its members in the selection of parliamentary candidates than is true of the Labour or Conservative Parties. Both of these, like the SNP, make up a candidate list and the leadership maintains control over it. On the other hand the National Executive of the SNP does not direct constituencies which candidate to select. In by-elections the NEC has the power to name a candidate because of the need for swift action but this is always done in consultation with the constituency party and there is no record of a conflict on this issue. In the other parties the actual selection of the candidate is done by the constituency party without any general consultation of the general membership except in so far as they are represented by their delegates to the constituency party. There is no procedure whereby all the membership are formally consulted as in the SNP nor even an arrangement whereby all the members have the opportunity to meet the members on the short list.

Part Three

Finance

We turn now to another aspect of party organisation which illustrates the importance of the grass roots organisations in the SNP: the raising of finance. In discussing the relation between the branch and constituency party I pointed out that the basic fund raising body was the branch. Although attempts have been made to make the constituency the central fund raising unit, this has not been accepted.[18]

There is no doubt that since the life of the party was in the branches, they were able to run the normal sort of activities: jumble sales, dances, socials and so forth. If there had been nothing more the party would have been much poorer than it is but the financial base would still have been in the branches. In fact there was a great deal more in the form of Alba Pools.

Alba Pools was launched on 4 January 1965 and very soon became immensely successful. By March it was being used by sixty branches and there was a weekly sale of 6,000. Prize money totalling £120 was paid out and there was a regular income to headquarters. In the first twenty weeks of operation there was a total income of £3,000 to the branches and £1,000 to headquarters. By the end of 1966, 32,000 tickets were printed weekly, of which about 70 per cent were regularly sold. In June 1972 it was calculated that, since the beginning, Alba Pools had brought in £65,000 to headquarters and a great deal more than this to the branches.[19] There is no doubt that the peak years were 1968 and 1969 and, by the time this estimate was made, income from this source had begun to decline. Changes in the law and large increases in the cost of postage and stationery made it less attractive, but its major contribution was to build up party funds in the critical years of the 1960s. More than this, the party unit which was built was the branch.

Although, as we have seen, the level of income from Alba Pools is now much lower, it is still true that the branches have no rivals as centres of financial support for the party. Whereas the Labour Party has the trade unions and the Conservatives have contributions from the management or ownership of industry, for the Nationalists there is only income from individual members fed in through their branches. In terms of Duverger's discussion of the role of finance in party structure we would have to say that the SNP was by far the most 'mass orientated' political movement in Scotland. Since concentration of these mass contributions is at the low level of the branch, the financial base of the movement is very much at the grass roots. Just as in 1964 when constituencies were being inaugurated, there was an attempt to make constituencies the major fund raising body, so in 1969 there was an attempt to make branches hand over to constituency parties for elections all but what was necessary for their own running expenses.[20] This was not successful. There are several implications of their distribution of financial power. One of the most striking is the unwillingness of the branches to commit money to build up party headquarters. I have already commented that, compared with other parties, there was a much smaller proportion of full-time senior headquarters staff. Another indication is that, if there is a need for money, the party leaders must carry along the branches by persuading them that it is necessary. In mounting any of the campaigns which the SNP has organised; the oil campaign for example, the funding has been done by a levy on the branches. Such a technique was only successful because of the informal consultation with branches which secured their co-operation.

The industrial structure of the party

If the SNP cannot depend on the trade unions for money, industrial organisation is a major consideration for the party. Any study of the organisation or policy of the party must take account of what the party has done to move into this area.

There are several reasons why this is particularly important for the SNP. One is that several important party members are on the left or are radical on issues of industry and employment. Thus, Billy Wolfe, the Chairman of the party, has always taken an interest in these matters and was a supporter of a special association together with other trade unionists: the Association of Scottish Nationalist Trade Unionists. Margo Macdonald has also been active in meeting industrial workers and even those who are not automatically associated with left wing ideas, like Gordon Wilson, have supported these initiatives. This is a tradition which goes back into the history of the party. There were many members in the 1920s and 1930s who had been in the ILP or who were sympathetic to working class needs in general, but the party in the 1960s has made an effort to organise this concern in an effective way. The reasons for the change are, of course, that there are now leaders in the party who appear to have these organisational skills. At least as important is the realisation that, if the SNP is going to win a majority in Scotland, it must take a

283

large number of industrial seats. Scotland has a manual working class population which is proportionally larger than that of England. Moreover this social group is particularly important in the major centre of Scottish population: the industrial west central belt. In the immediate past the effect of this has been that Scotland has been a Labour stronghold and towns like Glasgow, Paisley, Dumbarton and the semi-urbanised areas like Lanarkshire have been overwhelmingly socialist. The distribution of parliamentary seats in the Scottish population ensures that the Nationalists must break this western Labour stronghold if they are to win a majority of seats in Scotland. At the moment it is the Labour Party which is overwhelmingly the party of the Scottish manual working class. To achieve their objective the SNP has to become an alternative working class party in Scotland. It is this which makes their concern for industrial affairs and industrial organisation so important.

There is no doubt that the party is committed to building up an industrial organisation. At the same time there are Nationalists who are uneasy. The SNP in Glasgow has always had a reputation of being rather more based on a working class membership. Before the war, when the party was based in Glasgow, there were conflicts with for example the Edinburgh branch, which were partly founded on this issue. It is important not to underestimate the influence, direct and indirect of the Fianna na h-Alba on the Glasgow membership. This was almost exclusively based on working class boys. In the tiny organisation which the SNP was at that time, the proportion coming from the Fianna was not inconsiderable and, even where there was no direct link, the 'rebel' atmosphere of the Fianna was fairly strong. The class composition of the city is a sufficient explanation for the fact that the party in Glasgow was more working class than in the east or the north. As the party increased its support in Scotland, the importance of the Glasgow organisation with the headquarters and the old branches slipped away. Suspicion of Glasgow is a feature of Scottish life, and it may have been part of the reason why the headquarters of the party was moved from Glasgow to Edinburgh. What is certainly true is that there has been a subsequent and very marked attempt to rectify the balance between east and west. By the facts of geography, the industrial organisation of the SNP has concentrated its main attention to the West.

One of the first attempts to attract industrial workers to the SNP was the Association of Scottish Nationalist Trade Unionists (ASNTU). This was set up in January 1965, mostly on the initiative of William Johnson of Clydebank, and has the status of an organisation affiliated to the party. The aim was to encourage SNP members to take part in the normal duties of their trade union branches and to advise the party on industrial conditions. Despite the support of Billy Wolfe, it has not been a success. Part of the reason may have to do with personalities, in that the individuals who started it do not seem to have had sufficient contacts with trade unionists. They also appear to have dominated the organisation. For whatever reason there has been little increase in the membership since the beginning. There was an attempt in 1972 by the ASNTU to set up district committees but this too was unsuccessful.[21]

In 1975 a new type of industrial organisation was established.[22] It was resolved to support a trade union and industrial officer to be a senior member of staff reporting, like other senior members of staff, to the NEC executive. At the same time it was decided to tidy up the constituency and branch organisations for dealing with industrial matters. At the moment, every constituency has an industrial organiser and there are often industrial organisers in branches too. The latter report to the constituency industrial organiser as well as to the branches.

Both the headquarters organisation and that of the grass roots organisation have to be seen in the context of the policy to recruit industrial workers. The change of emphasis from the ASNTU is important. The Association encouraged ordinary branch members who happened to be trade unionists to be more active in their trade unions. One reason for its failure may have been that the SNP activist, whether a trade unionist or not, is usually busy on the normal political activities of leafletting, canvassing and so forth. The new organisation concentrates much more on the industrial situation itself.

The system works from the top down and the bottom upwards. The industrial officer sends each constituency industrial organiser a list of all establishments in his area employing more than one hundred workers. In turn the local industrial organiser keeps headquarters informed about the industrial situation in his area. From 1975 a new tear-off section of the membership card is filled out when the year's subscription is paid. It includes information on the trade union, type of work done and the place of work, so that there is a record of all the industrial associations of SNP members. Clearly this is much more systematic than the voluntary nature of the ASNTU.

Having identified those members who are trade unionists they are encouraged to attend trade union branch meetings and to stand as shop stewards and conveners. Since branch meetings are badly attended and since most workers would consider it a chore to be a shop steward it is relatively easy to have some success in this field. The movement also aims at the recruitment of existing shop stewards and conveners. It is unlikely that recruitment would be successful at higher levels since such a person would be on the first steps of the ladder of professional trade unionism and, as such, would be firmly tied into the Labour or the Communist Party network. It is then, at the lowest level of trade union organisation that the effort has been directed and this is now done through a new organisation: the industrial group. This is, perhaps, the most direct organisational indication that the party's emphasis in its industrial policy has moved. Instead of being interested in industrial matters through attracting people into party branches, the party has now gone to the work place to organise there. It should not be taken from this that the SNP is moving to a cell organisation of the type described by Duverger.[23] The basic organisation is still the branch and the groups are not used for discussion on policy matters other than, occasionally, for a discussion on the particular conditions under which they work. On the contrary, groups operate during election times and during campaigns in order to mobilise members to distribute leaflets and do the basic jobs in their work places. On the other hand, the existence of an industrial group does mean that members are encouraged to attend their trade union meetings and identify themselves as SNP members; if only by handing out a pamphlet, and other trade unionists recognise that there are SNP members working alongside them who are prepared to be active in union activity. There is, of course, a similar Conservative organisation of trade unionists. It is in a different position from that of the SNP organisation; first, in that there is much greater sympathy of workers for nationalist propaganda and secondly, in the fact that the Conservative organisation is not really used for work place activity.

The SNP also encourages its trade union members to attend trades councils. This too is an opportunity for publicity since trades councils are important platforms. They often organise industrial campaigns and demonstrations themselves but, as in the case of union branch meetings, these are not well attended. A few SNP spokesmen can make a considerable impact. The system of industrial groups and activity on trades councils is still in its infancy but, because of their importance in recruiting the industrial votes, they are likely to develop.

The industrial groups are not the only industrial activity of the SNP. Indeed, they are in their infancy compared with other activities of the party. A number of 'industrial campaigns' have been run including one on shipbuilding and another on oil. These have been successful in bringing publicity. The whole concentration on industrial matters has had a pay-off in the extent to which trade unionists now seem ready to contact the SNP on issues such as the loss of jobs, or generally in the resolution of industrial disputes. The shop stewards at the Marathon oil rig building yard on the Clyde approached the SNP when they feared that the only way to get an order for a new rig was to persuade the government to intervene. Similarly stewards at the Dalzell Works of the British Steel Corporation approached the party when they suspected that their plant was to be run down in favour of lower cost mills at Scunthorpe and on Teesside. Other meetings with shop stewards have included those at Rolls Royce in East Kilbride, Weir's of Cathcart, Babcock and Wilcox and many others. In all, the practice of turning to the party in such circumstances seems to have become a regular pattern. This is certainly not to argue that the stewards involved are all joining the SNP. The majority of them probably regard the party in a purely instrumental way. Nevertheless, with a little judicious publicity, it probably has the effect of increasing sympathy for the party. This was admitted in a statement by Hugh d'Arcy, the Communist Chairman of the Scottish Trade Union Congress who, while in a delegation to safeguard Scottish jobs, told government representatives that if things continued as they were there would be little that could be done to prevent workers voting for the SNP in overwhelming numbers.[24]

The other associations

The ASNTU is not the only organisation associated with the SNP, but the others are like it in not being of great importance, at any rate for the moment.

The Fletcher Society takes its name from Fletcher of Saltoun who was one of the best known and most effective opponents of the Union in 1707. It was founded in 1974 by a number of people among whom Professor David Simpson of the University of Strathclyde and

Professor Tom MacRae of the University of Bradford were prominent.

Its aims are 'to promote research, discussion and publication of policy alternatives regarding an independent Scotland'. This last aim is implemented by the publication of Fletcher of Saltoun Papers of which there have been, up to now, five.[25]

The Fletcher Society is independent of the party, its only formal link being that its office bearers, but only its office bearers, must be party members. It meets monthly and frequently invites speakers who are not party members. It does not exist, therefore, as a group within the SNP with a particular line of its own as, for example, the Bow Group or the Fabian Society sometimes express group views. The Fletcher Paper views are those of their authors alone. At the end of 1976 there were some 200 members.

The Federation of Student Nationalists is rather different from the Fletcher Society in that it is an affiliated organisation with representatives on the National Council and the right to put down resolutions at Conference. In view of the great part which the Glasgow University Student Nationalists played in the 1920s and the traditional place of students in nationalist movements, it is necessary to say that this is not a strong organisation. Nationalism is not strong among the Scottish students; the causes of Mao, Trotsky and even Stalin seem to be rather better subscribed.

Although there have been various attempts to create nationalist youth groups both inside and outside the SNP, the party now is firmly against a Young Nationalist type of organisation. Most members are sensible of the embarrassments caused to the Labour Party by the Young Socialists. There is an organisation called the Young Scots but there are few branches and there is no suggestion that it should be built into a youth wing. It is more in the form of a club for children attracted to the nationalist movement rather than for teenagers and those in their early twenties.

In a similar way there is no women's organisation in the SNP. This has been suggested at various times but never accepted. There is SWIFT: Scottish Women's Independence Fund Trust, but this is purely a money raising device.

Conclusion

The third strand in my explanation of the SNP's rise was the effectiveness of their organisation. It is not easy to demonstrate this.

Nevertheless I have, in these last four chapters, shown the weakness of early organisation and the ways in which this has been strengthened since 1960. A great deal of attention has been paid to organisation and this seems to have paid off. It is significant that in Glasgow where organisation is weakest the party strength is also at its lowest ebb. In Glasgow there are still several constituencies with only one branch in them and Glasgow has been the hardest place to increase Nationalist support. It is not a necessary part of my argument to say that this is always a cause and effect relationship but the co-existence of these two conditions is striking. Table 14.1, prepared for the NEC, shows the relationship between performance at the 1966 election and the development of branches in the constituencies. It is significant that it is in the constituencies with the most branches that deposits were saved and in other constituencies where the party did not contest but later won, there was a higher than average number of branches: in Hamilton, East Dunbartonshire and Argyll, for example.

Table 14.1   Numbers of branches in constituencies

Constituency	No. of branches
Not contested in 1966	
Glasgow, Bridgeton	1
Cathcart	1
Central	—
Gorbals	—
Govan	1
Hillhead	1
Kelvingrove	1
Pollok	1
Provan	1
Scotstoun	1
Paisley	1
Greenock	1
Renfrewshire, East	1
Renfrewshire, West	—
Coatbridge and Airdrie	1
Bothwell	1
Hamilton	4
Motherwell	2

289

Table 14.1 Numbers of branches in constituencies (continued)

Constituency	No. of branches
Ayr	1
Bute and North Ayrshire	4
Central Ayrshire	2
Kilmarnock	1
South Ayrshire	2
Galloway	—
Edinburgh, Central	—
East	1
Leith	1
North	1
Pentlands	—
West	2
Berwick and East Lothian	1
Roxburgh, Selkirk and Peebles	1
Dundee East	—
Dundee West	—
Angus, South	1
Angus, North and Mearns	—
Aberdeen North	1
Aberdeen South	—
Aberdeenshire, West	—
Moray and Nairn	3
Banff	2
Argyll	3
Inverness	4
Ross and Cromarty	2
Western Isles	1
Caithness and Sutherland	1
Orkney and Zetland	—

Deposit lost 1966

Glasgow, Craigton	2
Maryhill	1
Shettleston	1
Springburn	1
Woodside	1
Rutherglen	2

Table 14.1   Numbers of branches in constituencies (continued)

Constituency	No. of branches
Lanark	4
Dunbartonshire, East	4
Edinburgh, South	1
Aberdeenshire, East	3
Deposit saved in 1966	
Dunbartonshire, West	4
Dumfries	6
Stirlingshire, West	7
Clackmannan and East Stirling	6
West Lothian	9
Midlothian	10
Dunfermline	3
Kirkcaldy	3
Fife, West	4
Fife, East	7
Kinross and West Perthshire	8
Perth and East Perthshire	3

When all is said and done, however, this chapter is rather more speculative than the others. It is worth while re-emphasising a few things.

The first is the branch structure which has proved to be peculiarly suited as an instrument for attracting community support. The SNP is a party whose strength comes from social contacts and these activities are centred more effectively on the branch than they would be on the larger and less community-oriented parliamentary constituency.

Secondly, while the branch is an excellent unit for mobilising support, it is not immediately useful at election times. It was inevitable, with the electoral success of the past, that there should have been a desire to reflect electoral geography in party organisation. That this has not been carried to its logical conclusion is a reflection of the grass roots base of the movement and the strength of its grass roots organisation. This is closely related to the open style of decision making in the party. It cannot be denied that there are influential members and that the members of central bodies like the

NEC and the National Council are very much more important than the rank and file activist. On the other hand these points of decision are more accessible to the SNP member than are the equivalent organisations in other parties as I hope I have shown.

The third point concerns the efforts which the party has made to develop an industrial base. The SNP realises that it can only be successful if it captures the industrial west and its efforts in this direction show a strong sense of political awareness.

Finally the party could not have arrived at the present situation had it not been for the financial base which was built up through Alba Pools and other lesser money raising ventures.

In all, the organisation has in the past been a major ingredient in the SNP's recipe for success and in the future this seems likely to continue.

15 Conclusion

In this short concluding chapter I shall restate my explanation of the rise of the SNP vote in the light of the historical and other data which I have put forward. I shall also deal briefly with one or two recent discussions of the subject.

There are two broad types of theory to account for the rise of this nationalist movement. One attributes the rise to conditions obtaining over Britain as a whole or even in Europe: the decline of the left, the crisis of imperialism, the collapse of the two party system. There are many possibilities. On the other hand there are those theories which attribute the situation to the rise of national consciousness in Scotland, which, in turn, has led to a demand for national self-determination. My position is that a satisfactory explanation requires the conjunction of both of these approaches.

Evidence for the growth of alienation from the existing British political system can be had from many sources. I have quoted several of them in this book. This is not to argue that Britain is on the edge of a revolution, but it is an undeniable fact that the major parties have lost the virtual hegemony which they once had and that major institutions such as Parliament and the Civil Service no longer enjoy the same public esteem as they once did. All this is linked, no doubt, with the loss of imperial grandeur. It also appears to be connected with Britain's sad economic performance and the inability of politicians of any party to deal with the situation. Among those who supported the Labour Party in order to improve their position there seems to have been a particularly high level of disillusion. Thus the people who had once put their trust in the main political parties or who had thought that the British system was the best in the world, were now faced with unavoidable evidence of decline. Where once it had been in their material interest to support British institutions, this was no longer self-evident.

It was, however, not just the economic or imperial position of Britain which had changed. Another 'Britain-wide' movement must also be taken into account. Whereas in the years before 1939 some of the old respect for authority and the traditional ruling class still lingered, the Second World War and the advent of a strong Labour government greatly reduced the status of the traditional leaders. Their position had, of course, been eroded long before this but the years after 1945 saw a further weakening of respect for the traditional order. A rather more open society grew up in which opportunity for the gifted child was at least perceived to be more open, and with this went a new self-confidence for people in the lower ranks of society. This was one contributor to the process of modernisation in British society. This self-confidence gained official recognition in, for example, the modern planning orthodoxy which emphasises the appearance if not the reality of participation. In the 1960s and 1970s it led to various schemes for community councils and schools councils and student participation, all of which were supposed to consult the interests of those concerned at grass roots level. The movement for grass roots participation and the rise of nationalism were both children of the 1960s. Both suggest that there was an awakened interest in involvement with decision making, especially in one's own community.

This explanation for the rise of nationalism is all very well so far as it goes. As I argued earlier, it does not account for the rise of a nationalist movement in Scotland, because it only explains why voters turned away from the old institutions, particularly the parties. We still have to explain why they should turn to precisely this new form of political expression. In the second part of this book I have illustrated the ways in which Scotland became a more important social and political entity for the Scottish people in this century. In the years up to the First World War, the main political identity which people in Scotland undoubtedly had was that of being British. The explanation given above only suggests why the strength of this identification and others, such as that with the working class, may have declined. It was the major function of the second part of the book to suggest that there were also 'positive' reasons why it was specifically the Scottish identification which was the beneficiary.

It has to be said first of all that the Scottish identity was always recognised by the Scots although its political implications in the sense of self-government for the nation were not recognised or supported. Secondly, as I have shown in the short discussion of Scottish history, there were always institutions such as the Church and the educational system which would have provided the basis for a rebirth of nationalist feeling. Indeed one of the puzzles which it is outside the scope of this book to tackle is why, given the existence of this 'basic equipment of the nation', Scottish nationalism did not emerge in the nineteenth century along with Polish, Bohemian and other nationalist movements. In the mid-twentieth century, however, the existence of these institutions and of a distinctive popular culture helps us to understand why the identity of Scotland as a distinctive unit within the United Kingdom was preserved.

But to understand this is not enough. This foundation of institutions and social practices had, after all, existed for centuries. What happened in the 1950s and 1960s to make so many Scotsmen identify politically with Scotland rather than with a social class? Despite the tenor of a great deal of Marxist and socialist writing, there was nothing automatic about the fact that so many voters from the poorer sections of society or from among manual workers should find their primary identification in a social class. They might equally seek it in a religious group or in a much more restricted economic stratum: skilled workers as against unskilled. These loyalties have, after all, been characteristic of other countries.

In the second part of this book I have, therefore, tried to suggest the ways in which Scottish voters were persuaded that their primary political identification was with Scotland rather than as 'working men and women' or as those 'with a stake in society' or any other group. In exactly the same way the working class had to be persuaded of the primacy of its class membership over other ties; without this, Labour and socialist parties would have achieved no success. What has to be studied is the nature of the change in this self-image.

In Chapter 14 I have pointed to the very important role played by organisation. Whereas the machines of the Conservative and Labour parties were run-down and undermanned in the 1960s, the SNP managed to put together a first rate workforce. It is, however, no denigration of this organisation to say that it alone cannot explain

295

the growth of the SNP vote. It was necessary for the organisers to have a starting point. My contention is that this starting point was provided by the growing awareness that their feeling of Scottish identity could have political implications. In Chapters 4 to 6 I have pointed out some of the ways in which this happened. When one looks at the picture presented there, there is no inevitability about the process. It might well be that a nationalist movement would have taken off without precisely the conjunction of circumstances described, but I have argued that several elements were responsible for making the SNP vote as strong as it became.

One important feature which contributed to the situation was the operation of the Scottish Press and television. The arrival of Scottish Television (STV) meant that more Scottish material was presented and with it more Scottish news and current affairs. Partly forced by this, the BBC also increased the amount of coverage which was given to Scottish affairs. As a secondary effect, when the SNP victories at Hamilton and Govan came along they were given extensive treatment and this increased the impact of these events.

This press and television presentation of Scottish affairs certainly helped to make people aware of the political side of Scottish identification but it was not a primary cause and it did not work alone. Why should the media take more interest in Scotland? One of the most important reasons for their renewed interest lay in the economic disaster which overtook Scotland after the First War. In Chapter 5 I have shown how there gradually came about a realisation that the situation in Scotland was particularly bad. Government intervention was demanded and schemes were developed to encourage the Scots to help themselves. The studies which were done by Bowie and others, and the activities of such bodies as the Scottish Economic Committee and Tom Johnston's organisations, all contributed to this awareness of Scotland as an economic and political unit.

The major factor contributing to a consciousness in Scotland was, therefore, an awareness of a particularly bad economic situation in Scotland. Immediately after the end of the First World War there seems to have been little attempt on the part of the Press, the government, or even those affected, such as the trade unionists and the industrialists, to present the problem as, in particular, a Scottish one. For various reasons, including the activities of academics like Bowie and industrialists like Weir, who were certainly not nationalists, the situation came to be perceived as a Scottish one. Although the people whom we have just mentioned did not advocate a solution in terms of home rule or independence, they did concentrate the attention of the interested public on its Scottish aspects.

A further process reinforced this perception. Whereas at the beginning of the century governments had not believed that they could affect the economy, by the 1930s attempts were being made to mount some minimum programme for the diminution of unemployment. It gradually became a commonplace that the state of the economy was in some sense the responsibility of the government. When the British economy in general and the Scottish economy in particular did not seem to respond to various sorts of treatment prescribed by various sorts of government, the governments themselves were held to be incompetent. When economic policy started to have a regional aspect and when one of these regions was Scotland with, by this time, a well articulated public opinion, the stage was set for regional politics. In Smelser's terms this process can be seen as the creation of a generalised belief system. As such it provided one basis for the growth of nationalism.

There is another social process which has to be mentioned. There had been economic disasters in Scotland before the First World War, and in the 1920s and 1930s although economic conditions were worse the nationalist organisations nevertheless put up a poor performance. I believe that one of the crucial factors which contributed to the later success of Scottish nationalism was the modernisation which took place after the Second World War. Many writers on modernisation write as if it were a process which started with the introduction of the industrial and social processes characteristic of Britain in the nineteenth century and ceased when the old peasant society had been relegated to a minor position in the economy. In practice, modernisation is a process which goes on all the time. The traditional nineteenth century industries gave way to those based on a new technology and this in turn may lead to a whole series of different life styles. Such a process occurred in Scotland, admittedly in very restricted areas, to a lesser extent than in England, but we can observe the development classically in such areas as the new towns. The collapse of the old industries meant that, through no choice of the workers, their life styles had to change. More important than this, however, was the fact that, even in the slower changing Scottish conditions, massive alterations were taking place. Although there was poverty it was not grinding poverty for any except the very few. The National Health Service meant that the sick were cared for in a humane way and lack of money was a smaller barrier to medical care than it had been before the war. Perhaps most important of all, the Education Acts created a situation in which there was much more opportunity for an able child to get the training and education he or she needed without too much attention to his or her economic situation. There were still massive problems. The poor still were not able to take as much advantage of their opportunities as those who were better off but there was a great improvement over the situation which had existed before the war.

What these circumstances seemed to breed was a self-confidence among many Scots and a feeling that their opinions were worth listening to. If the old political organisations were not able to produce an improvement then one should not be afraid to try new solutions. It would be ridiculous to suggest that such people were the norm among Scots in the 1950s and 1960s, but they were there in sufficient numbers to start the move towards nationalism.

Before ending this chapter I feel it is very important to clear two misconceptions about the rise of nationalism in Scotland. Both of them have been referred to in the Press and by politicians, but they have also been present in the academic discussion and it is to this that I should like to address myself.

In an excellent series of essays, Tom Nairn distinguishes between the old and the new Scottish nationalism.[1] He identifies the rise of the present nationalist wave as a result of 'uneven development' and suggests that the arrival of North Sea oil brought about a process of capitalist exploitation in Scotland to which the rise of nationalism was a reaction.

Nairn's argument is complicated and suggestive and does, therefore, deserve to be explored. The bases for his thinking about nationalism are partly Marxist and partly developments of some points made by Ernest Gellner. Nairn is concerned to present a materialist rather than an idealist explanation for the rise of this movement in Scotland. In order to do this he points to the perception of economic position on the part of those who might join the nationalist movement:[2]

The *real* point has always lain in the objective fact that, manifestly one nationality has never been even remotely as good as, or equal to, the others which figure in its world view. Indeed the purpose of the subjectivity (nationalist myths) can never be anything other but protest against the brutal fact: it is mobilisation against the unpalatable, humanly unacceptable truth of grossly uneven development.

The key to Nairn's approach is uneven development. As far as the comparison between Scotland as a whole and England as a whole is concerned his argument is undoubtedly valid, but why should uneven development form the basis of a nationalist movement? Nairn argues that, in the collapse of the ex-imperialist state, it is the 'smaller nationalities [who] have lost faith in the old state long before its social opposition. More rapidly and decisively than either the mainstream English intellectuals or the English working class, they have acknowledged the genuinely predictable verity of British state history', because they have an 'alternative historical reality and a potentially different vision of things'.[3]

There is nothing wrong with Nairn's argument as far as it goes. The problem is that he does not explain the situation fully enough. The Scottish people had an alternative view of history and social reality long before nationalism became strong. Why did it suddenly take on a political significance? It is not enough to argue that the British state is foundering, because, as I pointed out in Chapter 2, the reaction to this collapse of the old institutions could have taken many forms other than that of support for Scottish nationalism. I have argued that since the beginning of the century, slowly and in a non-political way at first, Scottish interest in Scotland itself has grown, and it is a major part of my argument that the present political situation cannot be understood except in terms of these diverse processes and events. Nairn, on the other hand, puts forward an argument in terms of what he calls 'neo-nationalism'.[4]

It still poses a threat (or more exactly, a combined promise *and* threat) of modernisation, 'imperialistic' disruption of old ways and so on. But this now occurs at a far more advanced stage of general development, in areas which long ago emerged from the absolute 'backwardness' just referred to. Located on the fringe of the new metropolitan growth zones, they suffer from a relative deprivation and are increasingly drawn to political action against this. This action is analogous to old style nationalism, above all in its ideology. But, precisely because it starts from a higher level and belongs to a more advanced stage of capitalist evolution—to the age of multinationals and the effective internationalisation of capital—its real historical foundation will be different. The impact of the oil industry on

Scotland and of the US multinationals on the French *Midi* is
provoking a new Scottish and Occitanian separatism.

It may be that Scottish nationalism has many new features but it
is impossible to explain its rise by appealing to the activities of
multinational oil companies. The table in Chapter 1 shows quite
clearly that the growth of the SNP vote started well before 1971, the
year in which the public first learned that oil exploration was going
on in the North Sea. It is arguable that the discovery of oil speeded
the movement to the nationalists, but it certainly did not spark it off,
however convenient this argument is for the logic of neo-Marxism.

My final point concerns the relation between the rise of the
nationalist vote and support for independence or devolution. It has
been argued that, at least at some stage in the increase of SNP votes,
the Scots have been persuaded that devolution would be a possible
answer to their problems or at least that it would be one component
in a general package to improve their situation. I showed in Chapter
10 that the level of support for devolution or home rule of some sort
has stood at around 75 per cent for a very long time: from the period
before the large increase in the nationalist vote. It does, therefore,
seem implausible that the rise of the nationalist vote should be
explained by support for devolution or any other institutional
change, since there has been little or no change in the independent
variable, while the dependent variable has changed dramatically in
its value. As late as the ORC poll in the *Scotsman* on 26 October
1976 the level of support for any form of legislature, subordinate or
independent, in Scotland was 73 per cent, much as it had been in
earlier years.

There is only one way in which the levels of support for devolution
could be important in explaining the nationalist vote, and that
would be if, for the Scottish voters, the whole issue had become more
important: i.e. in earlier years they supported the idea of devolution,
albeit with a very low priority, but in the late 1960s and the early
1970s it became of primary importance. The evidence is totally
against this. The report of the ORC poll published in the *Scotsman*
on 26 October 1976 give the replies to the question 'What do you
yourself feel are the most important problems the government
should do something about?' The issues which seemed to be most
important were prices (mentioned by 57 per cent) and unemployment
(mentioned by 35 per cent of the sample). Many other issues were
mentioned far more often than devolution or independence, which

together were mentioned by only 7 per cent of the respondents. During the period when this question has been asked in the ORC poll, the highest proportion of the Scottish sample mentioning devolution or independence as the most important question has been 11 per cent, in December 1975.

Support for the SNP has risen, therefore, not because there has been a change in the level of significance given to the policies of that party concerning a Scottish Parliament. In the same way, the increased support is certainly unrelated, in the crucial initial stages at any rate, to multinational companies' exploitation of North Sea oil or anything else. The crucial connection seems to have been forged by a gradual restructuring of the political consciousness of the Scottish electorate in such a way that they began to perceive themselves as Scots in terms of their political interests rather than as, for example, members of the working class. Thus the party which stood for Scotland was the one which began to get their support, just as the poorer parts of the British population turned to the party of the working man in the earlier part of this century. In doing so they did not necessarily agree with the policies of the party in detail or even know about them. More important than anything else was their identification of their own position in political terms. The growth of Scottish identification in this sense grew out of the earlier non-political consciousness and led to the SNP breakthrough.

Appendix A/
National Party
of Scotland
Constitution,1931

1. NAME:	The National Party of Scotland.
2. OBJECT:	Self-government for Scotland with independent national status within the British group of nations, together with the reconstruction of Scottish National life.
3. POLICY:	The Party shall pursue the achievement of its object by all such methods as shall be determined by the Party assembled in National Conference or by the National Council from time to time according to current requirements; but the Party shall contest Parliamentary and Local Government Elections, and shall present a Nationalist programme for the reconstruction of Scottish National life.
4. MEMBERSHIP:	The Party shall be strictly non-sectarian, and its objects and policy shall be promoted primarily by means of Branches, and such Federations or Area Councils as from time to time may be authorised by the National Council.
	All persons who signify their adherence to the Object and Policy of the Party shall be eligible

for membership either of Branches, or where no Branches exist as individual members of the National Organisation.

5. ORGANISATION: (a) *Branches*—A group of members in one district, or belonging to a public institution approved of by the National Council having been obtained.

(b) *Federation of Branches*—A group of Branches within a Parliamentary constituency, or other district, the boundaries of which shall have been defined by the National Council, but no such Federation shall be formed without the sanction of the National Council having been obtained.

(c) *Area Councils*—Office Bearers or such other instructed representatives of Branches within a particular area, the boundaries of which shall have been defined by the National Council, but no Area Council shall be formed without the sanction of the National Council having been obtained.

(d) *National Conference*—National Officials together with such of the assisting National Officials as the Conference may deem to be necessary and representation from the Branches on the following basis:—

One representative from each Branch whose Membership does not exceed thirty; two representatives from each Branch whose membership exceeds thirty but not one hundred; three representatives from each Branch whose membership exceeds one hundred, but not one hundred and fifty; and additional representatives from other Branches on the basis of one additional representative for every fifty or part thereof over one hundred and fifty.

The National Conference shall be the supreme governing body of the Party and shall meet in June of each year on a date to be arranged by the National Council.

(e) *National Office Bearers*—A President, a Chairman of National Council, a Vice-Chairman of National Council, a National Treasurer, a National Secretary, together with such assisting officials as the Conference may deem necessary. All National Office Bearers shall be elected at each annual Conference of the Party.

(f) *National Council*—The National Office Bearers together with such of the assisting National Officials as the Conference may deem necessary and twelve other Councillors from among the members of the Conference. The National Council shall always be subject to the authority of the Conference, but shall have the power to deal with matters of emergency, routine, and the more immediate and more urgent Executive work of the Party.

(g) *Other National Committees*—The National Council may delegate such of their powers and duties as they deem necessary to Sub-Committees and may co-opt on such Sub-Committees members of the Party who may not be members of the National Councils or Conference.

6. AMENDMENT OF CONSTITUTION: Notice of amendment of Constitution shall be given in writing to the National Secretary at least two months prior to the date of the Annual Conference, and shall be endorsed by a Branch or by the National Council. Any amendment to become effective shall be passed by a majority of not less than two-thirds of the members present at the annual Conference.

Appendix B/ SNP Constitution, 1948

NAME

The Scottish National Party.

AIM

Self Government for Scotland.

The restoration of Scottish national sovereignty by the establishment of a democratic Scottish government whose authority will be limited only by such agreements as will be freely entered into with other nations in order to further international co-operation and world peace.

MEMBERSHIP

Membership is open to all who endorse the aim of the Party and make payment annually of the minimum subscription fixed by the National Council or Branches as the case may be. Members of the National Council and Branch Office-Bearers may not at the same time be members of any other political party.

ORGANISATION

(a) *Branches*—A Branch may consist of any number of members but no Branch shall be formed without the sanction of the National Council having been obtained.

Members shall be entitled to vote in one branch only, and shall be included in the affiliation list of one branch only.

Groups may be formed, under approval of the appropriate Area Council, or of the National Council, with a membership of any number, where the creation of a Branch is not practicable; and may appoint an official known as a Local Secretary who will maintain liaison with the National office-bearers, will sit on the Area Council and will vote only in terms of the Area Council Constitution.

(b) *Federations of Branches, Area Councils and Associations*—The National Council shall set up such Federations, Area Councils or Associations as it shall deem necessary in consultation with the Branches.

(c) *Area Councils*—Area Councils shall consist of members elected by Branches within a given area to the number decided upon by the said area.

(d) *Annual National Conference*—The Annual National Conference shall consist of:—

Representatives from each Branch on this basis:—one representative from each Branch whose membership does not exceed thirty; two representatives from each Branch whose membership exceeds thirty but not sixty; three representatives from each Branch whose membership exceeds sixty but not one hundred; and additional representatives from each Branch on the basis of one additional representative for every additional fifty members or part thereof. No Branch shall be entitled to more than ten delegates.

The Chairman of the National Council, the National Secretary, the National Treasurer, together with all National officials and members of the Council shall ex officio be members of the Conference but with the exception of the Chairman, Secretary and Treasurer, may vote only as delegates on the election of National office-bearers and Council.

Voting at the Annual Conference shall be on the basis of one vote for each delegate or member of the Conference and no voting by proxy shall be allowed.

The Annual National Conference shall be the supreme governing body of the Party and shall meet each year on a date and at a place to be arranged by the National Council.

(e) *National Office-Bearers*—The National Office-Bearers shall be a President, a Chairman of the National Council, two Vice-Chairmen, a National Secretary, a National Organising Secretary and a National Treasurer, together with such other office-bearers or conveners of

National Committees as the Annual National Conference may deem necessary. All National Office-Bearers shall be elected at each Annual National Conference of the Party, and must be duly accredited members of the Party and nominated by Branches thereof.

(f) *National Council*—The National Council shall consist of:—

  i The National Office-Bearers (as in paragraph (e) above);

  ii One Area Representative to be elected by each Area Council from its own Area Council members;

  iii Twenty ordinary Council Members to be elected by the Annual National Conference from party members other than National Office-Bearers and Area Representatives, or such smaller or larger number of Ordinary Council Members as the immediately preceding National Conference may have determined.

(g) *Other National Committees*—The National Council may delegate such of its powers and duties as it shall deem necessary to an Executive Committee or to other Committees—and may co-opt on such Committees members of the Party, who need not be members of the National Council.

Notes

Chapter 1 The Nature of the Problem and its Background

1 The election data in this section are drawn from *The Times Guide to the House of Commons*, London, Times Publishing Company; for each election year and, for pre-war years, from *British Parliamentary Election Results 1918-1949*, F. W. S. Craig, Glasgow, Political Reference Publications, 1969.

2 These polls were carried out by the Opinion Research Centre, London, for the *Scotsman* and by Systems Three, Dundee, for the *Glasgow Herald*.

3 See L. Dion, 'Anti-Politics and Marginals', *Government and Opposition*, vol. 9 (Winter 1974), pp. 28-41.

4 Data taken, as noted above, from *The Times Guide to the House of Commons* for each election year.

5 R. Rose and D. Urwin, 'Social Cohesion, Political Parties and Strains on Regimes', *Comparative Political Studies*, vol. 2 (1969).

6 See J. Madeley, 'Scandinavia: The End of the Middle Way', *New Society*, vol. 28, no. 611 (20 June 1974), pp. 699-701.

7 R. Inglehart, 'The Silent Revolution in Europe', *American Political Science Review*, vol. LXVII, no. 1 (1971).

8 See A. Miller, 'Political Issues and Trust in Government 1964-1970', *American Political Science Review*, vol. LXVIII, no. 3 (1974).

9 D. Butler and D. Stokes, *Political Change in Britain*, London, Macmillan, 1969.

10 In Brittany, for example, see R. Dulong, *La Question Bretonne*, Paris, Fondation National de Science Politique, 1975.

Chapter 2 The Substance of Nationalism

1 L. Pye, *Politics, Personality and Nation Building*, New Haven, Yale University Press, 1963.

2 S. Rokkan, *Citizens, Elections and Parties*, New York, Wiley, 1970.

3 A. Lijphart, 'Cultural Diversity and Theories of Political Integration', *Canadian Journal of Political Science*, vol. 4, no. 1 (1971).

4 N. Glaser and D. Moynihan, *Ethnicity*, Cambridge, Mass., Harvard University Press, 1975.
5 E. Kedourie, *Nationalism*, London, Hutchinson, 1961 (2nd edn); H. Kohn, *The Idea of Nationalism*, New York, Macmillan, 1945.
6 See H. Hanham, *Scottish Nationalism*, London, Faber, 1969.
7 Edinburgh, Scottish National Party, 1974.
8 We shall see that the appeal is, in fact, mixed.
9 *The Union of 1707 and its results*, Glasgow, Morrison, 1892.
10 Kohn, op. cit., p. 16.
11 Ibid., p. 45.
12 See A. Raum, *Germany 1789-1919*, London, Methuen, 1967.
13 E. Kamenka, *Nationalism*, Canberra, Australia, National University Press, 1973, pp. 6-7.
14 See W. Ferguson, *Scotland: 1689 to the Present*, Edinburgh, Oliver & Boyd, 1968.
15 J. Barbour (Archdeacon of Aberdeen), *The Bruce*, Oxford, Early English Text Society, 1870.
16 Blind Harry, *Schir William Wallace*, Edinburgh Text Society, 1889.
17 K. Wittig, *The Scottish Tradition in Literature*, Edinburgh, Oliver & Boyd, 1958.
18 See, for example, the account in Ferguson, op. cit., p. 96.
19 Ibid., p. 102.
20 See A. M. Stoddart, *John Stuart Blackie: A Biography*, 2 vols, Edinburgh, Blackwood, 1895.
21 J. G. Herder, *Über den Ursprung der Sprache*, Stuttgart, Freies Geistesleben, 1965.
22 See J. G. Fichte, *The Vocation of Man*, New York, Bobbs Merrill, 1958.
23 See T. K. Derry, *A History of Modern Norway*, Oxford, Clarendon Press, 1963.
24 See D. R. Elston, *Israel: the Making of a Nation*, Oxford University Press, 1963.
25 According to the 1971 census 1·7 per cent of the Scottish population spoke Gaelic as well as English.
26 See H. MacDiarmid, 'Towards a Synthetic Scots', in *Contemporary Scottish Studies*, Edinburgh, *Scottish Education Journal*, 1976 (reprint). In the present work the name Hugh MacDiarmid will be used.
27 See H. MacDiarmid, 'The Case for Synthetic Scots', *Scots Observer*, vol. 6, no. 310 (September 1932).
28 Kedourie, op. cit., p. 47.
29 See D. Buchan, *A Scottish Ballad Book*, London, Routledge & Kegan Paul, 1973.
30 See R. Roteberg, *The Rise of Nationalism in Central Africa*, Cambridge, Mass., Harvard University Press, 1966.
31 With the exception of the Nationalist Party of Scotland, to be referred to in Chapter 13.
32 See Appendix B for the Constitution of the SNP.
33 See N. Azikiwe, *Renascent Africa*, London, Cass, 1968.

Chapter 3   The Rise of the SNP: Some Theories

1 They are well summarised in J. Wilson, *Introduction to Social Movements*, New York, Basic Books, 1973.
2 M. Pinard, *The Rise of a Third Party*, Englewood Cliffs, N. J., Prentice Hall, 1971.
3 Wilson, op. cit., p. 8.

4 N. Smelser, *Theory of Collective Behaviour*, London, Routledge & Kegan Paul, 1962.
5 See, for example, the grass roots nature of both movements.
6 R. Inglehart, 'The Silent Revolution in Europe', *American Political Science Review*, vol. LXVII, no. 1 (1971).
7 The most recent account of the events leading to the Union is given in W. Ferguson, *Scotland's Relations with England: A Survey to 1707*, Edinburgh, John Donald, 1977.
8 Thus, for example, there had been a Secretary of State for Scotland from 1707 until 1745, but after the rebellion of that year the Lord Advocate had become responsible and effectively governed Scotland in consultation with a coterie of Edinburgh advocates. From 1828 until 1885 the Home Secretary was in charge although the Lord Advocate was still responsible.
9 H. Hanham, *Scottish Nationalism*, London, Faber, 1969, ch. 4.
10 Ibid., p. 44.
11 E. O. Henry, *The Rise of Sinn Fein*, Dublin, Talbot Press, 1923.
12 S. Rokkan, *Party Systems and Vote Alignments*, New York, Free Press, 1967, p. 41.
13 See W. D. Burnham, 'Theory and Voting Research', *American Political Science Review*, vol. LXVIII, no. 3 (September 1974), pp. 1002-23.
14 See I. Crewe and B. Sarlvik, *Partisan Dealignment in Britain 1964-1974*, mimeo, Essex.
15 We shall explore this with reference to folk song clubs and the churches as well as other organisations.
16 This has been widely commented upon by, for example, I. Macleod, 'The Rise and Fall of the SNP', *Political Studies*, vol. 18, no. 2 (1970), pp. 357-72.
17 Pinard, op. cit., pp. 32-3.
18 R. T. Mackenzie and A. Silver, *Angels in Marble*, London, Heinemann, 1968, p. 119; D. Butler and D. Stokes, *Political Change in Britain*, London, Macmillan, 1969.
19 E. Gellner, *Words and Things*, London, Gollancz, 1959.
20 E. Kedourie, *Nationalism*, London, Hutchinson, 1961 (2nd edn), p. 64.
21 See A. de Tocqueville, *The Old Regime and the French Revolution*, New York, Doubleday, 1955.
22 A. Campbell *et al.*, *The American Voter*, New York, Wiley, 1960, p. 436.
23 Pinard, op. cit., p. 96.

Chapter 4   The Political Background

1 V. Zander, 'Resistance and Social Movement', *Social Forces*, vol. 38, no. 2 (1959). See also C. Tilly, *History and Thought*, Princeton University Press, 1973.
2 See J. Kellas, *Modern Scotland: The Nation since 1870*, London, Pall Mall, 1968, pp. 126-8.
3 W. Stewart, *J. Keir Hardie*, London, Independent Labour Party, 1921, p. 40.
4 Including some, like Tom Johnston, who became prominent in later years.
5 A policy which the Communist Party abandoned in 1938.
6 It is well known that Stalin's approach to nationalism in the Soviet Union was particularly repressive.
7 *Labour and the New Social Order*, London, Labour Party, 1918.
8 Rev. Campbell Stephen, MP, and David Kirkwood, MP, for example.
9 *Scots Independent*, vol. III, no. 8 (June 1929).
10 See R. Dowse, *Left in the Centre*, London, Longmans Green, 1966, and R. K. Middlemas, *The Clydesiders*, London, Hutchinson, 1965.

11 See W. Kendall, *The Revolutionary Movement in Britain 1900-1921*, London, Weidenfeld & Nicolson, 1969, pp. 105-42 and pp. 351-61.

12 A copy is to be found in the National Library of Scotland.

13 *Strike Bulletin*, Glasgow, Clyde Workers Committee, 12 February 1919.

14 N. Milton, *John Maclean*, London, Pluto Press, 1973, p. 194.

15 *Conference on Devolution*, Letter from Mr Speaker to the Prime Minister, Cmd 697, HMSO, 1920.

16 See J. MacCormick, *Flag in the Wind*, London, Gollancz, 1955.

17 See R. L. Mowat, *Britain Between the Wars*, London, Methuen, 1955, p. 125.

18 See J. McCaffrey, 'The Origins of Liberal Unionism in the West of Scotland', *Scottish Historical Review*, vol. 50, no. 149 (1971), pp. 47-71.

19 See MacCormick, op. cit., p. 80.

20 *The New Scotland*, Glasgow, London Scots Self-Government Committee, 1943.

21 Ibid., p. 10.

22 Ibid., p. 19.

23 Ibid., p. 22.

24 *Scottish Reconstruction*, Glasgow, Scottish Reconstruction Committee, vol. 2, no. 1 (1944).

25 T. Johnston, *Memories*, Glasgow, Collins, 1952, p. 149.

26 Johnston, op. cit., p. 66.

27 *New Scotland*, no. 3, 1946.

28 *Scottish Affairs*, Cmd 7308, HMSO, 1948.

29 R. H. Crossman, *Labour in the Affluent Society*, Fabian Pamphlet no. 325, London, Fabian Society, 1960.

30 Commission on the Constitution, Minutes of Evidence, vol. 4, HMSO, 1970.

31 *Glasgow Herald*, 30 October 1973.

32 *Glasgow Herald*, 23 March 1974.

33 *Sunday Times*, 18 August 1974, and *Glasgow Herald*, 19 August 1974.

34 *Democracy and Devolution*, Cmd 5732, HMSO, 1974.

35 R. Boothby, *My Yesterdays Your Tomorrow*, London, Hutchinson, 1963.

36 Royal Commission on Scottish Affairs, Cmd 9212, HMSO, 1954.

37 See M. Sissons, *The Age of Austerity*, Penguin, 1962.

38 So called by bringing together the names of Hugh Gaitskell of the Labour Party and R. A. Butler of the Conservatives, who were thought of as the main examples of the conflation of the two parties' policies.

39 D. Butler and D. Stokes, *Political Change in Britain*, London, Macmillan, 1969; I. Crewe and B. Särlvik, paper presented to the Political Studies Association Conference, Nottingham, 1976.

40 M. J. Keating, 'The Role of the Scottish MP', PhD Thesis, Glasgow College of Technology, 1975.

41 Ibid., especially pp. 84-5.

42 Scottish Office Memorandum to the Select Committee on Scottish Affairs, Edinburgh, Scottish Office, 1969.

43 *Scottish Affairs*, Cmd 7308, Session 1947-8, HMSO, 1948.

44 O. D. Edwards, 'The Scottish Grand Committee 1958-1970', *Parliamentary Affairs*, vol. XXV, no. 2, London, 1972.

45 Keating, op. cit., p. 232.

Chapter 5   The Scottish Economy

1 Theory is not always followed in Russian practice, however. See F. C. Barghoorn, *Soviet Russian Nationalism*, New York, Oxford University Press, 1956.

2 M. Hechter, *Internal Colonialism*, London, Routledge & Kegan Paul, 1975.
3 See T. C. Smout, *A History of the Scottish People 1560-1830*, London, Collins, 1969.
4 The early nationalists were conscious of this. See H. Hanham, *Scottish Nationalism*, London, Faber, 1969, ch. 8.
5 T. Devine, *The Tobacco Lords*, Glasgow, Donald, 1975.
6 See West Central Scotland Plan, Report vol. 1, Edinburgh, Scottish Development Department, 1974.
7 W. Slaven, *The Development of the West of Scotland*, London, Routledge & Kegan Paul, 1975.
8 Queen Victoria, *Our Life in the Highlands*, London, Kimber, 1968 (originally published London, 1868).
9 See Smout, op, cit., pp. 397-403.
10 See J. B. Russell, *Public Health Administration in Glasgow*, Glasgow, Maclehose, 1905.
11 See H. Clegg *et al.*, *A History of British Trade Unions*, London, Oxford University Press, 1964.
12 R. H. Campbell, *Scotland Since 1707*, Oxford, Blackwell, 1965.
13 J. F. Handley, *The Irish in Modern Scotland*, Cork, 1945, p. 1.
14 See, for example, *The East End Study*, Glasgow District Council, 1976.
15 Slaven, op. cit., p. 232.
16 W. H. Marwick, *Scotland in Modern Times*, London, Cass, 1964, p. 158.
17 J. Firn, 'External Control and Regional Policy', in G. Brown (ed.), *The Red Paper on Scotland*, Edinburgh University Student Publications Board, 1975.
18 *Final Report on the Fourth Census of Production* (*1930*), HMSO, 1933.
19 G. M. Thomson, *Scotland, that Distressed Area*, Edinburgh, Porpoise Press, 1935.
20 G. M. Thomson, *Caledonia, or the Future of the Scots*, London, Kegan Paul, 1927.
21 According to a letter from Thomson to A. Dewar Gibb, National Library of Scotland Dep. 6951/1.
22 J. A. Bowie, *The Future of Scotland*, Edinburgh, Chambers, 1939.
23 *Annual Survey of Economic Conditions in Scotland*, Glasgow, Clydesdale Bank, 1934.
24 For example, *Review of the Economic Conditions of the Highlands and Islands of Scotland*, Glasgow, Scottish Economic Committee, 1938.
25 The Committee on Scottish Administration.
26 Campbell, op. cit., p. 275.
27 *Report on Scottish Administration*, Cmd 5563, HMSO, 1937.
28 Marwick, op. cit., p. 107.
29 East Kilbride was designated in 1947 and Cumbernauld was started in 1956.
30 Campbell, op. cit., p. 7.
31 *Annual Survey of Economic Conditions in Scotland 1958*, Glasgow, Clydesdale Bank, 1958.
32 G. MacCrone, *Scotland's Future: the Economics of Nationalism*, Oxford, Blackwell, 1969.
33 K. J. W. Alexander, *The Political Economy of Change*, Oxford, Blackwell, 1975, p. 116.
34 In the *Three Banks Review*, no. 14 (June 1952).
35 *Inquiry into the Scottish Economy 1960-1*, Edinburgh, Scottish Council (Development and Industry), 1961.
36 *Central Scotland: a Programme for Development and Growth*, Cmd 2218, HMSO, 1963; *The North East: a Programme for Regional Development and Growth*, Cmd 2206, HMSO.

37 H. B. Myers, *The Quebec Revolution*, Montreal, Harvest House, 1964;
T. Sloan, *Quebec, the Not So Quiet Revolution*, Toronto, Ryeson, 1965.
38 Alexander, op. cit., p. 116.
39 A. O. Hirshman, *Exit Voice and Loyalty*, Cambridge, Mass., Harvard
University Press, 1970.
40 The major facts of the situation produced by the discovery of this oil are
discussed in D. I. MacKay and G. A. MacKay, *Political Economy of North
Sea Oil*, London, Robertson, 1975.
41 Alexander, op. cit., p. 116.
42 D. I. MacKay and G. A. MacKay, op. cit., p. 12.
43 J. Craigen, 'The Scottish Trade Union Congress', Edinburgh, Heriot Watt
University (unpublished MLitt dissertation), 1974.

Chapter 6   The Effects of Literary Nationalism

1 See M. Brown, *The Politics of Irish Literature*, London, Allen & Unwin, 1972.
2 L. S. Senghor, *Nocturnes*, London, Heinemann, 1969.
3 E. Arndt (1770-1860), *Lieder für Deutschen*, Leipzig, 1813; B. Auerbach
(1812-82), *Schwarzwälder Dorfgeschichten*, Mannheim, 1849.
4 See H. Cockburn, *Circuit Journeys*, Edinburgh, 1888.
5 The most recent literary history is M. Lindsay, *History of Scottish Literature*,
London, Robert Hale, 1977. See also K. Wittig, *The Scottish Tradition in
Literature*, Edinburgh, Chambers, 1958.
6 See, for example, T. Carlyle, *The French Revolution*, London, James Fraser,
1837.
7 See A. Turnbull (ed.), *The Poems of John Davidson*, Edinburgh, Scottish
Academic Press, 1973.
8 The visit was also satirised by radical poets, however: see Patrick Cadell's
article 'Royal Visitors' Book' in the *Scotsman*, 14 May 1977.
9 See J. MacQueen (ed.), *Poems of Ossian*, Edinburgh, James Thin, 1971.
10 See J. Boswell, *Journal of a Tour of the Hebrides 1773*, London, Charles Dilly,
1785.
11 Queen Victoria, *Journal of Our Life in the Highlands*, London, Kimber, 1968
(originally published London, 1868).
12 See also the interest in folk customs and songs referred to in Chapter 2, above.
This was the age of the great folk song collections.
13 *The Oxford Companion to English Literature* (3rd edn, 1946, p. 424) describes
the Kailyard School as follows: 'from "Kail Yard" a cabbage patch such as is
commonly attached to a small cottage. A term applied to writers of a recent
class of fiction describing with much use of the vernacular common life in
Scotland'.
14 See G. Blake, *Barrie and the Kailyard School*, London, Arthur Barker, 1951.
15 This can be seen from any standard economic history of Scotland. See, for
example, T. C. Smout, *A History of the Scottish People*, London, Collins,
1969.
16 See A. Drummond and J. Bulloch, *The Scottish Church 1688-1843: The Age of
the Moderates*, Edinburgh, St Andrews Press, 1973.
17 Perhaps this is best seen in S. R. Crockett's *The Stickit Minister*, London,
T. Fisher Unwin, 1895.
18 See T. H. Darlow, *William Robertson Nicoll*, London, Hodder & Stoughton,
1925.
19 In fact starting with 'Stormy Limits', written in 1934, MacDiarmid wrote a
great deal in English.
20 Was it for little Belgium's sake
Sae mony thoosand Scotsmen deed

And never ane for Scotland fegs!
Wi' twenty thoosand times mair need. (from *Towards a New Scotland*,
Edinburgh, Maclehose, 1935).

21 See Spence's article 'The Scottish Literary Renaissance' in *Nineteenth Century
and After*, vol. 100, no. DXCIII (July 1926), pp. 123-33.

22 See, example, V. Jacob, *Songs of Angus*, London, John Murray, 1915.

23 See preface to R. L. Stevenson, *Underwoods*, London, Chatto & Windus, 1887.

24 Through a device known as 'The Scots Secretariat'.

25 O. Spengler, *The Decline of the West*, London, Allen & Unwin, 1934.

26 Power was a well known Burns expert and in great demand as a speaker at
Burns Clubs.

27 See this even in an essay dealing principally with Scotland in 'The Caledonian
Antisyzygy', printed in *The Modern Scot*, vol. 2, no. 4 (January 1932), p. 335.

28 Fareweel to a' our Scotish fame,
Fareweel our ancient glory;
Fareweel even to the Scotish name,
Sae fam'd in martial story!
Now Sark rins o'er the Solway sands,
And Tweed rins to the ocean,
Tae mark whare England's province stands,
Such a parcel of rogues in a nation!

29 See Ramsay's poem 'The Vision' in *The Evergreen* or *Tartana and the Plaid*,
Edinburgh, T. Cadell, 1721.

30 See MacDiarmid's essay on Muir in *The Uncanny Scot*, London, MacGibbon &
Kee, 1968.

31 See 'Second Hymn to Lenin', in *The Criterion*, vol. II, no. 45 (July 1932).

32 One of the themes of *A Scots Quair*, London, Hutchinson, 1934, especially of
Cloud Howe, is the link between a farming family of the north east of Scotland
and the pre-historic inhabitants of the site.

33 See MacDiarmid's essay on Gibbon in *The Uncanny Scot*, pp. 154-63.

34 From 'On a Raised Beach', in *Stony Limits and Other Poems*, London,
Gollancz, 1934.

35 From *A Drunk Man looks at the Thistle*, Edinburgh, Blackwood, 1926.

36 See W. Souter, *Collected Poems*, London, Andrew Dakers, 1948.

37 For Fion McColla's novels see, for example, *The Albannach*, London, John
Heritage, 1932, or *And the Cock Crew*, Glasgow, William MacLellan, 1945.

38 See M. Lindsay, *Selected Poems 1942-1972*, London, Robert Hale, 1973.

39 See E. Muir, *Scottish Journey*, London, Heinemann, 1935 and *The Structure
of the Novel*, London, Hogarth, 1928.

40 E. Muir, *Scott and Scotland*, London, Routledge, 1936.

41 Ibid., p. 22.

42 A process which had begun by the middle 1930s.

43 *Scottish Scene or The Intelligent Man's Guide to Albyn*, London, Jarrolds,
1934.

44 H. MacDiarmid, *The Uncanny Scot*, p. 161.

45 See, for example, Neil Gunn, *The Silver Darlings*, London, Faber, 1948;
Highland River, London, Faber, 1937.

46 The Gunn collection of manuscripts is to be found in NLS Dep. 209.

47 See D. Glenn, *Hugh MacDiarmid and the Scottish Renaissance*, Edinburgh,
Chambers, 1964, p. 226.

48 Ibid., p. 219.

49 A. Sharp, *A Green Tree in Gedde*, London, Michael Joseph, 1965.

50 W. McIlvanney, *Remedy is None*, London, Eyre & Spottiswoode, 1966. See also
W. Bryden, *Benny Lynch*, Edinburgh, Southside, 1975.

Chapter 7 Youth and Nationalism

1 Perhaps the best known history text at the beginning of the century was P. Hume Brown, *History of Scotland*, 1st edn, 3 vols, Cambridge University Press, 1899-1909.
2 First published in 1827; Edinburgh, Cadell, 1928.
3 See, for example, his account of the battles of Bannockburn and Flodden.
4 P. Hume Brown, *A Short History of Scotland*, Edinburgh, Oliver & Boyd, 1907.
5 A. Muir Mackenzie, *Scotland in Modern Times 1720-1939*, Edinburgh, Chambers, 1942.
6 P. Hume Brown, *History of Scotland*, vol. 3, p. 74.
7 A. Lang, *History of Scotland*, 4 vols, Edinburgh, Blackwood, 1900-7, vol. 3, p. 110.
8 T. Wright, *A History of Scotland*, 3 vols, London, London Printing and Publishing Co., 1852-5.
9 B. Lenman, 'The Teaching of Scottish History in Scottish Universities', *Scottish Historical Review*, vol. 52, no. 154 (1973), p. 177.
10 This ran through many editions but seems to have been first published in 1869.
11 See, for example, W. Ferguson, *Scotland: 1689 to the Present*, Edinburgh, Oliver & Boyd, 1968; for Mackie's work see J. D. Mackie, *A History of Scotland*, Penguin, 1973.
12 P. Gaskell, *Morvern Transformed*, Cambridge University Press, 1968.
13 A. Ramsay, *The Tea-Table Miscellany*, Edinburgh, Arbuthnot, 1724.
14 W. Scott, *Minstrelsy of the Scottish Border*, Edinburgh, Black, 1802-30.
15 F. J. Childe, *The English and Scottish Popular Ballads*, Cambridge, Mass., Harvard University Press, 1882.
16 The Greig collection of ballads from the north-east of Scotland is still largely unworked. It is held in the University of Aberdeen, Manuscripts 701-90, 998, and 2732.
17 Some of the best-known Scottish songs were written by Lady Nairne. They include 'Will ye no come back again', 'The Laird o' Cockpen', 'The Auld Hoose', and 'The Land o' the Leal'.
18 Sung to the tune of 'Lily Marlene'.
19 Vol. IV, New York, Columbia.
20 Bo'ness Rebels Literary Society, Bo'ness, 1951.
21 Bo'ness Rebels Literary Society, Bo'ness, 1953.
22 *Rebels Ceilidh Song Book*, preface.
23 This chapter is based on the article in 'Rebel Songs of Scotland', in *Chapbook*, vol. 4, no 6.

Chapter 8 The Role of the Church, the Army and Football

1 G. Brenan, *The Spanish Labyrinth*, Cambridge University Press (2nd edn reprinted), 1964, p. 279.
2 See A. B. Philip, *The Welsh Question*, London, Routledge & Kegan Paul, 1976.
3 J. Highet, *The Churches in Scotland Today*, Glasgow, Jackson, 1950.
4 *Letters of Queen Victoria*, 2nd series iii, London, John Murray, 1926, p. 47.
5 J. H. S. Burleigh, *A Church History of Scotland*, London, Oxford University Press, 1960, p. 366.
6 R. Rose, *Governing without Consensus*, London, Faber, 1971.
7 *Scottish Affairs*, Cmd 7308, HMSO, 1948.
8 Church of Scotland, *Reports to the General Assembly 1948*, Edinburgh, Blackwood, 1948.

9 Ibid.
10 Royal Commission on Scottish Affairs, Cmd 9212, HMSO, 1954.
11 Commission on the Constitution, Cmd 5460, HMSO, 1973.
12 C. Mitchell, *Having Been a Soldier*, London, Mayflower, 1970.
13 D. W. J. Cuddeford, *And All for What*, London, Heath Cranton, 1933.
14 R. Nisbet, *Community and Power*, London, Oxford University Press, 1962.
15 J. Rafferty, *One Hundred Years of Scottish Football*, London, Pan, 1973.
16 J. Rafferty in I. Archer, *We'll Support You Evermore*, London, Hutchinson, 1976, p. 76.
17 Archer, op. cit., p. 213.
18 See, on the lack of efficacy of traditional institutions for sparking off nationalism, E. Gellner, *Words and Things*, London, Gollancz, 1959.

Chapter 9   The Scottish Press

1 See J. MacCormick, *Flag in the Wind*, London, Gollancz, 1955, p. 77.
2 M. Magnusson, *The Glorious Privilege*, Edinburgh, Nelson, 1967, p. 166.
3 *How Scotland Should be Governed*, Edinburgh, Scotsman Publications, February 1968.
4 *Glasgow Herald*, 23 February 1977.

Chapter 10   The SNP Vote: Some Relations and Conclusions

1 Published in the *Scotsman*, 31 May and 1 June 1975. Other polls were published in the *Scotsman*, 16 December 1975 and 26 October 1976.
2 D. Butler and D. Stokes, *Political Change in Britain*, London, Macmillan, 1969, and the subsequent work undertaken by I. Crewe and B. Särlvik, *Partisan Dealignment in Britain 1964-1974*, mimeo, Essex.
3 Carried out on Social Science Research Council Grant HR/1747. The sample size was 800.
4 The classical example is, of course, A. de Tocqueville, *The Old Regime and the Revolution*, New York, Doubleday, 1955.
5 W. G. Runciman, *Relative Deprivation and Social Justice*, London, Routledge & Kegan Paul, 1966.
6 Royal Commission on the Constitution, Research Study no. 7, HMSO, 1970, p. 49.
7 R. A. Brooks, 'Relative Deprivation and Social Mobility', unpublished PhD thesis, Michigan State University, 1975.
8 See J. Blondel, *Voters, Parties and Leaders*, Penguin, 1963, pp. 60-1.
9 J. Bochel and M. Denver, 'Religion and Voting', *Political Studies*, vol. 18 (1970), pp. 205-19.
10 Butler and Stokes, op. cit., pp. 124-34.
11 A., Lijphart, *The Politics of Accommodation*, Berkeley, University of California Press, 1968.
12 J. Highet, *The Churches in Scotland Today*, Glasgow, Jackson, 1950.
13 I. Budge and D. Urwin, *Scottish Political Behaviour*, London, Longmans Green, 1968, p. 40.
14 Royal Commission on the Constitution, Research Paper 7, p. 41.
15 Butler and Stokes, op. cit., ch. 16.
16 G. Pomper, 'From Confusion to Clarity', *American Political Science Review*, vol. LXVI, no. 2 (1972), pp. 415-28.
17 W. Miller *et al.*, 'The Connection between SNP Voting and the Demand for Scottish Self-Government', *European Journal of Political Research*, vol. 5, no. 1 (1977), pp. 83-102.

The Beginnings of the Modern Movement

1 N. Smelser, *Theory of Collective Behaviour*, London, Routledge & Kegan Paul, 1962.
2 See, for example, I. Macleod, 'The Rise and Fall of the SNP', *Political Studies*, vol. 18, no. 2 (1970), pp. 357-72.

Chapter 11 The Beginnings of Modern Nationalism

1 Indeed, even earlier than this; see, for example, G. W. S. Barrow's masterly study *Robert Bruce*, London, Eyre & Spottiswoode, 1965, for examples of something very like national feeling among Bruce's followers.
2 See for example, W. Ferguson, *Scotland: 1689 to the Present*, Edinburgh, Oliver & Boyd, 1968.
3 This was certainly the position of Lockhart of Carnwarth, who, as a Scottish member of the Commission to Consider the Union of 1707, had proposed a scheme of this sort.
4 See, for example, Mitchison, *A History of Scotland*, London, Methuen, 1970, p. 334.
5 Such as, for example, the Society for the Vindication of Scottish Rights and The Scottish Patriots.
6 Referred to in the *Scottish Home Rule Association Newsletter*, vol. 1, no. 1 (July 1920).
7 National Library of Scotland, Acc. 3721/17.
8 NLS, Acc. 6058/1, R. E. Muirhead to T. H. Gibson 18 June 1924.
9 These data are drawn from the various issues of the *SHRA Newsletter*.
10 General Council 16 September 1922 reports the resolutions to be put to the meeting on 22 September, NLS, Acc. 6058/2.
11 Ibid.
12 Reported in *SHRA Newsletter*, October 1922.
13 21 July 1923.
14 10 August 1923.
15 *SHRA Newsletter*, 13 January 1922.
16 J. Hunter, 'The Gaelic Connection', *Scottish Historical Review*, vol. LIV (2), no. 158 (October 1975), p. 178-204.
17 *Guth na Bliadhna*, vol. 1, no. 2, p. 303.
18 Ibid., vol. 2, no. 2, p. 300.
19 Ibid., vol. 2, no. 1, p. 28.
20 See H. MacDiarmid, 'In Memoriam McIlle losa', from *Stony Limits and Other Poems*, London, Gollancz, 1934.
21 See the pamphlet *Commun non Albanach*, Scots National League, London, 1909, from the private collection of Mr Iain Gilles, Oban.
22 *Liberty*, vol. 3, no. 1 (March 1921).
23 *Monthly Intelligencer*, July 1924.
24 NLS, Acc. 6058/2, T. H. Gibson to R. E. Muirhead, 16 June 1924.
25 Membership card and constitution in the National Library of Scotland, Acc. 6058/1.
26 *Monthly Intelligencer*, July 1924.
27 NLS, Acc. 6058/1.
28 See *Scottish Review*, vol. 3, no. 2 (Winter 1922).
29 See NLS, Acc. 6058/1.
30 See, for example, P. H. Brown (ed.), *The Union of 1707*, Glasgow, Outram, 1907, p. 119.
31 See NLS, Acc. 6058/1.
32 Also in *Liberty*, vol. 2, no. 1 (May 1920).

33 N. Milton, *John Maclean*, London, Pluto Press, 1973, p. 245 n.: 'Erskine and Maclean that year founded the Scots National League, the object of which was "The (sic) resumption of Scottish national independence."'
34 *Scottish Review*, Spring 1919.
35 *Vanguard*, September 1920.
36 Including Art O'Brien, a friend of Gillies's, who ran the Irish Self-Determination League (linked to Sinn Fein) and who was on the Glasgow Committee of the SNL.
37 *Liberty*, vol. 2, no. 3 (March 1921).
38 *Freedom for Scotland*, Edinburgh, Scots National League Movement, 1926.
39 NLS, Acc. 5927/1.
40 See Minute Book, NLS, Acc. 5927/1.
41 NLS, Acc. 6058/1.
42 Ibid.
43 Ibid.
44 GUSNA Membership Card, Glasgow, 1927.
45 *Glasgow University Nationalist*, no. 3, Glasgow, 1928, p. 2.
46 A prize for debating presented by the *Observer* newspaper.
47 E. Hoffer, *The True Believer: Thoughts on the Nature of Mass Movements*, New York, Harper, 1951.
48 NLS, Acc. 6058/1, memo dated 11 February 1928.
49 Ibid.

Chapter 12   The National Party of Scotland

1 J. R. Roche and S. Sachs, 'The Bureaucrat and the Enthusiast', in B. McLaughlin (ed.) *Studies in Social Movements*, New York, Free Press, 1969.
2 National Library of Scotland, Acc. 6058, 11 April 1933.
3 D. C. Thomson, *Scotland in Quest of Her Youth*, Edinburgh, Oliver & Boyd, 1932.
4 NLS, Acc. 3721.
5 *Scots Independent*, vol. I, no. 1 (November 1926).
6 Ibid.
7 NLS, Acc. 6058/1.
8 See, for example, NLS, Acc. 6058, 11 August 1928.
9 NLS, Acc. 6058/1.
10 H. Hanham, *Scottish Nationalism*, London, Faber, 1969, p. 157.
11 C. H. Douglas, *Social Credit*, London, Eyre & Spottiswoode, 1933.
12 See C. B. Macpherson, *Democracy in Alberta: Social Credit and the Party System*, 2nd edn, University of Toronto Press, 1962.
13 See J. Irving, *The Social Credit Movement in Alberta*, University of Toronto Press, 1959.
14 NLS, Acc. 6058.
15 For example 11 August 1928, NLS, Acc. 6058.
16 NLS, Acc. 6058.
17 *Free Man*, 6 February 1932.
18 *Scots Independent*, vol. III, no. 2 (December 1928).
19 *Glasgow Herald*, 3 September 1932.
20 *Glasgow Herald*, 17 September 1932.
21 *Free Man*, vol. I, no. 31 (3 September 1932).
22 *Free Man*, vol. II (new series), no. 8 (25 March 1933).
23 *Free Man*, vol. IV (new series), no. 12 (18 April 1935).
24 *GUSNA Handbook 1928-29*, Glasgow University Nationalists Association, 1928.
25 A. F. Tschiffely, *Don Roberto: being the account of the life and works of R. B. Cunninghame Graham*, London, Heinemann, 1937.

26 Ibid., p. 324.
27 *Scottish Daily Express*, 27 September 1932.
28 Papers in the private collection of Mr R. McEwen.
29 16 July 1928. From the private collection of Mr John Neil, Glasgow.
30 Ibid.
31 In a memorandum to be found in NLS, Acc. 6058.
32 A. D. Gibb, *Scotland in Eclipse*, London, H. Toulmin, 1930.
33 G. M. Thomson, *Caledonia, or the Future of the Scots*, London, Kegan Paul, 1927; and *Scotland, That Distressed Area*, Edinburgh, Porpoise Press, 1935.
34 NLS, Dep. 217/1.
35 NLS, Acc. 5927/1.
36 NLS, Dep. 217/1.
37 *Bulletin*, 13 June 1932.
38 *Scottish Daily Express*, 6 September 1932.
39 *The Times*, 15 November 1932.
40 NLS, Acc. 6058/4.
41 NLS, Dep. 217/2.
42 Reported in the *Free Man*, vol. I, no. 37 (15 October 1932).
43 NLS, Acc. 3721/193.
44 NLS, Acc. 6058, November 1939.
45 As can be seen from the proceedings of the conference in NLS, Acc. 6058/2.
46 NLS, 217/1.
47 Including R. E. Muirhead, NLS, Acc. 3721/5.
48 NLS, Dep. 217/1, 3 January 1933.
49 Ibid., 1 March 1933.
50 See NLS, Acc. 6058/2.
51 The agreed memorandum is in NLS, Acc. 6058/2.
52 *Free Man*, vol. 1 (new series), no. 40.
53 NLS, 3171/193.
54 NLS, Acc. 3421/5, 20 February 1935.
55 See H. Hanham, *Scottish Nationalism*, London, Faber, 1969, p. 159.

Chapter 13 The Scottish National Party

1 *Scots Independent*, vol. 3, no. 3 (new series), November 1937.
2 Ibid., vol. 2, no. 3 (new series), November 1936.
3 J. MacCormick, *Flag in the Wind*, London, Gollancz, 1959, pp. 102-3.
4 *Scots Independent*, vol. 3, no. 10 (new series), June 1938.
5 For example, over King Edward's title.
6 Evidence of this romanticism can be seen in the writings of both MacEwen and Gibb. See, for example, Sir A. M. MacEwen, *The Thistle and the Rose*, Edinburgh, Oliver & Boyd, 1932, pp. 1-37.
7 *Scots Independent*, vol. III, no. 9 (July 1929).
8 *Scottish Standard*, vol. 1, no. 2 (January 1936).
9 *Scots Independent*, vol. 2, no. 3 (new series), November 1936.
10 Ibid., vol. 3, no. 8 (new series), April 1938.
11 *Glasgow Herald*, 6 June 1938.
12 J. Howarth, 'The National Party of Scotland', Syracuse University, N.Y., DSS thesis, 1968, p. 139.
13 W. Wood, *Yours Sincerely for Scotland*, London, Barker, 1970, pp. 73-4.
14 Ibid., p. 74.
15 See especially, *Scots Independent*, vol. 2, no. 12 (new series), August 1937.
16 Ibid.
17 Ibid.
18 *Smeddum*, vol. 1, no. 1 (July 1937).

19 Ibid.
20 *The Anti-Conscription League*, 1 April 1936.
21 W. Wood, *I Like Life*, Moray Press, Edinburgh, 1938, p. 287.
22 *New Statesman and Nation*, vol. XXXV, no. 901 (2 August 1930).
23 *Daily Record*, 16 August 1933.
24 *Scotsman*, 17 April 1934.
25 National Library of Scotland, Acc. 3721/12.
26 NLS, Acc. 3721/15.
27 *Scots Independent*, vol. 3, no. 1 (new series), September 1937.
28 Ibid., vol. 3, no. 9 (new series), May 1938.
29 Ibid., vol. VIII, no. 97 (November 1934).
30 Ibid., vol. 1, no. 10 (new series), June 1936.
31 Ibid., vol. 3, no. 12 (new series), August 1938.
32 NLS, Acc. 6058/2, J. MacCormick to T. H. Gibson, 31 March 1933.
33 11 May 1935, reported in the *Glasgow Herald*, 13 May 1935.
34 *Daily Record*, 5 October 1936.
35 J. MacCormick, op. cit., p. 27.
36 NLS, Acc. 6058/2.
37 NLS, Acc. 5927/1, Minutes of Party Conference, 1932.
38 *Scots Independent*, vol. 1, no. 5 (new Series), January 1936.
39 Ibid., vol. 2, no. 11 (new series), July 1937.
40 *Glasgow Herald*, 3 May 1937.
41 *Scotland and the World Crisis*, Glasgow, SNP, 1938.
42 *Glasgow Herald*, 29 May 1939.
43 J. MacCormick, op. cit., p. 97.
44 *Scots Independent*, vol. 3, no, 12 (new series), August 1938.
45 Ibid., vol. 4, no. 7 (new series), March 1939.
46 Ibid., vol. 5, no. 5 (new series), January 1940.
47 Formed in 1939, according to the Muirhead papers, and going on until the 1950s when it merged with Scottish Congress.
48 The SNP was not the only Scottish organisation to express this fear. It was also referred to by the STUC, the Scottish Development Council and even Walter Elliot (a Conservative sitting for Glasgow, Kelvingrove) in the House of Commons on 6 August 1942.
49 *Scotsman*, 2 June 1942.
50 NLS, Dep. 217/2, 21 June 1942.
51 Secretary's statement to May National Council, NLS, Acc. 5927/1.
52 *Scotsman*, 1 and 2 June 1942.
53 Publicity was also given by the Scottish Secretariat, which circulated its pamphlets especially in the universities, where there was particular feeling against the war, e.g. *A Scot's Free Fight*, statement delivered at Glasgow Sheriff Court on 13 April 1942, Scottish Secretariat, Glasgow, 1942; *The Free-Minded Scot*, Scottish Secretariat, Glasgow, 1942.
54 NLS, Acc. 6419.
55 NLS, Scottish Convention Committee Minutes, 11 June 1942.
56 NLS, Scottish Convention Committee Minutes, 16 September 1942.
57 *Scots Independent*, vol. VI, no. 11 (September 1932).
58 NLS, Acc. 3711/66.
59 *The Wealth of Scotland* and *Scotland and the South* both by J. A. A. Porteous; *Scottish Convention, an Experiment in Democracy*, J. MacCormick, all published by Scottish Convention in Glasgow, 1947.
60 Personal communication to the author from Sheriff J. Bayne.
61 *Blueprint for Scotland*, Scottish Covenant Association, Glasgow, undated but probably 1947.

62 Ibid., pp. 2-3.
63 Copies are in the National Library of Scotland and the Edinburgh District Council public library.
64 *National Weekly*, 5 February 1949.
65 J. MacCormick, op. cit., pp. 139-40.
66 *National Weekly*, 24 March 1951.
67 *Scots Independent*, vol. 8, no. 11 (July 1943).
68 NLS, Acc. 3721/54.
69 *Scots Independent*, vol. 13, no. 11 (July 1948).
70 Ibid., October 1942.
71 December 1953.
72 NLS, Acc. 3721/8.
73 *Scottish Forward*, April 1959.,
74 Ibid., May 1962.
75 1955 Group information mimeo, 28 May 1955.
76 J. G. Pittendrigh to R. E. Muirhead, 10 May 1955, NLS, Acc. 3721/113.
77 *The English: are they human?*, Nationalist Party of Scotland, n.d.
78 NLS, Acc. 3721/113, August 1956.
79 *Scots Independent*, no. 92 (weekly series), 29 October 1955.
80 *Scottish Forward*, February 1961.
81 See Chapter 5, above.
82 *Scots Independent*, no. 256 (weekly series), 20 December 1958.
83 Ibid., no. 263 (weekly series), 7 February 1959.
84 For example R. H. S. Crossman, *The Diaries of a Cabinet Minister*, London, Hamish Hamilton, 1975.
85 *Scots Independent*, no. 482 (weekly series), June 1963.

Chapter 14   The Present Organisation of the SNP

1 R. Rose, *Problems of Party Government*, London, Macmillan, 1974, p. 129.
2 D. Butler and R. Pinto-Duschinsky, *The British General Election of 1970*, London, Macmillan, 1971.
3 J. Bochel and M. Denver, 'Religion and Voting', *Political Studies*, vol. 18 (1970), pp. 205-19.
4 R. Michels, *Political Parties*, London, Jarrold, 1915.
5 R. T. McKenzie, *British Political Parties*, London, Heinemann, 1959; or I. Bulmer-Thomas, *The Party System in Great Britain*, London, Phoenix House, 1953.
6 J. Bryce, *The American Commonwealth*, 3 vols, London, Macmillan, 1888, vol. 1, p. 54.
7 M. Duverger, *Political Parties*, London, Methuen, 1962.
8 Ibid., p. 71.
9 National Library of Scotland, Acc. 3721/92, 14 September 1934.
10 NLS, Acc. 6038, Confidential Memorandum to National Executive, May 1963.
11 National Executive Reports, 1963, 1965, 1967, 1969, 1971, Edinburgh, SNP, unpublished.
12 Rose, op. cit., p. 144.
13 NLS, Acc. 6038.
14 Minutes of the National Council, 11 March 1967, Edinburgh, SNP, unpublished.
15 M. Dalton, *Men Who Manage*, New York, Wiley, 1966.
16 S. Eldersfeldt, *Political Parties, a Behavioural Analysis*, University of Chicago Press, 1964, p. 9 and pp. 98-117.
17 Duverger, op. cit., p. 81.

18 See, for example, NLS, Acc. 6038, NEC meeting, December 1964.
19 National Council Minutes, 10 June 1972.
20 National Council, 6 September 1969.
21 National Council, 2 September 1972.
22 National Council, 14 June 1975.
23 Duverger, op. cit., pp. 27-36.
24 *Glasgow Herald*, 9 December 1976.
25 These 'Fletcher Papers' include G. Kennedy, *The Defence Budget of an Independent Scotland*, 1975; T. McRae, *North Sea Oil*, 1975; M. Slesser, *Scotland and Energy*, 1975; J. Hulbert, *Housing in Scotland*, 1976.

Chapter 15   Conclusion

1 T. Nairn, *The Break Up of Britain*, London, New Left Books, 1977.
2 Ibid., p. 96.
3 Ibid., p. 70.
4 Ibid., p. 128.

Index

323

Index

Howarth, J., 232
Hume, David, 92
Hunter, Dr James, 183
Hurd, Robert, 53, 221, 228, 240

Icelandic nationalism, 89
ideology, 32-3, 299
ILP, 28, 175, 176, 177, 186, 192, 197,
212, 216, 220, 228, 268, 283
see also Labour Party
Imperialism, 256, 293, 294
Indian National Congress, 253
'industrial campaigns', 287
industrial growth, consequences of,
70-1
industry, 23, 30, 61, 70, 71, 231, 284,
286-7, 297
Inglehart, Ronald, 5, 23, 30
'integral' nationalism, 13, 14
'Internal Colonialism' theory, 177
international relations, 49-50
International Scottish Home Rule
League, 216
Ireland, 15, 27, 46, 47, 103, 129, 131
Irish Home Rule movement, 9, 27, 40
Irish immigration, 72, 152, 153
iron and steel, 70, 72, 73, 81, 84, 287

jingoism, 46
Johnson, William, 285
Johnston, Russell, 51
Johnston, Tom, 43, 44, 48, 52, 54, 55,
56, 80, 81, 177, 296, 310

Kailyard School, 94, 95, 96, 109, 313
Kamenka, E., 11
Keating, M. J., 65, 66
Kedourie, E., 7, 16, 31
Kilbrandon Commission, 58, 133, 134,
148, 157, 161
see also Crowther Commission
Kinloch, J. L., 47, 171, 231
Kirkwood, D., 48, 310
Knox, John, 128
Kohn, H., 7, 10, 170
Korean War, 49, 82, 83, 251, 253

Labour Council for Scottish Self-
Government, 234
Labour Party, 20, 26, 28, 30, 33, 39,
41, 42, 43, 45, 48, 53, 57, 58, 61,
82, 86, 88, 102, 139, 170, 171, 174,
179, 181, 190, 197, 229, 235, 244,
247, 250, 251, 258, 268, 274, 284,
286, 288, 293, 294, 295

finance, 282
organisation, 268-9, 274
policy for Scotland, 51-2, 54, 56, 58,
59
vote, 4, 64, 146, 149, 150-3, 155,
156, 163-5, 260-2
see also ILP
Lallans (Scots), 15, 19, 101, 103
Lamont, Dr Archie, 47, 186, 224, 254
Landsmaal, 96
Lang, Andrew, 107
language, 14-15, 17, 89-105, 208
leadership, 266-7, 275, 276-80
League for the Independence of
Scotland (Comunn airson Saorsa
na h-Alba), 233
League of the Thistle and White
Heather, 234
League of True Scots, 233-4
Lenman, B., 108
Liberal Party, 20, 25, 26, 28, 39, 40,
41, 44, 45, 50, 64, 65, 129, 171,
174, 176, 181, 186, 216, 218, 220,
227, 228, 229, 236, 243
vote, 22, 23, 146, 149-53, 155, 156
Lindsay, Maurice, 99
Linklater, Eric, 210
Lipjhart, A., 7, 152
Lithgow, Sir James, 78
Lloyd George, D., 41
local government, 24, 25, 272
in Scotland Act (1929), 207
London Scots Self-Government Com-
mittee, 52, 53, 234-5, 311

McColla, Fion, 99, 105
MacCormick, Ian, 278
MacCormick, John, 48, 51, 56, 192,
193, 194, 197, 203, 207, 209, 210,
211, 212-5, 220, 221, 222, 223, 224,
226, 228, 229, 231, 232, 235, 236,
237, 239, 240-6, 248, 249, 250, 257,
265, 269, 277, 278, 279
MacCrone, G., 83, 84
MacDiarmid, Hugh (C. M. Grieve),
15, 47, 53, 90, 92, 96, 97, 98, 99,
101, 102, 103, 104, 105, 186, 193,
198, 206, 208, 241
MacDonald, Ian, 258, 259, 261
MacDonald, Dr John, 81, 231, 248,
257, 258, 259, 260, 277
MacDonald, Margo, 264, 278, 283
MacDonald, Ramsey, 42, 44, 48, 171
McDowall, J. Kevan, 216, 220, 226,
227

Index